Trans Identities in the French Media

Trans Identities in the French Media

Representation, Visibility, Recognition

Edited by Romain Chareyron

LEXINGTON BOOKS
Lanham • Boulder • New York • London

Published by Lexington Books
An imprint of The Rowman & Littlefield Publishing Group, Inc.
4501 Forbes Boulevard, Suite 200, Lanham, Maryland 20706
www.rowman.com

86-90 Paul Street, London EC2A 4NE

British Library Cataloguing in Publication Information Available

Library of Congress Cataloging-in-Publication Data Available

ISBN 978-1-66690-025-5 (cloth)
ISBN 978-1-66690-027-9 (pbk.)
ISBN 978-1-66690-026-2 (electronic)

I want to thank Judith Lakamper at Lexington Books
for her continued support throughout this process.
I also want to thank all the contributors for making this project come to life.
My deepest gratitude to Jeffrey Klassen,
whose input was instrumental in the completion of this book.

Contents

Introduction

Trans Identities in the French Media

Romain Chareyron

"LA QUESTION TRANS"

"*La Question trans*" took center stage on the radio show *Répliques* broadcasted on September 11th, 2021, by the French public radio channel *France Culture*[1] and hosted by French philosopher Alain Finkielkraut.[2] During the hour-long program, Finkielkraut led a debate on the issue of trans identities in contemporary French society with his two guests, Claude Habib[3] and Serge Hefez. Habib is a French academic who specializes in French literature from the eighteenth century, but who has strayed from her specialty with her most recent publication that also happens to be titled "*La Question trans*." Hefez is a French physician and psychiatrist as well as the Head of the Child and Adolescent Psychiatry Service at the Pitié-Sâlepétrière hospital in Paris. As the debate unfolded, two visions of trans identities were brought head-to-head. Habib advanced the idea that in recent times, the prefix 'trans' is mainly used in a declaratory manner, implying that the majority of people who use the term 'trans' today have not undergone gender reassignment surgery and have no intention to do so. Unlike former generations of trans people who underwent hormone therapy and gender reassignment surgery, Habib explained that younger generations have no qualms in declaring themselves 'trans' "without doing anything about it" ("sans rien faire"). For her, this attitude is symptomatic of a society in which social media offers a soapbox for individuals questioning social norms. For Habib, this is not a step toward greater acceptance in terms of gender diversity, but rather serves to hold people in

1

a state of indeterminacy that, according to her, could be highly detrimental to their well-being. Conversely, Serge Hefez explained that the emergence of concepts such as "nonbinary" and "gender fluid" were signs that younger generations were more comfortable questioning the validity of gender norms by refusing to adhere to socially imposed modes of behavior. While Hefez advocated for a reappraisal of the concepts of "gender" and "identity"—one championed by trans people—Finkielkraut and Habib's expressed a common fear that trans people's deconstruction of identity could lead to the negation of the male/female binary construct that has shaped most modern societies. Habib went so far as to employ expressions such as "*artificialisation des corps*" ("artificialization of the body") and "*agression de la nature*" ("assault on nature") when discussing trans identities.

In the light of what was said during this show, we are able to observe some of the dominant modes of thinking that have shaped public debates with regards to the question of trans identities in French society while bringing to light some of France's idiosyncrasies in terms of sexual citizenship. Habib and Finkielkraut's comments are indicative of a fairly restrictive stance with respect to trans people's material existence and daily life, understood here in purely medical terms. Their comments align with hegemonic views surrounding trans people in which they are expected to conform to the gendered norms of behavior and appearance instituted by society. This congruence or "sexual coherence" (Reeser 2013, 6) between an individual's self-identified gender and their physical appearance is essentially achieved through gender reassignment surgery and is commonly referred to by the term "transsexualism."[4] What Karine Espineira describes as an "acceptable and consensual" (Espineira 2014a, para. 20)[5] expression of trans identity has come to be perceived by trans people themselves as a form of oppression that denies them any agency.[6] This hegemonic viewpoint corresponds to a network of "nation-based discourses, institutions, and state-sanctioned forms of power" (Reeser 2013, 4) where bodies have come to be regulated by "a centralized health care system that [holds] sway over the ways 'healthy' bodies are produced and reproduced, and over the ways sexual reassignment surgery affects the lives of French people [. . .]" (4). Consequently, by passing judgment on people who call themselves "trans" while choosing not to undergo gender reassignment surgery, Habib perpetuates a damaging dichotomy. A division is established between "real" trans people—that is, people who elect to have gender reassignment surgery—and "fake" ones seen to "threaten" traditional gender roles—that is, people whose gender is different from the one assigned at birth but opt not to alter their bodies accordingly.[7]

It must be also noted that Habib and Finkielkraut's comments on trans identities convey an underlying fear of gender theory as a foreign import that threatens to alter and destabilize the foundations of French Republicanism.

Before we proceed any further in our exploration of media representations of trans identities, we therefore must take time to trace the origins of such conceptualizations of "gender" and "identity" in a French context. Indeed, the way citizenship is regarded in French society—that is, what is deemed acceptable or, on the contrary, considered too salient or divisive and therefore at odds with the country's republican universalism—will have a direct impact on the types of representations that have come to prevail in the media with regards to trans people.

WHAT IT MEANS TO BE FRENCH: PARTICULARISM VERSUS UNIVERSALISM

During the debate, Claude Habib uses the term "wokisme" several times to criticize the fact that, in today's society, a growing number of individuals are more at ease expressing an identity that does not correspond to one particular gender. A Gallicized version of the English word "woke"—which is broadly used to describe any individual that expresses an awareness of social inequalities, such as racism, sexism, or homophobia—"wokisme" has recently taken the French political and media world by storm. On October 13th, 2021, French Minister of Education Jean-Michel Blanquer launched a think tank whose goal was to fight "wokisme," which he perceives to be "a new cultural totalitarianism creeping in from the 'Anglosphere'" (Schofield 2021). The use of the term "Anglosphere" by the author of the article is not trivial, as it signals France's defiance toward any intellectual import from the anglophone world that is considered a threat to the country's republican values and universalism. The "wokisme" backlash is simply the latest iteration of this fear that "French identity as such is in danger of being consumed by 'non-French' [. . .] visions [. . .]" (Vilchez 2015, 115).

Another telling example can be found in the heated debates in the 2010s surrounding the introduction of gender theory to the French curriculum. In September 2013, then Women's Rights Minister (*Ministre des Droits des femmes*) Najat Vallaut-Belkacem implemented an experimental program called *ABCD de l'égalité* ("ABCs of Equality") in 275 primary schools. The goal of this programme was to combat sexism and gender stereotypes and "to teach children that some differences between the sexes are biological, but others are socially constructed" (Massel 2014, para. 1). While people on the left supported what they considered to be "an important step to promoting equality in France" (Massel 2014, para. 1), the program was met with great hostility from conservatives as well as religious groups. In January 2014, a group named *Journée de retrait de l'école* (which might be translated as "Take your Kid Out of School" day) promoted a campaign to pull children out of school one a day a month in order to protest the implementation of this program.[8] The group also launched a misinformation campaign, "announcing that schoolteachers were teaching boys to be girls and girls to be boys [. . .] Some went so far as to say that sexuality was being discussed with these primary schoolchildren, including how to masturbate" (Vilchez 2015, 114).[9] The public outcry against the program was so strong that, on June 29th, 2014, Vallaut-Belkacem announced its discontinuation. The magnitude of the protests as well as their repercussions compel us to look deeper at the grounds on which people object to gender theory being taught in schools. Such an analysis will also allow us to better understand the biases and misconceptions that come into play when discussing gender diversity.

As historian Camille Robcis notes, the staunch opposition against gender theory is part of a broader social upheaval that has intensified since 2013 and the passing of the bill granting same-sex couples the rights to get married and to adopt. Those who opposed the bill feared that institutions such as family and marriage, as well as gender roles, would be called into question:

> [. . .] the way I would put it is that the debate around the 'theory of gender' has resurfaced with particular intensity since the passing of the 2013 gay marriage law, known as 'Marriage for All' (*mariage pour tous*). Although the reform had been one of [French President] Hollande's campaign promises, it unleashed an opposition that surprised many commentators inside and outside of France [. . .] The 'theory of gender' [. . .] emerges as both the cause and the outcome of gay marriage. If homosexuals are allowed to reproduce, who will emerge from this process? What will the family look like, and more importantly, what will the future, the social, and the nation look like? Likewise, if children are taught to question gender stereotypes and to think about their sexual identity as more fluid with the help of this 'gender theory,' what kind of citizens will they become? What norms will govern our world? (Duong 2014)

As Robcis's comments bring to light, what the protests against gender theory and marriage equality have in common is a resistance toward anything that would disrupt a heteronormative vision of family, sexuality, and gender. The family in particular is seen as the cornerstone of French republicanism, as Robcis points out:

> [. . .] since the nineteenth century, French civil law and social policy have constructed the heterosexual family as constitutive of the social. In other words, the family figures as the best unit to organize solidarity and build political consensus, the most abstractable mode of social representation, and the purest expression of the general will [. . .] This history of thinking the heterosexual family as constitutive of the social and as synonymous with republicanism can help us better understand why the anti-gay-marriage protestors would

continually present gay marriage and the 'theory of gender' *as a foreign export* [. . .] (Duong 2014; *emphasis added*)

The expression "foreign export" used by Robcis is of particular significance, as it encapsulates a rhetoric adopted by conservative and religious groups in their attack against certain concepts that are seen as privileging the needs of specific segments of the population and thus going against the republican ideal "in which the individual as a unique and subjective identity is subsumed by the subject in his total and unique identification with the state" (McCaffrey 2005, 16). To do this, they point out the (often Anglophone, often American) origins of the concepts to deem them incompatible with their sense of a French collective identity. Stambolis-Ruhstorfer and Tricou sum up this attitude when they write:

> [. . .] anti-gender French activists [. . .] often used the English word 'gender,' rather than the French word *genre*, in order to portray 'gender' as a dangerous ideology imported from abroad. In France, intellectual anti-Americanism has a long history as an effective tool for delegitimizing the ideas of one's political adversaries [. . .] Rhetorically portraying ideas as 'American' is therefore useful when groups seek to derail legal changes they oppose in France. (Stambolis-Ruhstorfer and Tricou 2017, 86)[10]

While the authors' comments chiefly target the agenda of anti-gender activists, the same modus operandi could be found when participants of *La Manif pour tous* (Protest for Everyone) took to the streets to oppose the Socialist Party's bill for same-sex marriage that was eventually adopted in 2013, as noted by Bruno Perreau:

> France's anxiety about becoming Americanized is not just a simple question of loss of sovereignty. The idea of foreign cultural invasion is a direct echo of the fantasy of an enemy within, one who will multiply uncontrollably. Thus, it is directly linked to the idea of the propagation of homosexuality, which functions on many layers of discourse: contamination (which combines mental pathology and physiological illness), corruption (the destruction of the natural order through pagan practices), and conversion (enlistment in an activist movement not unlike a religious conversion) [. . .] the fantasy of the contagiousness of homosexuality underpins France's republican values even today [. . .] (Perreau 2016, 10)[11]

These remarks serve to highlight the profound social unrest stirred by any new reform that has the potential to alter centuries-old institutions like family and education. More generally speaking, what these social movements signal is the way identity is conceived of in a French context: not only—or,

should we say, not mainly—as the combination of physical and psychological traits unique to each individual, but as a willingness to adhere to France's
republican ideal whereby the expression of difference is curtailed in favor of
assimilation and sameness.[12] As summed up by Enda McCaffrey:

> This combination of transcendent qualities and self-abnegation have served to
> define French republicanism over recent centuries. (McCaffrey 2005, 16)

The fact that "[t]he French concept of citizenship has always intentionally neglected social and socioeconomic and cultural pluralist dimensions,
because of a fear of social fragmentation leading to the destruction of the
Republican ideology" (Lefebvre 2003, 15) is especially relevant when we
want to observe non-hegemonic gender expressions, their reception, and
subsequent representations.

DEFINING "TRANS IDENTITY" AND "REPRESENTATION"

To better understand the impetus behind the assembly of this volume, it is
important to clarify the terminology used in this introduction that also serves
as the backbone of the various texts that comprise said volume. The choice
of the term "trans identity" was made with a view to offer an approach that
is as inclusive as possible. It is also a direct reference to the French term
"transidentité" that allows for a diversity of life paths when regarding the
question of "trans." I will quote Karine Espineira whose work on trans
identities was instrumental in the conception of this volume. In the following quotation, Espineira clarifies the terms "transgender," "transsexual," and
"trans identity."

> A distinction is made between transgender and transsexual based on whether
> an individual has undergone hormone therapy and gender reassignment sur-
> gery. However, a survey conducted within the trans community reveals a
> more complex reality, as a number of people who identify as trans disprove of
> these categories. The terms 'transsexuality' and 'transsexualism' may be used
> when referring to a concept or a medical procedure [. . .] but when referring to
> people's lives and experiences, the terms 'transgender' or 'trans identity' are
> favored. The term 'trans identity' (*transidentité*) appears to be uniquely French.
> The word, coined by sociologist Heike Boedeker, was imported to France by
> the Strasbourg-based transgender-support group STS67 in the early 2000s. It is
> used as an umbrella term, in a way similar to the term 'transgender' [. . .] [The
> term 'trans identity'] emphasizes the identity-building process by shifting the

focus from the question of sexuality to that of gender. (Espineira 2015, 180; my translation)[13]

An additional explanation of the meaning of 'trans identity' can be found in an earlier publication by Espineira. She writes:

The prefix 'trans' has been combined with the suffix 'identity' since the early 2000s in a French context. Before that time, ['trans'] had been commonly associated with sexuality (transsexuality) since the 1950s and gender (transgender) since the 1970s. 'Trans identity' thus serves as an umbrella term that gathers together *transsexual and transgender people, as well as individuals who identify as trans but reject any formal categorisation.* (Espineira 2014b, 105; my translation, *emphasis added*)[14]

Using 'trans identity' as defined by Espineira precludes us from imposing rigid categories that would be detrimental to our purposes with this volume, which is to document the various meanings of 'trans' and the ways non-hegemonic gender identities are being expressed and represented in France today.[15] The same line of thinking informed our broad understanding of "media," considered here as any means of mass communication.

We now need to turn our attention to another term that is central to the texts that make up this volume, that of "representation." As defined by Stuart Hall, "[r]epresentation [. . .] implies the active work of selecting and presenting, of structuring and shaping: not merely the transmitting of already-existing meaning, but the more active labor of making things mean" (Hall 1982, 64). Central to Hall's comment is the idea that a *representation* is always an *interpretation*, since the act of representing is never neutral and requires a certain amount of selection and manipulation with a view to communicate a specific message. As we will soon observe, trans people have often been depicted in a negative light, as existing on the fringes of society, and are often tied to the societal issues of sex work and crime.[16] While some articles in this volume will explore the damaging effect of some contemporary representations of trans individuals, our objective is also to showcase the greater variety of voices found today that allow for a more nuanced and subjective approach of trans lives and trans identities. Before we do so, we must take into consideration another aspect of representation that, although obvious, is important to acknowledge: its communicative power.

Representation is always *for someone*, and the production of meaning that derives from a representation has real effects within society—it tends to shape people's understanding of individuals and phenomena. As noted by Kilo-Patrick R. Hart, "it has been acknowledged that media representations can be especially powerful in cultivating images of groups and phenomena about which viewers have little firsthand knowledge" (Hart 2000, 13). Hart uses the term "social construction" to define the variety of factors (cultural, historical, and medical, among others) that come into play when representing a complex and sometimes abstract phenomenon for public consumption. As a consequence, people's understanding of this phenomenon will primarily be based on the partial information that has been selected and presented to them. As noted by the author:

> Whether it occurs between small groups of people or millions, communication of social constructions serves as a primary means by which individuals influence others in their social world about various issues. As such, media representations of social phenomena contribute significantly to widely shared social perceptions. (7)

A similar connection is made by Cáel M. Keegan, Laura Horak and Eliza Steinbock when they discuss the significance of representation for trans visibility. For them, "media acts as a staging ground for the types of life that are permitted to become real and to shape reality in turn" (Keegan, Horak and Steinbock 2018, 7), which leads them to state that "[t]rans representation shapes public discourse and affects politics" (3). While tracing the history of the evolution of the representation of trans people is beyond the scope of this volume, a clear understanding of the major thematic trends that have accompanied the representation of trans people in mainstream media is essential. Doing so will allow us to better understand the (damaging) tropes that have been associated with trans people over time, how these tropes have been reclaimed by the media, and how the latter has conveyed representations of trans people that had a real impact on the social construction of this community by a cisgender audience.

TRANS IDENTITIES IN THE FRENCH MEDIA: THE PITFALLS OF REPRESENTATION

When discussing the question of trans identities in the media, the archival work done by Franco-Chilean sociologist Karine Espineira is foundational and deserves tribute. As the co-founder and co-head of *L'Observatoire des transidentités*, Espineira has played an instrumental role in analyzing the evolution of the representation of trans identities in the French media.[17] Her work focuses on trans identities on television, the scope of which includes television series, made-for-TV documentary films, talk shows, and news reports, and is based on 886 audiovisual records that cover the time period spanning from 1946 to 2010 (Espineira 2014a; Espineira 2014b; Espineira and Thomas 2014).[18] Her research brings to light the most common tropes that have prevailed at different points in time regarding the representation of trans identities, and what follows is an attempt at capturing what appears to be some of the defining moments of trans visibility in the French media.

Transsexuality first gained visibility through the transgender cabaret culture of the 1950s with renowned performers such as Coccinelle[19] and Bambi. Remaining within the confines of the cabaret, transsexuality was perceived as marginal and circumscribed to the domain of night life. However, Espineira notes, when it began to attract wider public attention through the highly mediatized gender reassignment stories of Christine Jorgensen[20] and Coccinelle, a shift occurred in the perception (and representation) of transsexuality, which seeped into the public sphere and gained wider media coverage.

From that moment on, a more negative and biased representation of trans people has dominated television. Espineira observes that, while the 1970s and 1980s saw an increased presence of trans people on television, this newfound visibility came at the expense of truthfulness and nuance. During the period, a number of talk shows broached the topic of transsexuality, but in a way that never allowed trans people to speak candidly about their life journey. As a matter of fact, the presence of people from the medical and psychiatric fields on these shows leveled out any of the specificities pertaining to each individual's life, confining their experiences to the harmful dichotomy mentioned in the opening pages of this introduction that pitted "real" trans individuals (those who embraced gender reassignment surgery) against "fake" ones (those whose trans identity was not dependent upon any medical intervention). The pathologization of trans people by the medical world,[21] denounced today by trans activists, found an outlet in those TV programs. Hence, the idea was perpetuated that the only acceptable expression of trans identity came from those who respected the gender binary once they had transitioned—a trans woman, for example, had to conform to the gender norms of femininity.

Espineira also explains that, from the 1980s to the 2000s, whenever a trans character was portrayed in a TV show, showrunners predominantly invoked the figure of the transvestite, demonstrating a narrow and limiting understanding of trans identities.[22] In addition, such characters never had recurring parts in the shows and were systematically presented as marginalized people, often linked to crime and sex work (the term used in the news reports at the time was "prostitution").[23] In a more recent article (2021), Espineira writes that, even in recent years, French television has been particularly tame and unimaginative in its portrayals of trans people. In addition to the fact that trans characters are offered very little visibility, the rare occurrences of trans representation are dated and obsolete. Such appearances show trans characters that are predominantly white, straight, middle-aged women. She laments the lack of diversity, visibility and complexity when it comes to the presence of trans characters on television when, in recent years, popular American shows such as *Orange is the New Black* (2013–2019), *Sense8* (2015–2017), *Transparent* (2014–2019), or *Pose* (2018–2021) have introduced their audience to a wide array of trans characters who are "[n]o longer represented as spectacular signifiers of gender variance [and] populate diverse narrative universes" (Koch-Rein, Yekani and Verlinden 2020, 3).

More generally speaking, she notices a disconnect between the prevailing representations of trans people in the media and the reality of trans identities. For example, the absence of trans men is one major hurdle for the representation of trans identities on French television according to Espineira.[24] In addition to the lack of media representation for trans men, aspects of trans identities that Espineira notes are conspicuously missing in the media include the activism found among trans people today together with their call for a depathologization of transsexuality and their questioning of the gender binary. While these observations offer a fairly concerning picture of how trans people are represented on French television—and are therefore conceived by a segment of the population—it was also the inception for this volume. Indeed, the texts that form this volume offer to extend Espineira's findings and explore how trans representations operate in (media-related) artistic fields such as television, cinema, literature, and graphic novels. Do we find the same problematic depictions as the ones noted by Espineira across all entertainment and artistic mediums? Are we witnessing the emergence of more complex and truthful representations where trans subjectivities can be expressed? Do "representation," "visibility," and "acceptance" go hand in hand, or does this triad require further examination? These are some of the questions at the heart of this volume.

ABOUT THE PRESENT VOLUME

The texts selected for this volume will provide readers with in-depth and innovative analyses that discuss the representation of trans identities in the French media, its main challenges, as well as the progress and pitfalls that shape these representations today. The broad scope of this volume was a purposeful choice. By understanding "media" as any means of communication through which news or information is disseminated, our objective is to observe how the question of trans identities has been dealt with in cinema and literature, but also in the news, TV series, or graphic novels. Because transgender and gender non-conforming people have many ways of understanding their gender identities, we believe that adopting such an inclusive stance does not dilute or lessen the impact of this project, but instead acknowledges the complexity and multi-layered meaning of the concept of "representation" when applied to the question of trans identities in a French context. With contributions from a diverse group of established and emerging scholars, this volume brings together specialists in fields such as comics studies, translation studies, women's and gender studies, queer studies, and media studies. The expertise and insight of these authors constitute a valuable body of work that helps to position Trans Studies within a French context. Reflecting on the questions of trans visibility and recognition, each contribution showcases the works of artists who offer ground-breaking ways of conveying non-hegemonic gender identities. This volume finds its cohesiveness in the contributors' sustained endeavor to "complicat[e] a supposedly straightforward understanding of both 'trans' and 'representation' and thereby avoid the 'trap of the visual' that equates more [. . .] representation with more societal recognition" (Koch-Rein et al., 5).

In other words, these essays offer a nuanced approach toward the relationship between "representation" and "visibility." Indeed, the increased visibility of trans individuals requires serious examination, as a greater number of representations of a social group does not necessarily bring about a better understanding of said group. As was previously mentioned, these representations might be fraught with misconceptions and biases, such that the interpretative lens through which the public perceives trans individuals could potentially be detrimental to these very individuals. Anson Koch-Rein, Elahe Haschemi Yekani and Jasper J. Verlinden perfectly sum up the need for realistic depictions of trans people that do not sensationalize them and leave room for their voices to be heard: "[. . .] representing trans is a crucial debate that includes concerns about who can speak *for* trans people and *how* trans lives should be represented. But it is also testament to the fact that representation expands the realm of the intelligible" (Koch-Rein, Yekani and Verlinden 2020, 2).

This volume therefore seeks to understand the question of who controls the cis gaze and how this might influence the representation of trans identities and our subsequent perceptions. Similarly, the essays take a critical stance toward the belief that representation automatically entails visibility and acceptance. As noted by Koch-Rein et al., "[. . .] visibility cannot simply be equated with social acceptance" (3). Along the same line, the essays of this volume choose to delve into this tension between "representation," "visibility" and "recognition" by questioning what "representation" entails. In certain situations, it might operate "in a dichotomous system of 'good' vs 'bad" (Koch-Rein et al. 2020, 5) that leaves little agency to the characters portrayed. In others, it might achieve what José Esteban Muñoz refers to as "disidentification," understood as "a strategy that works on and against dominant ideology" (Muñoz 1999, 11). With such a strategy, "minoritarian subjects perform in encounters with existing forms of representation that can be reframed, re-imagined, and undone to a certain extent in order to produce new ones" (Koch-Rein et al., 5).

In their article "Trans Kids in France: Unpacking the Media Frenzy," Charlie Fabre analyzes the recent and ever-growing attention from the French media toward the narratives of trans youth. Fabre's study draws on the premise that the increased exposure of trans youth we are witnessing in the media—as well as the negative and often transphobic discussions it gives rise to—is first due to a misrepresentation of trans issues from the media in the twentieth and twenty-first century. After offering a brief overview of the evolution of the representation of trans individuals over time, Fabre focuses more specifically on two recent examples of trans youth narratives that, according to him, shone light on some of the most common dilemmas when it comes to the representation of trans kids *as seen through a cisgender gaze.* Using the examples of Lilie—an eight-year-old trans girl struggling alongside her family for her legal recognition as a girl—and Sasha—a young trans girl facing similar struggles and whose journey was caught on camera by French director Sébastien Lifshitz for his documentary *Petite fille*—Fabre highlights the fact that most stories about trans youth tend to give primacy to the adults in their lives, whether it be their parents or medical and psychological professionals. In so doing, Fabre argues, such narratives deprive the viewer from gaining direct access to trans kids' subjectivity and personal journey, choosing instead to focus on the parents' struggles and the psychologists' assessment. Fabre thus suggests that the first step toward better representation is to carve out a space where an individual's subjectivity can be freely expressed, rather than having it related and defined by others.

"Mobile Desires: Paul B. Preciado's *Un Appartement sur Uranus* and the Marginal Western Subject" by Leah E. Wilson focuses on the work of trans philosopher Paul B. Preciado. *Un Appartement sur Uranus* compiles a series of articles written by Preciado for the French newspaper *Libération* between March 2013 and January 2018. During this period which saw Europe undergo a series of sociopolitical crises, Preciado chronicled societal events such as the rise in far-right nationalism, the fall of democracies and the rise of anti-gender campaigns through the anti-normative perspective of refusing gender categorization or national ties. According to Wilson, what emerges from Preciado's writings is that issues such as migration, capitalism, and democracy are all connected to questions of gender and sexuality. Wilson understands *Un Appartement . . .* as providing valuable insights into the way hegemonic categorizations have produced inequality and instigated violence for Others in modern Western societies. As the collection of articles documents Preciado's journey around the globe, Wilson's article explores the connections between Preciado's nomadic position and the author's ability to bring to light the political and economic systems that cause worldwide harm.

Wilson postulates that Preciado's writings advocate for solidarity among the oppressed (i.e., marginalized subjects such as refugees and animals) and call for revolution.

Brian J. Troth's article "Multiple Bodies: The Digital and the Physical in Arthur Cahn's *Les Vacances du petit Renard* (2018)" takes the prefix 'trans-' at its most literal meaning of being 'on the other side' or 'crossing' in order to analyze the type of body-switching that occurs in Cahn's novel. The fiction focuses on 14-year-old Paul who, during his summer stay at his aunt's in the south of France, decides to download the dating app Grindr to try to connect with Hervé, his aunt's 45-year-old best friend. While Troth acknowledges that the main protagonist is not transgender or transsexual, he is interested in exploring how Paul's use of Grindr to create a cyberself that is a collage of other men's pictures and identities operates along the line of "gender performativity" as conceptualized by Judith Butler. More particularly, Troth is interested in analyzing how the different avatars created by Paul cast new light on Butler's theory by incorporating the idea that all gender is a performance in today's digital world. By endorsing different digital identities, Paul creates multiple bodies that are both real (the images he uses can be traced back to actual people) and created (the men he pretends to be do not exist), which prompts Troth to write that, through his actions, this protagonist pushes the theories of gender performativity as well as the "body without organs," as defined by Gilles Deleuze and Félix Guatari. In so doing, Troth posits, Cahn's protagonist questions reality or, more precisely, what we deem as "real," and how today's connected world further complicates the ways we think of and conceptualize gender and identity.

Justine Huet's "Dubbing *Transparent* (2014–2019): A 'Ballsy' Translation?" brings an original take on the question of trans identities by focusing on the translation choices made for the French dubbing of Jill Soloway's ground-breaking series. By choosing to discuss the translation of transgender characters, her work analyzes an area of translation studies that has been given little academic attention so far. Using Lawrence Venuti's concept of "domestica-tion"—referring to the original version's "foreignness" and its manipulation and adaptation for the target audience—as the premise of her work, Huet interrogates to what extent the dubbing of the show is able to reflect the lived experience of the French transgender community. After highlighting some of the most salient sociocultural and political differences between France and the United States regarding transgender issues, Huet provides comparative analyses of the show's original dialogues and their dubbed version. What ensues from these analyses is that the choices made by the translation team reflect the fact that French society remains unfamiliar and resistant to non-normative identities. For Huet, the inconsistencies found in the dubbed version of *Transparent* are mainly rooted in France's conception of "citizenship" that is based on the ideology of universalism and its rejection of *"communita-risme"* understood as the action of putting forward the interests of a specific group or community at the expense of *"le bien commun"* (the common good) that has served as the foundation of French republicanism for centuries.

R. Cole Cridlin's "Trans(ing) the Rural: Metronormativity and Melancholia in Sébastien Lifshitz's *Wild Side* (2004)" analyzes the significance of the film's urban and rural settings in connection to the main character's subjectivity as a transgender woman who leaves Paris to return to her hometown in northern France to care for her dying mother. While other academic texts have discussed the representation of trans identity in Lifshitz's film, Cridlin's article casts light on an aspect of the film that has rarely been addressed, focusing on the relationship between the main character—Stéphanie—and her rural upbringing. According to Cridlin, the rural setting is significant in that it allows the viewer to catch a glimpse of Stéphanie's subjectivity, something that we are denied access to when she is represented in her urban setting. Complicating the concept of "metronormativity" coined by Jack Halberstam that describes the rural-to-urban migration narrative undertaken by most queer individuals, Cridlin explains that these two geographical settings need not be considered as irrevocably separate. For him, the use of flashbacks as a narrative device indicates that Stéphanie has never been able to leave her past behind altogether and that she therefore lives her life in a sort of limbo: unable to move past her rural childhood, she cannot fully inhabit the present time. Her existence is therefore defined by melancholia. The return to her roots will allow Stéphanie to grieve for a past that was still burdening her as an adult, allowing her to move forward with her life.

Laurel Iber's "Transfeminine Embodiment in the Films of Sébastien Lifshitz and Lukas Dhont" contemplates the representation of trans identities in Lifshitz's *Bambi* (2013) and *Petite fille* (2020) and Dhont's *Girl* (2018) to examine the cinematic staging of transfeminine embodiment through the lens of the following couplings: invisibility/visibility, reality/fiction, and lived identity/performance. While different in genre (two of the selected works are documentaries, while the other is a fiction) and tone, Iber posits that all three films present the viewer with stories centered around the tension between interiority and exteriority, the discontinuity between the two posing significant epistemological, ontological, and existential problems. Tying these films together is also the fact that each of the main characters alternatively experiences being unseen and excessively scrutinized, thus casting into relief the relationship between lived identity and gender performance.

In his article "Circus Freaks and Pretty Monsters: Fighting and Reclaiming a Transphobic Stigma," Arthur Ségard turns his attention to the rhetoric that has associated trans people with "monsters" or "freaks" in order to better understand the reversal of the stigma operated in some contemporary trans discourses. While offering a historical overview of transphobic stigma, Ségard observes how, from the nineteenth century to their public appearances in contemporary mainstream media, trans people were constructed as both monstrous and spectacular beings, the latter term being positively reclaimed by the cabaret culture of the 1950s, when the majority of performers (then called "*travestis*") adopted a strategy of visibility based on extravagant performances. Since the 1990s, Ségard observes, some trans intellectuals and activists have gone further by reclaiming the very discursive strategies that ostracized them and designated them as radically Other. The disruptive power of the monster, as someone who cannot be assigned a specific position within society, has been used by some trans people as a means of upsetting binary norms and carving out a space where subjectivities can be expressed. However, as Ségard notices, what now appears as a deliberate choice used to be an imposition from a patriarchal, heteronormative society. He thus offers caution as to the possible danger that could ensue from such linguistic reappropriation, as the stigma can still be used to reassert the dominance of the ruling class. This is especially true in a French context where any claim from specific groups or individuals can be perceived as a possible threat to republican universalism.

Annick Pellegrin approaches the questions of gender and sexuality through the medium of the *bande dessinée* (graphic novel) with her article "*Peau d'homme*: A Different Kind of Happy Ending." Focusing on the acclaimed work of the late graphic novelist and colorist Hubert, Pellegrin sets out to analyze how the use of the archetypal structure of the fairy tale allows Hubert to critique contemporary societal issues linked to LGBTQ+ rights in French society. Set in the Cinquecento, Hubert's *Peau d'homme* tells the story of Bianca, the daughter of a rich merchant, and Giovanni, the man she is promised to. Lamenting the fact that she never got to know the man she is supposed to marry, Bianca is given a "human skin"—the titular *peau d'homme*—from her godmother, in the form of a male bodysuit than enables her to transform into a man. According to Pellegrin, putting his protagonist in a position in which she can move freely between sexes and genders allows Hubert to offer a commentary on contemporary gender injustice, using the tropes of the fairy tale to make his message more appealing to a broader audience. Through its questioning of gender, sexuality, marriage, and family, Hubert's work can be seen as a response to the wave of protests that accompanied the legalization of same-sex marriage and adoption by same-sex couples in France in the early 2010s. As she demonstrates how Hubert resorts to the structure of the fairy tale to incorporate contemporary societal issues, Pellegrin also observes how *Peau d'homme* modernizes some traditional aspects of the fairy tale. Chiefly among them is its subversion of the traditional "happy ending."

NOTES

1. www.franceculture.fr/emissions/repliques/repliques-emission-du-samedi-11
-septembre-2021

2. It is to be noted that, prior to this debate, Finkielkraut had expressed his views on the question of trans identities in an interview he gave to Elisabeth Lévy in 2013 for the conservative magazine "Causeur." In this interview, Finkielkraut refers to the Romanticism movement and its conception of humanity to assert his idea that gender should not be understood as a cultural construct, but as a deeply historicized process that needs to be acknowledged and respected as such. For him, gender studies—through its questioning of gender as a binary construct—represents a denial of such historicity as well as an erasure of the concept of "otherness" which he perceives as a threat to identity formation. In the same interview, Finkielkraut also communicates his disapproval of gender theory being taught in primary schools, along with the questions of homosexuality and homophobia. (www.youtube.com/watch?v =qEBc6P9BvvE)

3. Two of Claude Habib's essays have attracted public attention over the years: *Le Consentement amoureux*, published in 1998, and more particularly *Galanterie française*, published in 2006. In the later work, Habib defends her vision of relationships between men and women steeped in the French concept of "galanterie" (gallantry) as it was established during the seventeenth and eighteenth centuries. Her ideas have come under attack in recent years, especially after the criminal case against Dominique Strauss-Kahn and the allegations of sexual assault and attempted rape made by Nafissatou Diallo, a housekeeper in his hotel suite. The concept of "galanterie" put forward by Habib has been strongly criticized as antifeminist and forming the bedrock of rape culture.

4. As noted by Karine Espineira in her text "Le Sein dans une perspective transgenre et intersexe," in French, the terms "transsexualité" and "transsexualisme" are used when referring to a medical procedure, namely that of gender reassignment surgery. She adds that, whenever we are referring to the lived experiences of trans people, the terms "transgenre" and "transidentité" are preferred. Espineira explains that the term "transidentité" tends to be favored among trans people, as it shifts the focus from the sexual to the personal and the identity formation process (see Espineira 2015, 179–98). More information will be provided further in this chapter regarding the terminological choices made.

5. "[une] transidentité acceptable et consensuelle."

6. While an in-depth analysis of this particular topic goes beyond the scope of this volume, it is important to mention that the stronghold of the medical and psychiatric fields over the destiny of trans people has long been criticized by the trans community. In August 2018, the radio show "LSD (La série documentaire)," broadcasted by the French public radio channel *France Culture*, dedicated a 4 hour-long series to trans identities in France. What makes this program particularly significant is that all the participants belong to the trans community. They were thus able to tell their own stories instead of having them co opted by cisgender people. The second installment of the series focused more particularly on the lasting impact of the state-mandated

procedures trans people had to conform to in order to undergo gender reassignment surgery. As a matter of fact, until 2016, "the nation state requir[ed] a number of normalizing criteria for an official change of sex—including sterility (e.g. a transman cannot get pregnant) and heterosexuality (e.g. a transwoman cannot be a lesbian)" (Reeser 2013, 6). In addition to this, some of the participants of the radio show mention the fact that certain medical procedures, such as vaginoplasty, were poorly executed, resulting in a number of medical complications such as necrosis.

7. A growing number of trans activists are refuting the idea that all trans people want to pass as either male or female. For many of them, gender identity and expression are not about conforming, and they consciously choose to present themselves in a way that does not conform to one of only two genders. Queer activist and theorist Sam Bourcier expressed this idea when he said, "passing is oppressive" and reinforces the gender binary (Bourcier 2005, 238).

8. Politicians also opposed the implementation of gender theory in the French curriculum on different occasions. As noted by Michael Stambolis-Ruhstorfer and Josselin Tricou: "In 2011, Philippe Gosselin, a conservative French MP, sounded alarms about a Ministry of Education plan to teach high school biology students the difference between sex and gender: 'The appearance of 'la théorie du genre' in biology textbooks [. . .] affirm[s] that gender identity is not a biological given but a social construction. This theory, born in the United States [. . .] [must] not be incorporated into biology textbooks'" (Stambolis-Ruhstorfer and Tricou 2017, 79).

9. One aspect of the curriculum decried by the protesters was the decision to include Céline Sciamma's film *Tomboy* (2011) to introduce schoolchildren to the socially constructed and performative aspect of gender. As Jennifer Vilchez writes: "the film is treated as a propaganda piece that would potentially instill the idea into the young students' mind that they can freely choose to be boys or girls regardless of sex—what gender theory is understood by the opponents of the film as promoting" (Vilchez 2015, 116).

10. The same idea is put forward by Camille Robcis when she says: "[. . .] the use of the English term 'gender' in France suggests that the concept is fundamentally alien to French society, ultimately untranslatable" (Duong 2014).

11. Stambolis-Ruhstorfer and Tricou note that, while the bill allowing same-sex marriage and adoption was passed, a significant percentage of the French population remained opposed to same-sex parenting: "[. . .] before 2008 and during the same-sex marriage debates in 2012 and 2013, majorities ranging from 67 to 54% of French respondents stated that they did not think same-sex couples should be allowed to adopt [. . .]" (Stambolis-Ruhstorfer and Tricou 2017, 83). Bruno Perreau reaches a similar conclusion when he writes: "[. . .] gay marriage ushered in a new legal era but did not alter the immunological impetus behind the way French national identity has been forged. The national body remains defined by its efforts to 'immunize' itself against minority cultures, in particular homosexuals [. . .] despite legal reforms, the 'straight mind'—that is, a mode of thought based on a reification of the difference between the sexes—continues to function as a political totem in France and the majority conceptualization of citizenship is as operative today as it was prior to marriage for all [. . .]" (Perreau 2016, 2–6).

12. The most recent example of this trend is the outcry that followed the inclusion of the gender-neutral pronouns "iel, ielle, iels, ielles" in the online edition of the French dictionary *Le Robert*. In a tweet dated from November 16th, 2021, Minister of Education Jean-Michel Blanquer expressed his disapproval, claiming that gender-inclusive writing was not the future of the French language ("L'écriture inclusive n'est pas l'avenir de la langue française"). For more information, see: theconversation.com/no-need-to-iel-why-france-is-so-angry-about-a-gender-neutral-pronoun-173304

13. "Les personnes transgenres sont distinguées des personnes transsexuelles selon le fait qu'elles aient recours ou non aux hormones et opérations. L'étude du terrain associatif et militant montre que la réalité est bien plus complexe et que les auto-identifications contredisent cette distinction. L'usage des termes transsexualité et transsexualisme peuvent être convoqués si l'on parle d'un concept et d'une pratique médicale [. . .] mais s'agissant des vécus et expériences identitaires, l'usage des termes 'transgenre' et 'transidentité' est préféré. Le terme transidentité semble être une spécificité française. Le mot est forgé par la sociologue Heike Boedeker, il est importé en France par le collectif strasbourgeois STS67 au début des années 2000. Tout comme le terme transgenre, il est à la fois un terme refuge ou parapluie [. . .] Il met en avant la construction de l'identité et s'attache au genre en se distinguant de la sexualité."

14. "Le préfixe 'trans' est associé au suffixe 'identité' depuis les années 2000 dans le contexte français, après avoir été associé à la sexualité (transsexualité) depuis les années 1950 et au genre (transgenre) depuis les années 1970 dans un contexte international. Ainsi, le terme de 'transidentité' est un terme parapluie dans lequel se reconnaissent des personnes transsexuelles et transgenres, ainsi que d'autres identités trans alternatives."

15. Arnaud Alessandrin and Karine Espineira clearly express this when they say that "[. . .] trans identity is plural, and [. . .] any attempt at trying to define it is limiting and subject to blind spots." ("[. . .] la transidentité est plurielle et [. . .] toute tentative définitionnelle se solde forcément par la consécration de points aveugles") (Alessandrin and Espineira 2015, para. 1).

16. In an article called "Les personnages trans dans les séries françaises" Karine Espineira analyzes some of the recurring thematic components that come into play when portraying trans characters in French TV shows. Her work reveals that trans characters are almost always associated with night life and tend to have a dramatic story arc, as they often end up being murdered or being a murderer themselves. She also writes that these TV shows almost exclusively tie trans people to transvestism (Espineira 2021).

17. On the topic of transidentities in the media, see the following works by Espineira: *La Transidentité. De l'espace médiatique à l'espace public* (L'Harmattan, 2008); *Quand la médiatisation fait genre. Médias, transgressions et négociations de genre* (L'Harmattan, coll. "Cahiers de la transidentité," 2014); *Médiacultures: La transidentité en télévision. Une recherche menée sur un corpus de l'INA* (1946–2010) (L'Harmattan, 2015).

18. Her work is based on audiovisual material found at the INA (National Audiovisual Institute), a repository of all French, radio, and television archives.

19. A famed performer, actress and singer, Coccinelle (1931–2006) is known as the first post-war gender reassignment patient in Europe.

20. Christine Jorgensen (1926–1989) was the first person to be widely known in the United States for having gender reassignment surgery.

21. As noted by Dwight B. Billings and Thomas Urban: "[. . .] transsexualism is a socially constructed reality which only exists in and through medical practice [. . .] The legitimisation, rationalisation, and commodification of sex-change operations have produced an identity category—transsexual [. . .]" (Billings and Urban 1996, 99–100).

22. While this goes beyond the scope of our analysis, it is interesting to note the comments made by Anson Koch-Rein, Elahe Haschemi Yekani and Jasper J. Verlinden about some of the dominant archetypes regarding the portrayals of trans people in American cinema as well as on television, in order to see how French and American productions diverge but also echo each other. They write: "For the longest time trans representations were closely tied to narrow and problematic depictions of gender non-conforming people as either dangerous psychopaths and sexual predators (e.g., *Silence of the Lambs* [1991] but also *Nip/Tuck* [2003–2010]) or as victims with little agency. These stories often relied heavily on now widely criticized 'wrong body' tropes of storytelling that reduced trans to transition" (Koch-Rein, Yekani and Verlinden 2020, 2).

23. Espineira's work on the representation of trans identities in the French media is particularly rich and wide-ranging, and cannot be circumscribed to the elements I chose to extract for the purpose of this introduction. However, regarding the connection established by the media between trans people and sex work, Espineira and Maude-Yeuse Thomas note that, between 1988 and 1992, news reports about "Le Bois de Boulogne" often associated trans people with sex workers and the AIDS pandemic (see Espineira and Thomas 2014, para. 24–25).

24. Koch-Rein et al. notice a similar imbalance regarding the representation of trans men in the American media: "[. . .] trans visibility remains often deeply and conflictingly gendered in a binary. This binary has long been characterised by a disproportionate, sensationalized visibility of (certain kinds of) trans femininities and a comparative lack of media attention to trans masculinities" (Koch-Rein et al. 2020, 4).

REFERENCES

"Alain Finkielkraut: la théorie du genre." *YouTube* video, 17.46. June 6, 2013. www .youtube.com/watch?v=qEBc6P9BvvE

Alessandrin, Arnaud, and Karine Espineira. 2015. "Des 'psys,' des theories et de la transphobie." In *Sociologie de la transphobie*. Pessac: Maison des Sciences de l'Homme d'Aquitaine. http://doi.org/10.4000/books.msha.4833

Billings, B. Dwight, and Thomas Urban. 1996. "Construction of Transsexualism. An Interpretation and Critique." In *Blending Genders: Social Aspects of Cross-Dressing and Sex-Changing*, edited by Richard Ekins and Dave King, 99–118. London: Routledge.

Bourcier, Sam. 2005. *Sexpolitiques, Queer zone 2*. Paris: La Fabrique.

Duong, Kevin. 2014. "Gender Trouble in France. An Interview with Camille Robcis." *Jacobin* (December 8, 2014). www.jacobinmag.com/2014/12/gender-trouble-in -france/

Espineira, Karine. 2021. "Les personnages trans dans les séries françaises." *Le Genre & l'écran* (October 31, 2021). www.genre-ecran.net/?Les-personnages-trans-dans -les-series-francaises

Espineira, Karine, and Maud-Yeuse Thomas. 2014. "Les Trans comme parias. Le Traitemtn médiatique de la sexualité des personnes trans en France." *Genre, sexualité & société* n°11 (July 1, 2014). doi.org/10.4000/gss.3126

Espineira, Karine. 2014a. "La Médiatisation des politiques transgenres: du statut de contre-public à l'inégalité de la representation." *Revue française des sciences de l'information et de la communication* 4 (January 1, 2014). doi.org/10.4000/ rfsic.695

Espineira, Karine. 2014b. "La Sexualité des sujets transgenres et transsexuels saisie par les médias." *Hermès, La Revue* n°69: 105–9.

Espineira, Karine. 2015. "Le Sein dans une perspective transgenre et intersexe." In *Le Sein: des mots pour le dire*, edited by Martine Sagaert and Natacha Ordioni, 179–98. Toulon: Laboratoire BABEL.

Hall, Stuart. 1982. "The Discovery of 'Ideology': Return of the Repressed in Media Studies." In *Culture, Society, and the Media*, edited by Michael Gurevitch, 56–90. London: Methuen.

Hart, Kylo-Patrick R. 2000. *The AIDS Movie. Representing a Pandemic in Film and Television*. New York and London: The Haworth Press.

Keegan, Cáel M., Laura Horak and Eliza Steinboch. 2018. "Cinematic/Trans*/Bodies Now (And Then, and to Come)." In *Somatechnics* 8 (1): 1–13.

Koch-Rein, Anson, Elahe Haschemi Yekani and Jasper J. Verlinden. 2020. "Representing Trans: Visibility and Its Discontents." In *European Journal of English Studies* 24 (1): 1–12.

Lefebvre, Edwige-Lilian. 2003. "Republicanism and Universalism: Factors of Inclusion or Exclusion in the French Concept of 'Citizenship.'" In *Citizenship Studies* 7 (1): 15–36.

Massel, Simon. 2014. "France Gives Way to Opponents of 'Gender Theory' in Schools." *The Conversation* (July 7, 2014). theconversation.com/ france-gives-way-to-opponents-of-gender-theory-in-schools-28641

McCaffrey, Enda. 2005. *The Gay Republic: Sexuality, Citizenship and Subversion in France*. Farnham, UK: Ashgate.

Muñoz, José E. 1999. *Disidentifications. Queers of Color and the Performance of Politics*. Minneapolis: Minneapolis University Press.

Perreau, Bruno. 2016. *Queer Theory: The French Response*. Stanford: Stanford University Press.

Reeser, Todd W. 2013. "*Trans*France." *L'Esprit créateur* 53 (1): 4–14.

Schofield, Hugh. 2021. "France Resists US Challenge to Its Values." *BBC News* (December 13, 2021). www.bbc.com/news/world-europe-59584125

Stambolis-Ruhstorfer, Michael and Josselin Tricou. 2017. "Resisting 'Gender Theory' in France: A Fulcrum for Religious Action in a Secular Society." In *Anti-Gender Campaigns in Europe: Mobilizing Against Equality*, edited by Roman Kuhar and David Paternotte, 79–98. Lanham, MD: Rowman & Littlefield.

Vilchez, Jennifer. 2015. "The Controversy Around *Tomboy*: The Aversion to Gender Theory in French Education and Culture." *Культура/Culture* 5 (12): 111–20.

Chapter 1

Trans Kids in France

Unpacking the Media Frenzy

Charlie Fabre

A cursory search for trans[1] youth within the history of French media quickly leads to the conclusion that it is a recent topic. Indeed, in a 2016 article, Arnaud Alessandrin traces this recent media crescendo back to a specific movie: Céline Sciamma's *Tomboy* (2011) with its character Mickaël, a nine-year-old child who decides to present as a boy despite their assigned gender after moving to a new neighborhood. In interviews, Sciamma has stated she does not perceive herself as an *avant-gardist* regarding the representation of trans children in the French media: she does not consider her movie to be about a trans child. According to her, "childhood is a time when we all play pretend [. . .] I wanted the transition from the personal to the universal to be able to continuously unfold" (Dokhan 2011; my translation).[2] Nevertheless, even if the director did not consider the film to constitute a "trans movie," this is the way it was perceived by the audience. The instant trans children became a cultural focus, however, they also became a target for conservatives in France. In particular, *Tomboy* caught the attention of certain political groups when the film became part of elementary school curricula in September 2012. By the end of 2013, a parent's letter pointing out the "dangers" of the movie soon led to a petition that gathered more than 15,000 signatures (Fabre 2011). As Bruno Perreau states in his book *Qui a peur de la théorie queer?* (2018), the reaction was mostly led by conservative movements such as "La Manif Pour Tous," a group known for its virulent opposition to marriage equality (59). Other alt-right movement such as L'UNI (*Union Nationale Interuniversitaire*) attempted to trace a link between *Tomboy* and "*la théorie du genre*" (Caillaud 2013). At the time, many media outlets took part in questioning the "controversial" (Doiezie 2013) aspects of the movie and the "scandal" (Brizard 2014) that emerged from it.

It is no surprise that telling a queer story rooted in childhood provokes reactions in society. Childhood often "appears to be the ideal vehicle for directors to reflect upon today's society and some of its most sensitive issues" (Chareyron 2019, 8). Queer children, both "feared and admired," (Perreau 2018, 59) therefore find themselves at the heart of controversy. A study by Alessandrin (2016) identifies only two instances in the media in the four years following *Tomboy* in which trans youth constitute the central theme: one online article in the French edition of *Slate* and one reality show (*Les Maternelles*).[3] It is therefore clear that despite the point of departure established by Sciamma's film, it did not immediately represent an explosive moment in the French media. The topic was subsequently brought to light with the documentary *Devenir il ou elle* (Debaisieux 2017), but it was only at the end of 2020 and the beginning of 2021 when trans youth began to receive a large amount of media attention.

The current article examines this recent and sudden shift of the public eye which on one hand can be characterized by the normalization of trans existences through the *born-this-way* narrative. As stated by Simon Copland in *The Guardian*:

> Over the past decade the idea that we are "born this way"—or that our sexuality is genetic—has become increasingly important. The mantra has become a political strategy, in particular for gay and lesbian communities, who see it as a way to protect themselves from discrimination. (Copland 2015)

Although science offers no strong answers to the theory, it is still widely popular, especially in mainstream media, and is applied to trans communities as well. Nevertheless, a heated public debate currently unfolds regarding trans children's very existence, creating a sense of anxiety that further fuels the media attention directed toward this group.

The current article also raises ethical questions regarding the representation of trans children in the French media. Indeed, in 2008, the CSA (*Conseil Supérieur de l'Audiovisuel*, the French public authority in charge of regulating audiovisual content) published guidelines regarding "the involvement of minors on television."[4] There are two aspects of this charter that will be especially important for our study. First, it emphasizes the "sensitivity and vulnerability of children" and sets ground rules for their safety, stating, for example, that TV shows involving minors should neither dramatize nor mock a child's personal story. Furthermore, it specifies that the narrative surrounding a minor's involvement should not be reduced to the difficulties the child faces in their life. We highlight these two specific points because they rarely seem to be respected when it comes to the representation of trans children. One important example we will examine is the media coverage surrounding Lilie, an eight-year-old trans girl. In 2020, Lilie and her supportive parents struggled for her legal recognition as a girl.[5] The family suffered discrimination from Lilie's school and the judiciary system, both refusing to recognize her chosen name. Eventually, the school accepted. Her official documents, however, still bear her deadname.[6] We will explore how Lilie's story evolved from a single TV report to a media frenzy, and how the coverage was solely focused on her struggles, therefore often leading to a melodramatization of her story.

Finally, the notion of "cis gaze" will be a key element of our analysis:

> The *cis gaze* defines the way in which trans people are represented in film, aiming to titillate the cis audience and the cis-normative gaze while never calling into question the hegemony of this gaze. Such stereotypical representations conform to the established range of acceptance towards trans people in a society. (Fabre 2020)

A cis-centered narrative meant for a cis audience leads to biased media coverage of trans children's stories. We will see the pernicious way this normative bias applies when trans children are not granted the power of self-expression.

Before examining the shift that occurred in 2020 and the elements that brought us to that observation, we will place our very recent corpus into a historical, social and political context. In order to do so, we will examine the events surrounding trans representation in the French media, drawing upon the work of Karine Espineira on French TV archives. We will also consider the current social and political context surrounding the existence of trans children, often subject to the obsessive attention of alt-right groups. After establishing the context, we will move on to our main corpus concerning the media coverage around Lilie's story. After a discussion of Sébastien Lifshitz's documentary *Petite Fille* (Arte, December 2nd, 2020), we will clarify the importance of social media as well as the media treatment of young trans women's deaths. In the end, this will allow us to unpack the current relevance of trans youth media representation.

CONTEXTUALIZING TRANS YOUTH EXPOSURE

A common reaction to the increased visibility of trans communities is to deny that trans children existed before this heightened exposure (Levin 2021). Their "novel" existence is instead argued to be the result of what conservatives have coined the *trans lobby*, imported from American individualism

(Flavigny 2021) and in opposition to French universalism (Fassin 2001, 215–32). While the idea is mainly rooted in alt-right ideology, it has infused a broader portion of the population. Media coverage surrounding trans issues in the twentieth and early twenty-first century had an important part to play in that misconception, shaping today's discourses about trans children.

1946–2021: From Invisibility to Hypervisibility

When it comes to examining trans representation in the French media, Karine Espineira's work on TV archives (2015) from 1946 to 2010 cannot be overlooked. The French-Chilean researcher examines different periods in the representation of trans individuals and trans identities, as determined by sociopolitical context (Espineira 2015, 76–78). Her work shows that, through time, trans representation has undergone a semantic change in the way it has been addressed in the media, first occupying the space dedicated to minor news items (*"faits divers"*), then those for social issues (*"faits de société"*), and finally finding a place within the larger equal rights movement (see Espineira 2014, 35–47). Espineira advocates for media representation that "goes beyond voyeurism" (see Espineira 2014, 35–47). Nevertheless, a mismatch emerges between the mediatization of trans identities and that of children that limits any advancement in the representation of trans children. Espineira's research reveals a marked absence of trans young people in the French media coverage of trans identities from 1946 to 2010. This lack is perhaps explained by the topics most central to the corpus—sex work and political battles, for the most part[7]—which tend to exclude children. Even so, such are the topics upon which trans visibility was developed for decades, making it even harder to include the question of trans childhood. If trans kids have always existed, they have not been portrayed, let alone given the space to speak for themselves in the French media.

Yet, as stated in our introduction, the situation has shifted, slightly at first, between the years of 2011 and 2016, and then more abruptly in the last months of 2020. The term "hypervisibility" refers to a notion coined by Julianne Pidduck in order to describe the "sea change in the [. . .] re/production and dissemination of images of same-sex desire and identity" (Pidduck 2011, 9). She writes:

> In contrast with cultural and historical contexts where same-sex desires and lesbian and gay identities are or were invisible (or unspeakable), the prefix "hyper" points to a new order of excessive visibility. (Pidduck 2011, 9)

It seems like that idea of an abrupt change leading to a broad and sudden visibility very accurately describes the situation of trans children's visibility in the French media. Because it appears that we are at (the beginning of) a key moment, our corpus focuses on very recent instances of trans child representation (between 2020 and the first half of 2021). However, before visiting the corpus, we will take a moment to describe the violent reactions faced by trans kids when their visibility increases, as excessive exposure can imply harm.

WHEN MORE EXPOSURE MEANS MORE HATRED

The topic at hand takes on a new significance in a political and social climate in which right-wing politicians and so-called feminist movements[8] have been trying (sometimes successfully) to harm trans children's rights. Such was the case in the United States when Arkansas banned hormones and puberty blockers for trans minors the day before the International Trans Day of Visibility in 2021(Scheffer 2021), and in the United Kingdom, when the Bell vs. Tavistock case led to forbidding minors' access to hormonal treatments and puberty blockers before the decision was successfully appealed (mermaidsuk.org 2021).

In France, the political focus on trans youth is mainly visible through the media coverage of the matter. Indeed, during my research on trans children's representation in the country's media, I became sidetracked by an endless spiral of transphobic articles. There would be a lot to say about the obsession for trans youth held by certain newspapers. For instance, the subject was widely discussed in *Marianne* (a left-wing news magazine) in 2020 and the first months of 2021. One editorial expounds upon "The evolution of 'gender dysphoria' diagnoses on children in the last ten years" and how important it is for us, as a society, to "regain our sense of responsibility [. . .] in order to protect our young people" (Cognet, Eliacheff, and Masson 2021). Additionally, I witnessed a pervasive sense of worry among many people, based on a limited view of trans. One article stated there was "a misunderstanding of what is happening among children and teenagers who feel uncomfortable in their male or female bodies. They are claimed to be 'transgender,' or victims of what American culture sees as Nature getting it wrong: putting a boy's soul in a girl's body, or vice versa" (Flavigny 2021). Another article was convinced of a movement where "if a little boy likes to play with his kitchen set, his body will be chemically corrected to look like a little girl" (Go 2021). On May 27th, 2021, the alt-right magazine *Valeurs Actuelles* struck hard with its cover about "the transgender delusion," an issue containing articles about the "transgender madness" (D'Ornellas 2021) and more.

Throughout this biased rhetoric, we must point out that none of the authors of these articles is a specialist in trans studies. If they were, they would know that no trans activist has ever said that if a boy played with a kitchen set, he should go on HRT immediately. They would also be aware of the fact that French legislation does not allow children to undergo "chemical correction" until at least the age of sixteen. Puberty blockers can be taken earlier but both these and hormonal treatments require the approval of all legal guardians. Furthermore, minors' transitions are even more closely monitored by medical and psychiatric professionals than adults' (Folden 2020). The authors of these articles are giving their opinions on a subject they have no more knowledge on than I might have about soccer. In any case, just like the polemical debates that emerged following *Tomboy*, they represent ignorant reactions to our subject, and do not constitute the direct representation of trans children in the media. They simply serve as an indicator of the political and social climate in which this article was written.

Moreover, those articles exist in a context in which intolerance against trans people seems to be the norm in France. In August 2021, the country ranked at the bottom of a British study on the acceptance of LGBT+ people by members of their own families. According to that study, less than half of the French population were sure as to whether they would be supportive of a family member coming out as trans, while 27 percent stated they would not be supportive at all (Nolsoe 2021).

TRANS YOUTH MEDIA COVERAGE
BETWEEN 2020 AND 2021

This research is in part motivated by the context and an intuition that we are at a historical turning point[9] in trans representation, one that is focused on children. The basis of this intuition is one specific story—Lilie's—which took on enormous proportions in local and national media during the second half of 2020. These months were also marked by the release of the documentary *Petite Fille*. In this movie, Sébastien Lifshitz follows Sasha, a very young trans girl, and her family. Just as in the case of Lilie, the mother occupies a central role in the story as it follows her learning more about her child and about transness. Finally, while all this was trending, social networks also played a role in bringing trans youth into the public eye. This section focuses on these elements to reveal the significance the subject holds in the current climate. We will also make a direct link with the media coverage around the suicide of two young trans women that occurred in the same period.

LILIE AND SASHA: HOW LITTLE GIRLS BECAME
ICONS OF TRANS KIDS' STRUGGLES

Lilie's story was indeed the spark that led mainstream media to focus their coverage on the various views surrounding trans minors. Whether it was TV, radio, newspapers, or social media, a large number of headlines were focused on Lilie's story. The exposure was especially important at two key moments: between September and December 2020, after Lilie's mother's first appearance on *BFMTV* (a French news channel) in order to increase awareness of her family's struggle, and around March 8th, 2021, when the legal decision to refuse Lilie's name change was announced. The table on the following page details the media coverage at those two moments.

The table shows an important variety in the media coverage of Lilie's story. Evidently, there is diversity in the medium used, but not only that. It is apparent that the story captured the attention of regional media (*La Provence*, *France Bleu*) as much as national outlets (*L'Obs*, *C8*, *TF1*), global media (*Le Monde*, *Le Parisien*), and magazines (*Marie Claire*, *Terrafemina*, *Parents Magazine*). We can also point to the political diversity of the sources. The story was all over the spectrum, from far-right (*Valeurs Actuelles*) and right-wing media (*Le Figaro*) to centrist (*Le Monde*) and publications on the left (*L'Obs*).[10]

The headlines, however, were not as varied and mostly made specific reference to Lilie's age, especially in March's occurrences. Indeed, nine media sources among the twenty-six from March mention her age. The others use vocabulary such as "*petite fille*" or even "*fillette*" which both can be translated as "little girl," the second form being more informal and even slightly pejorative. The focus on her young age is not simply a statement of fact: it can also be perceived as a means to emphasize her youngness. Displaying this information in a headline enables online readers to react strongly without having read the article. As the information is propagated, it acquires more and more viewers, generating mass anxiety around the idea that 8 years old is "too young to be trans." The media exposure of her parents plays into this angst as it leads people to search for a rational explanation: Lilie is too young, but her parents are not; perhaps it is their fault. Another, more sympathetic, interpretation views the presence of a parental figure as reassuring: maybe Lilie is "too young to be trans," but at least her parents love her, and she will be fine.[11] In any case, we can note that the first TV appearances on *BFMTV*, *Quotidien* and *Sept à Huit* laid bare Lilie's parents' story and struggle as much as Lilie's.

Finally, returning to the language used by the headlines, it can be observed that certain outdated expressions are still popular among journalists. Among all the quoted headlines about Lilie, eight of them mention that *she used to be*

Table 1.1. Media coverage of Lilie's story between 2020 and 2021

	Television	Radio	Newspaper	Social Media
Last half of 2020	**September 9th, 2020,** BFMTV **September 13th, 2020,** Sept à Huit, TF1 **October 6th, 2020,** Quotidien, TF1 **November 13th, 2020,** ça commence aujourd'hui, France TV	**September 9th, 2020,** RMC Découverte	**September 10th, 2020,** La Provence **September 11th, 2020,** Terrafemina **September 17th, 2020,** Le Monde **October 7th, 2020,** Valeurs Actuelles **October 8th, 2020,** Le Figaro **October 16th, 2020,** Marianne **November 5th, 2020,** L'Obs **December 15th, 2020,** Le Point	**September 10th, 2020,** aufeminin.com **September 11th, 2020,** PositivR **September 23rd, 2020,** Konbini
March to May, 2021	**March 9th, 2021,** BFMTV **March 11th, 2021,** France 3 PACA **March 21st, 2021,** Touche pas à mon poste, C8	**March 9th, 2021,** RMC Découverte **March 9th, 2021,** France Bleu	**March 9th, 2021** • L'Obs • Ouest France • Le Parisien • La Nouvelle République • Le Dauphiné Libéré • La Voix du Nord **March 10th, 2021,** • Marie Claire • Sud Ouest • La Dépêche • Actu Marseille • Femme Actuelle • Le Journal des Femmes • Midi Libre • Magic Maman **March 11th, 2021** • Parents Magazine • Terrafemina • Supers Parents	**March 10th, 2021,** Oh My Mag

a boy, she has the body of a boy or that *she was born a boy*. We can also note that, even though French is a highly gendered language, the media are some-times capable of neutralizing gender when it does not suit them to employ a trans person's correct pronouns and gender agreement. For instance, even without the eight headlines that explicitly misgender Lilie, we are left with seventeen headlines that refer to her as a *trans child* or using transgender as a noun[12] instead of asserting that she is a girl or at least a trans girl. Out of the thirty-nine occurrences included in the study, only fourteen affirmed Lilie's true gender.

As shown in the table, a lesser amount of TV coverage is observed during the second period, but a larger variety of media sources are present. We can also note that some media such as *BFMTV, RMC Découverte* (radio broad-casted on BFM's website) *Terrafemina* or *L'Obs* appear in both periods, per-haps indicating a more attentive approach that necessitated a follow-up story. Finally, it is also interesting to note that afterwards, in their articles about trans youth that had nothing to do with Lilie, some media outlets kept using her pictures in their headings, as was the case for *Valeurs Actuelles*.

The number of occurrences (sixteen during the first period, twenty-three during the second) is substantially noteworthy compared to the overall vis-ibility of trans issues in general. This bolsters our view that this constitutes an event of significance. By comparison, Espineira's discussion of the peak media coverage surrounding trans sex-workers in *le bois de Boulogne* between 1988 and 1992 estimates an average number of twenty-one instances per year (Espineira 2015, 76). If we consider September 2020 to March 2021 as a peak for trans youth representation, Lilie's story alone represents almost twice that amount.

Finally, our tools of study are not able to reveal something that was in fact quite important to the impact of that story: the numerous private pages and organizations who shared it on their networks especially thanks to social media coverage. In order to estimate the importance of such social networks, it may be considered that *Konbini*'s original video about Lilie was viewed 5,831,648 times. To put it in perspective, that is more than the number of people who went to see Marvel's *Avengers: Infinity War* (2018), in France (5,044,429).[13]

A second story was at the center of trans children's representation in December 2020, that of Sasha, the main character of Sébastien Lifshitz's documentary, *Petite Fille*. The movie benefited from wide media coverage following its first screening on Arte's website and TV channel[14] and later its appearance on the French Netflix catalog (March 15th, 2021). Once again, the media coverage of the subject brought it to the radio (*France Inter*, December 2nd, 2020), online media (*Slate*, December 2nd, 2020; *Mediapart*, December 28th, 2020), specialized newspapers (*Télérama*, December 2nd, 2020) and ones in general circulation (*Le Monde*, November 24th, 2020), from the left (*Libération*, November 29th, 2020) to the right political spectrum (*Causeur*, March 26th, 2021).

With *Petite Fille*, Lifshitz portrays Sasha with the gaze of an adult cisgender man. This can be seen through the multiple scenes in which we see Sasha getting dressed, the amount of dialogue given to adults as opposed to Sasha, the emphasis on the mother's struggle, and the scenes of vulnerability in which Sasha is depicted (crying, getting naked and dressed, etc.) The intention of the film is to build empathy for the daughter and her family. To do so, the director emphasizes Sasha's struggles, not only going against the CSA's principles but also aligning his film to a history of trans representation focused on the community's struggles. Here, we can evoke the cis gaze as such a narrative satisfies the cisgender audience's assumptions about a trans story: that trans lives should be full of difficulty and strife, not only for the individual but also (if not mostly) for their relatives, and that trans people's bodies are not their own to protect. These beliefs stand out even more so in the context of trans children as children's bodies and lives are perceived as belonging to their parents rather than to themselves.

Both Sasha and Lilie are young girls from supportive families contending with authorities who refuse to recognize their true identities. This moment could have served as an opportunity to deepen the conversation about the work left to do on a political level regarding trans rights, but instead the discourse remained quite shallow. In particular, the highly charged reactions on social media were infused with alt-right ideas, such as those mentioned earlier. Public opinion seemed to be torn regarding the question of trans identity in childhood. For example, a quick internet search for "articles about *Petite Fille*" gives us headings lauding the documentary as "a trans child's radiant origin story" (Mendelbaum 2020) or "brilliant portrait of a unique kid" (Ekchajzer 2020) while others issue warnings about its dogmatic "proselytism" (Lebreton 2020). The coverage wavers between praise and terror. Such appeals to sentiment never question the system leading these two families to reach out for media visibility as they lack the basic resources required to help their daughters.

The use of the word "icon" to describe Sasha and Lilie earlier in this article was a very conscious choice on our part. The media capitalized on their pictures, their names, and, as we saw earlier, the "trans child" tagline. As seen in the headlines and content, it is clear that the media across the political spectrum misappropriated their stories with questions and viewpoints founded on preconceived notions. They gave more space to the daughters' parents and to doctors and psychologists than to the actual subjects, and in so doing, they rendered the girls hypervisible. Indeed, Lilie and Sasha were very much seen, but never heard. The girls never became torchbearers or spokespeople for the cause as they were not granted a space to express themselves and their needs, nor did their visibility make ground for political progress. Instead, the impact of their media coverage appears to be much more superficial.

The end of 2020 emerges as a turning point regarding the media coverage of trans kids, with the far-reaching media coverage surrounding Lilie in the last half of 2020, the release of *Petite Fille*, along with various other stories.[15] As after any media craze, the trend lingered, and in the beginning of 2021, the topic still received airtime on major national TV channels such as *TF1*[16] or *France 5*.[17] A second peak materializes in March 2021, once again linked to Lilie's story. All the while, the input of social media on the matter was quite important throughout the whole period.

THE IMPACT OF SOCIAL MEDIA

Social media content creators such as Brut,[18] Konbini,[19] or the LGBTIAQ+ video creator PAINT[20] helped to drive the (hyper)exposure of trans youth in the media. A common theme can often be identified throughout the comments, in the depiction of the content or in the content itself: normalization. At a first glance, it may seem that there is no harm in wanting to normalize the very existence of a part of the population that has been, and still is, wounded by structural transphobia. Normalizing and dismantling prejudices about a marginalized community can be a way to decrease the uneasiness surrounding it. We will turn a critical eye to the phenomenon of normalization by discussing the videos created by PAINT media, which represent both trans young people and their parents or family members.

While Lilie's story circulated in the media, a series of videos entitled "Mom/Grandma, I am transgender" were released by PAINT from September to December, 2020.[21] Being a LGBTIAQ+ organization, PAINT's videos and headlines are entirely focused on LGBTIAQ+ content. The "Mom/Grandma, I am transgender" videos were part of a larger campaign that was not solely about trans people, as it was also featuring content like "Mom/Grandma, I am gay." PAINT's explicit goal is to normalize LGBTIAQ+ narratives through visibility and the telling of everyday stories. With this in mind, we can more closely examine the three videos, "Mom, I am non-binary," "Grandma, I am transgender" and "Mom, I am transgender," which represent three trans-masculine teenagers whose ages are not explicitly mentioned but appear to be between 14 and 17 years old. In many ways, those videos correspond to what a cisgender audience might expect when encountering a trans person, as illustrated by the commonalities that emerge:

- two of the three videos start with the teenagers defining certain terms (what is transgender? non-binary? cisgender?);
- all three feature coming-out stories;
- all three highlight the mental health struggles the teens went through before coming out;
- all three videos emphasize the parents' struggle ("I birthed you as a girl," "I saw you being born a girl," "I called you that name for fourteen years") and the efforts they have taken (the idea of making mistakes but "being careful" is repeated almost word-for-word in every video);
- in all three, the parents talk about how "unimaginable" it is to reject your kids for who they are.

The last two points are key elements in capturing the essence of the normalization narrative. By aiming its attention on the parents, the narrative is meant to help cisgender people understand transness. However, the type of empathy that is fostered when the audience is met with individuals onscreen who have a limited understanding of trans (but still love their trans kids regardless) tends to be overly simplified. It seems easier for cisgender people to feel close to other cisgender adults than to a trans child alone. Here, a link can be drawn to the French government's social awareness campaign in May 2021, bearing messages such as "yes, my granddaughter is trans."[22] In the posters, the face of the girl is hidden, and only the smiling face of the grandmother is visible, garnering sympathy from the cis public. Moreover, even if the intended audience in these cases seems evident, we can offer further critique by calling attention to the fact that presenting trans teens with their mothers or grandmothers serves only to infantilize them.

The bias inherent to narratives that center around trans people's relatives is not specific to France nor the news media. For example, it is very often the case in fiction. To return to our very first example of the film *Tomboy*, even though the film's protagonist is Mickaël, the reaction of the mother plays an important role in the cisgender audience's reception of the film. We can find further evidence in our corpus: in Lifshitz's documentary, it is the mother who is given the most speaking time, and we saw earlier the importance of motherhood in the coverage surrounding Lilie.

To see a parent reacting in a negative way or being allowed to misgender their child because it is hard for them to change (in PAINT's videos, one mother even tells her child it is as hard as transitioning) is the kind of thing other cisgender parents might rely on to satisfy their confirmation bias. This focus on the trans person's relatives is also part of a broader approach taken by the media that is entangled with a cis-centered gaze (see Fabre 2020). Whether the parents are supportive or not, the media tends to give priority to their feelings to the detriment of the trans children. The same disregard is even more apparent in the case of the trans children's thoughts and opinions.

GRIEVING AND DEMANDING RESPECT:
HOW THE MEDIA TREATS OUR DEAD SISTERS

What we have seen from the analysis of trans youth visibility so far is an absence of the voices of the most involved. The media coverage of young people might be a way of normalizing trans lives by essentializing them through the reinforcement of the "born-this-way" theory, but those who are brought into the open are disowned from their own narrative. This approach also allows the media to exclude all political aspects from trans existences. While young trans people remain at a higher risk of dying by suicide than the rest of the population,[23] our (here referring the trans community to which I belong) lives are used to reassure cis people by allowing them *to talk about us without us*. As Jules Gill-Peterson—a scholar of transgender history—puts it in her *Guardian* interview: "children are really easy targets, because we don't grant them the privilege to speak for themselves and defend their own interests." (Levin 2021). This notion is conspicuous throughout the current article, as we evoked the ways in which Sasha and Lilie were denied the power to speak for themselves, as were the teens interviewed for PAINT whose voices simply served to reassure cis people about their understanding of transness.

Above all this, when the media talks about young trans people more than usual, it is often after a young trans person has died. Between September and December 2020, the time points used in our corpus, at least two young trans girls, Doona and Fouad, died by suicide. Their deaths set off large protests in the trans community as they were disrespected in the media who employed their deadnames and gender assigned at birth. This occurred even after the AJL (*Association des Journalistes LGBTI+*) had released a public guide meant to help the media with the treatment of trans subjects. In this guide, it is specified, for example, that "in France, legal status is very often only modified months or even years after trans people have legally changed their names" (AJLGBT 2019) and highlights the fact that using a trans person's deadname is harmful and counterproductive.

In Doona's case, most media outlets changed their articles and headlines after dozens of trans people sent them messages calling them out on their transphobia. After her suicide, one local newspaper, *Metropolitain Montpellier*, admitted they had only changed their headline because they had been "harassed," not out of respect for the victim who, according to them, was "still a man as there had been no official process of becoming a woman."

They also accused the trans community of not respecting the family's grief.[24] I am compelled to articulate the devastating violence of not being able to grieve as a community because you must worry whether the media will offer the proper respect to the person who has just died.

The point here is not to treat Doona and Fouad like children by placing them in comparison with Lilie and Sasha; however, they were also young women. As Karine Espineira puts it, the media are still looking for what is "reasonable and consensual" to show when talking about trans youth. It seems it is not reasonable to bring up the structural discrimination, the political violence, the transphobic administration, etc., in such terms.

SO, WHAT IS THIS ALL FOR?

The present observations lead us to wonder what the goal was when the media decided to extend their coverage to trans children if it was not to amplify their voices nor provoke reactions beyond public (uneducated) debate. None of the media coverage, whether it was centered around a family's fight for their children's rights or around suicide, resulted in political decisions that could prevent such situations from happening in the future.

Certainly, it is not the media's responsibility to take up the fight for trans causes, but they are guilty of choosing not to give visibility to organizations that do. They are guilty of endangering the public image of transness by disengaging it from any political or communitarian perspective, and of often placing the burden of an entire societal issue on a single person, often a very young one, simply for views, clicks, and reactions. The current media coverage of trans children in France increases exposure without dealing with the growing vulnerability that is its inevitable result. The media reap the benefit from a hot-button issue without moderating the social media conversation or caring about who they give a platform to. For example, the French television show *Quotidien*, who promoted Lilie's story, later invited French historian and psychoanalyst Elizabeth Roudinesco on stage to speak about a "pandemic of transgenders" (Coutures 2020). Such examples, added to the openly transphobic articles we examined earlier, make us question the normalization tactic. There seems to be a strong denial surrounding the existence of trans children and as such, a strong denial of their rights from a large part of the population. Instead of bringing society to a greater acceptance and understanding of transness, it gives certain individuals more space to brandish their uninhibited transphobia. To those people, we can do no better than to quote Julia Serano as she writes, "if you are actually concerned about transgender and gender non-conforming people—whether they be children or adults—then I suggest that you stop fretting over the 'cisgender-people-turned-transgender' trope, and instead work to help end transphobia once and for all" (Serano 2016).

The cases examined in the current article offer support to our initial intuition: we are indeed at a turning point for trans representation, and that turning point involves an increased representation of trans children. Trans youth media visibility as it exists right now enables transphobic discourses to intensify without meeting real opposition, but trans kids should not be deprived of visibility as a result. Indeed, trans youth is a reality and always has been. Trans youth visibility is therefore vital and should be allowed to exist, as it allows more trans people to come to a fuller understanding of themselves. Unlike what is happening in the current moment, trans kids should not be used by the media as a pretext to secure more viewers. Trans children should be given a voice instead of being seen as objects. They should never be instrumentalized and used to silence the political existence of the trans community. Most importantly, we must turn the tables on transphobic discourses that frame trans youth as a societal problem.

NOTES

1. The term "trans" will be used to cover all identities that fall outside the cisgender binary logic.

2. Unless indicated otherwise, all translations of French texts are mine.

3. The article, called "La Souffrance des entrants trans" was published on December 11, 2014 (http://slate.fr/story/95615/les-enfants-trans) and the TV segment dedicated to trans children and called "Mon fils voudrait être une fille" was broadcasted on October 22, 2015.

4. For more information, see "Charte du 24 novembre 2008 relative à la participation de mineurs à des émissions de télévision," CSA, November 24, 2008, www.csa .fr/Arbitrer/Espace-juridique/Les-relations-du-CSA-avec-les-editeurs/Chartes/Charte -relative-a-la-participation-de-mineurs-a-des-emissions-de-television-Novembre -2008

5. For all information regarding the topics of name and gender identity under the French legislation, refer to chrysalide-asso.fr/identite/

6. The deadname of a trans person is the name they were given at birth but which they may choose not to use after finding a name that better fits their identity, at which point the name no longer corresponds to the person. Using a person's deadname is a common form of transphobia.

7. Espineira's analysis shows fourteen occurrences of trans-related content between 1975 and 1977. That's three more than during the 1946 to 1974 period. She links it with the media coverage of sex work in Marseille. There was later, between 1988 and 1992, a broad media coverage of *le Bois de Boulogne*, a well-known place of sex work, and then again it can be linked to a growth in trans occurrences in media

(twenty-eight in 1992 while only seven in 1993). In 1995, with the media coverage surrounding the creation of the first organizations for trans rights, the numbers went from seventeen (1994) to fifty-five (1995). The same logic is observed until 2010. (Espineira 2015, 76–77)

8. See Caroline Ffiske's article, published in 2020, "Keira Bell has led. The rest of us must follow, or collude in harm," discloses a trans-exclusionary discourse. The TERF (Trans Exclusionary Radical Feminism) movement is well-known for its rhetoric, depicting trans people (and especially trans women) as gender traitors and/ or predators. They tend to present trans identity as a threat to the class of women (for example Ffiske wrote another article titled "Who will defend women's rights from the trans lobby?") and young people. Ffiske's article is just an example of such beliefs. Her rhetorics can be linked with other TERF groups or individuals such as the Radfem collective, well-known for its essentialist positions.

9. The idea of a *turning point* in trans representation was used by the *Time Magazine* in 2016 to talk about the growing cultural impact of trans figures in the United States. For more information, see Karine Espineira's article "La médiatisation des 'enfants et ados trans': des écrans télés aux chaînes YouTube, se raconter et s'affirmer au présent" (62–63).

10. That political compass is based on French political orientations. A list of media political orientation can be found on: www.integrersciencespo.fr/orientations -politiques-de-la-presse-etrangere-et-francaise#Orientations_des_journaux_francais

11. Those comments can be found on the Facebook page of *Konbini News* (www .facebook.com/konbininews/videos/lilie-8-ans-n%C3%A9e-avec-un-genre-qui-nest -pas-le-sien-reportage/631524110818998/).

12. "Transgender" is meant to be used as an adjective.

13. According to *Allociné*'s data on *Avengers: Infinity War* (www.allocine.fr/film/ fichefilm-218265/box-office/).

14. When it was first broadcasted on television, on December 2, 2020, *Petite fille* achieved the best audience of the year for a documentary in primetime, with 1,375,000 viewers.

15. Agathe Lecaron, "Mon enfant est transgenre," *La Maison des Parents, France 5*, October 14, 2020.

16. Harry Roselmack, "Le combat des enfants transgenres," *Sept à Huit, TF1*, February 28, 2021.

17. Anne-Elisabeth Lemoine, "La nouvelle vie de Stella, enfant transgenre," *C à vous, France 5*, February 25, 2021.

18. Pauline Normand, "7 questions très simples sur la transidentité," *Brut*, November 27, 2020.

19. Mathieu Habasque and Jean-Victor Houët, "Lilie, 8 ans, née avec un genre qui n'est pas le sien," *Konbini news*, September 20, 2020.

20. Instagram account of the social media PAINT: @ paint.official.

21. "Maman, je suis non-binaire," *PAINT*, September 2, 2020 (www.youtube.com /watch?v=IJjpl6XDTbs);

"Mamie, je suis transgenre," *PAINT*, September 30, 2020 (www.youtube.com/ watch?v=3oxTW9p1P-s);

"Maman, je suis transgenre," *PAINT*, December 15, 2020 (www.youtube.com/watch?v=vF9Zrt7nR0s)

22. A copy of the poster can be accessed at the following link: www.santepubliquefrance.fr/docs/oui-ma-petite-fille-est-trans.-affiche-60x80cm

23. Every year the trans community mourns on Trans Day of Remembrance for all those who killed themselves or were murdered because of transphobia. In 2020, at least 350 trans people, mostly women, were on that list.

24. Screen captures of the conversation were posted on the Facebook page "Support Your Local Girl Gang" on September 24, 2020: www.facebook.com/supportyourgirlgang/photos/pcb.803933727021852/803933663688525/

REFERENCES

AJLGBT (Association des journalistes lesbiennes, gays, bi.e.s, trans et intersexes). 2019. "Respecter les personnes trans." October 17, 2019. www.ajlgbt.info/informer-sans-discriminer/respecter-les-personnes-trans/

Alessandrin, Arnaud. 2016. "Mineurs trans: de l'inconvénient de ne pas être pris en compte par les politiques publiques." *Agora débats / Jeunesses* n°73: 7–20.

Brizard, Caroline. 2014. "*Tomboy* diffusé dans les écoles, un scandale?"*L'Obs*, January 7, 2014 www.nouvelobs.com/education/20140107.OBS1639/tomboy-diffuse-dans-les-ecoles-un-scandale.html

Caillaud, Lise. 2013. "*Tomboy*: la théorie du genre fait son cinéma à l'école." *Observatoire de la théorie du genre*, November 12, 2013. www.theoriedugenre.fr/

Chareyron, Romain. 2019. "Disparate Lives: Representations of Youth in French and Francophone Cinema." In *Screening Youth, Contemporary French and Francophone Cinema*, edited by Romain Chareyron and Gilles Viennot, 1–17. Edinburgh: Edinburgh University Press.

Cognet, Anna, Caroline Eliacheff, and Céline Masson. 2021. "Transgenrisme: 'Avec cet effacement des limites, c'est la suprématie des sentiments qui guide les conduits.'" *Marianne*, March 16, 2021. www.marianne.net/agora/tribunes-libres/transgenrisme-avec-cet-effacement-des-limites-cest-la-suprematie-des-sentiments-qui-guide-les-conduites

Copland, Simon. 2015. "Born This Way? Society, Sexuality and the Search for the 'Gay Gene.'" *The Guardian*, July 10, 2015. www.theguardian.com/science/blog/2015/jul/10/born-this-way-society-sexuality-gay-gene

Coutures, Alix. 2020. "Dans *Quotidien*, Elisabeth Roudinesco choque avec des propos sur les personnes trans." *Huffington Post*, March 11, 2020. www.huffingtonpost.fr/entry/dans-quotidien-elisabeth-roudinesco-choque-avec-des-propos-sur-les-transgenre_fr_6049c78fc5b65bed87d84e19

Doiezie, Mathilde. 2013. "*Tomboy*, sa projection controversée dans les écoles." *Le Figaro*, December 24, 2013. www.lefigaro.fr/cinema/2013/12/24/03002-20131224ARTFIG00339--tomboy-sa-projection-controversee-dans-les-ecoles.php

Dokhan, Julien. 2011. "*Tomboy*: Interview avec Céline Sciamma." *Allociné*, April 20, 2011. www.allocine.fr/article/fichearticle_gen_carticle=18603428.html

D'Ornellas, Charlotte. 2021. "Quand la folie transgenre s'attaque aux enfants." *Valeurs Actuelles*, May 28, 2021. www.valeursactuelles.com/clubvaleurs/societe/quand-la-folie-transgenre-sattaque-aux-enfants/

Ekchajzer, François. 2020. "*Petite Fille* sur Arte: le portrait solaire d'une enfant unique en son genre." *Télérama*, December 2, 2020. www.telerama.fr/ecrans/petite-fille-sur-arte-le-portrait-solaire-dune-enfant-unique-en-son-genre-6747078.php

Espineira, Karine. 2021. "La médiatisation des 'enfants et ados trans'—des écrans télés aux chaînes YouTube, se raconter et s'affirmer au present." In *Jeunes trans et non-binaires, de l'accompagnement à l'affirmation*, edited by Denise Medico and Annie Pullen Sansfaçon, 62–77. Montréal: Éditions du remue-méninge.

Espineira, Karine. 2015. *Médiacultures, la transidentité en television*. Paris: L'Harmattan.

Espineira, Karine. 2014. "Les constructions médiatiques des personnes trans - Un exemple d'inscription dans le programme 'penser le genre' en SIC." *Les Enjeux de l'information et de la communication* 15 (1): 35–47.

Fabre, Charlie. 2020. "Le cis gaze, en bref." *Représentrans*, November 2, 2020. representrans.fr/2020/11/02/le-cis-gaze-en-bref/

Fabre, Clarisse. 2011. "Une pétition s'oppose à la projection de *Tomboy* dans les écoles." *Le Monde*, December 21, 2011. www.lemonde.fr/culture/article/2013/12/21/une-petition-s-oppose-a-la-projection-de-tomboy-dans-les-ecoles_4338625_3246.html

Fassin, Éric. 2001. "Same Sex, Different Politics: 'Gay Marriage' Debates in France and the United States." *Public Culture* 13 (2): 215–32.

Ffiske, Caroline. 2020. "Keira Bell Has Led. The Rest of Us Must Follow, or Collude in Harm." *The Article*, December 2, 2020. www.thearticle.com/keira-bell-has-led-the-rest-of-us-must-follow-or-collude-in-harm

Flavigny, Christian. 2021. "Une campagne gouvernementale entretient des jeunes dans le leurre d'une 'transidentité.'" *Marianne*, July 27, 2021. www.marianne.net/agora/tribunes-libres/une-campagne-gouvernementale-entretient-des-jeunes-dans-le-leurre-dune-transidentite

Folden, Menica. 2020. "Commencer un traitement hormonal quand on est mineur." *Wiki Trans*, June 21, 2020. wikitrans.co/ths/mineur/

Go, Julie. 2021. "Tous les enfants devraient pouvoir mettre des robes, quel que soit leur sexe, sans avoir à altérer leurs corps." *Marianne*, August 6, 2021. www.marianne.net/agora/tribunes-libres/tous-les-enfants-devraient-pouvoir-mettre-des-robes-quel-que-soit-leur-sexe-sans-avoir-a-alterer-leurs-corps

Lebreton, France. 2020. "*Petite fille*: je crains le prosélytisme." *La Croix*, December 12, 2020. www.la-croix.com/Famille/Petite-fille-Je-crains-proselytisme-2020-12-12-1201129727

Levin, Sam. 2021. "Trans Kids Are Not New: Historian on the Long Record of Youth Transitioning in America—Interview with Jules Gill-Peterson." *The Guardian*, April 1, 2021. www.theguardian.com/us-news/2021/apr/01/trans-children-history-jules-gill-peterson-interview

"Maman, je suis transgenre." YouTube video, 6:16. December 15, 2020. www .youtube.com/watch?v=vF9Zrt7nR0s

"Maman, je suis non-binaire." *YouTube* video, 9:09. September 2, 2020. www .youtube.com/watch?v=IJjpl6XDTbs

"Mamie, je suis transgenre." YouTube video, 6:38. September 30, 2020. www .youtube.com/watch?v=3oxTW9p1P-s

Mandelbaum, Jacques. 2020. *"Petite Fille*: histoire de l'éclosion lumineuse d'un enfant transgenre." *Le Monde*, November 24, 2020. www.lemonde.fr/culture/article /2020/11/24/petite-fille-histoire-de-l-eclosion-lumineuse-d-un-enfant-transgenre _6060888_3246.html

Mermaidsuk.org. 2021. "Mermaids statement on the Bell vs. Tavistock appeal." September 17, 2021. mermaidsuk.org.uk/news/ mermaids-statement-on-the-bell-v-tavistock-appeal/

Nolsoe, Eir. 2021. "International Survey: How Supportive Would Britons Be of a Family Member Coming Out?" *YouGov*, August 31, 2021. yougov.co.uk/topics/international/ articles-reports/2021/08/31/international-survey-how-supportive-would-britons-

Perreau, Bruno. 2018. *Qui a peur de la théorie queer?* Paris: Presses de Sciences Po.

Pidduck, Julianne. 2011. "The Visible and the Sayable: The Moment and Conditions of Hypervisibility." In *Cinematic Queerness: Gay and Lesbian Hypervisibility in Contemporary Francophone Feature Films*, edited by Florian Grandena and Cristina Johnston, 9–40. Bern: Peter Lang.

Scheffer, Nicolas. 2021. "L'Arkansas adopte l'une des lois anti-trans les plus radicales jamais passées à l'échelle de l'État." *Têtu*, March 30, 2021. tetu.com/2021/03/30/ larkansas-adopte-lune-des-lois-anti-trans-les-plus-radicales-jamais-passee-a- lechelle-dun-etat/

Serano, Julia. "Detransition, Desistance, and Disinformation: A Guide for Understanding Transgender Children Debates." *juliaserano.medium.com*, August 3, 2016. juliaserano.medium.com/detransition-desistance-and-disinformation-a- guide-for-understanding-transgender-children-993b7342946e

Chapter 2

Mobile Desires

Paul B. Preciado's
Un Appartement sur Uranus *and*
the Marginal Western Subject

Leah E. Wilson

In 2013, Paul B. Preciado, a francophone trans* philosopher, began writing for a regular column, "Interzones," in the French newspaper, *Libération*, and in 2019, a collection of these contributions was published as a volume, *An Apartment on Uranus* (*Un Appartement sur Uranus*).[1] In the initial articles that appeared in *Libération* and in the compilation, Preciado presents his subjectivity as anti-normative, refusing gender categorizations and national ties as he critiques the rise in far-right nationalism, the fall of democracies, and the failures of late-stage capitalism. Indeed, Preciado's chronicles cover a period in which Europe is in crisis. As economic and migration catastrophes rattle Europe, particularly in the period Preciado's collection covers (March 2013–January 2018), anti-gender campaigns have risen in France and other European countries, such as the *Manif pour Tous* protests against same-sex marriage in France (Corrêa, et al. 2018).[2] Preciado's attention to a variety of humanitarian concerns demonstrates that issues of migration, capitalism, and democracy are intricately connected with questions of gender and sexuality.

Preciado's perspective is particularly significant during this time as global upheavals and anti-gender campaigns compound to harm LGBTQIA+ (Lesbian, Gay, Bisexual, Transgender, Queer, Intersex, Asexual) people. Indeed, the Global North has experienced an onslaught of assaults against LGBTQIA+ human rights. With public (and viral) attacks by so-called gender critical feminists in the United Kingdom, laws that target trans* youth in the United States, epidemic violence against LGBTQIA+ people in Europe, and the reports of abuse trans* asylum-seekers face while in limbo in Greece and Turkey, a trans* voice that explains the intertangling of global emergencies and anti-LGBTQIA+ attacks is much needed (Burns 2019; Krishnakumar 2021; Committee on Equality and Non-Discrimination 2021, 14–15; Tsaggari 2018). Moreover, *An Apartment on Uranus* has, as of June 2021, sold over 14,000 copies, which marks Preciado's popularity among younger queer and trans* French readers who regale him and his work as revolutionary (Dryef 2021). Indeed, as Thomas Liano (2020) explains, the journalistic style and the brevity of the entries that form the volume, while limiting the detail Preciado can provide on any one topic, nevertheless make his work accessible to broader audiences and expands the collection's radical capacity, attesting to the significance of the way he portrays his trans* subjectivity during our current period (144–45).

Preciado, recording his journeys across dozens of cities around the globe, is in a unique position to comment on contemporary world calamities. This essay examines the way Preciado embodies a nomadic position and deploys his individual location to find what Chandra Talpade Mohanty (2002) calls "common differences," with other marginalized subjects, such as refugees and animals, to reveal the political and economic systems that cause world-wide harm, to build solidarity among the oppressed, and to call for revolution (518). I first argue that Preciado's transnational, trans*feminist work links our current hypercapitalist, neoliberal era to nineteenth century Western epistemologies to show how binary thought creates rigid categories that generate global inequalities. Preciado's vision for a "Uranian" identity thus challenges dichotomous thinking to illustrate the desirability of a mobile position by disrupting sexual, gender, national, and human/nonhuman borders. I then discuss how his use of metaphors allows him to make connections between marginalized subjects as he idealizes disidentification and multiplicity as a method for realizing transnational solidarity. Yet, I next contend that, as Preciado's self-theories that romanticize mobility produce modes of resistance for some marginal subjects, his anti-normative vision for revolution centers Western positionality and his analogies entail exploitation. As Preciado's media influence crosses over francophone borders with the translation of his works into English, it is imperative to evaluate how Preciado's contributions contest capitalist, heteronormative, and colonial notions of identity and yet also perpetuate modes of being that privilege Western subjects.

TWENTY-FIRST CENTURY CRISES AND
THE CALL FOR REVOLUTION

In the published collection of his *Libération* articles, Preciado begins with an introduction that traces the creation of Western philosophy's binary thinking to the nineteenth century and explains how, inspired by Karl Heinrich Ulrichs, his volume will disrupt the gender, sexual, and national categories fashioned by dichotomous theorizations. Preciado exemplifies, as scholars such as Siobhan Somerville have done, the ways in which nineteenth century sexologists influenced contemporary notions of sexuality and gender (Somerville 2000, 37–38). Detailing the story of Ulrichs and his invention of the word "Uranian" as a way to claim a "third sex" that explains his sexual attraction to other men at a time when homosexuality was illegal in Germany, Preciado (2019) lauds Ulrichs's defiance of binary categorization (21–23). He writes, "He invented a new language and a new scene of enunciation. In each of Ulrichs's words addressed from Uranus to the Munich jurists resounds the violence generated by the dualist epistemology of the West" (2020, 27).[3] However, despite Ulrichs's declaration that rebelled against binary thinking, Preciado explains that he unintentionally influenced conceptions of homosexuality and heterosexuality that molded how sexuality and reproduction would be biopolitically managed well into the twentieth century and shapes how we discuss sexual and gender identities in dualistic terms today (2019, 25–26). In this introduction, Preciado dares his readers to consider the way these binaries limit their own imaginations and the way of organizing Western society, writing:

> How can you, how can we, organize an entire system of visibility, representation, right of self-determination and political recognition if we follow such categories? Do you really believe that you are male or female, that we are homosexual or heterosexual, intersexed or transexual? Do these distinctions worry you? . . . If you feel your throat constricting when you hear one of these words, do not silence it. It's the multiplicity of the cosmos that is trying to pierce through your chest. (Preciado 2020, 28)[4]

In the twenty-first century, Preciado explains, the nineteenth century categorizations we have inherited are unsatisfactory and a return to "Uranian" thinking that validates multiplicity is desirable. Furthermore, illuminating that gender and sexual categories are generated through scientific and medical fields, Preciado urges readers to question the identities we have been assigned (such as male and female) and also the sexual and gender identities we claim.

For Preciado, it is necessary to dispute dichotomous thinking and these imposed categories as they shape how nations manage their citizens through exclusive systems. As Dean Spade (2015) expounds, gender and sexual definitions are reified through state administrative processes that dictate who can have access to government IDs, social security, employment, health care, and determines whether or not a person can pass through national borders and gain citizenship (73–78).[5] In France, these administrative hurdles require, according to Alain Giami and Emmanuelle Baubatie's (2014) study on gender affirming procedures in France, that trans* individuals undergo "sex reassignment surgery" to change their civil status, which prevents trans* individuals from claiming their specific identities (1499). Indeed, during the majority of the time that Preciado's writes his chronicles, trans* people in France were still mandated to be sterilized before they could legally transition, and la Cour européenne des droits de l'homme (CEDH) condemned France for this requirement in 2017 (*Le Monde* avec AFP 2017).[6] Preciado (2019) illuminates these obstacles with his discussion of administrative processes that make his crossing between countries difficult as a trans* man and underscores that these barriers also limit the mobility of asylum-seekers and migrants (212–14).

These categorizations and ways of organizing societies, economies, nations, and governments establish ideologies of exclusion that depend on definite categories and have caused global catastrophe. In his chronicles, Preciado reports on the fall of democracies in the West, Catalonia's fight for independence, the rise of far-right nationalism globally, the popularization of "anti-gender" ideologies in Europe, the bullying of trans and queer students, the Greek austerity measures, and the suffering of migrants, among other disasters, to highlight the harm of these exclusionary logics and to associate the Western hegemonic system with the failures of late-stage capitalism (Preciado 2019, 65–68; 119–20; 48–53; 182–86; 178–81; 150–54). Readers see this particularly when Preciado discusses the choice to hold the 2017 documenta 14, an art exhibit usually held in Kassel, Germany, that started in 1955 as a way for Germany to celebrate its art after WWII, in both Kassel and Athens amid the height of Greece's debt crisis (Documenta). Controversy surrounded the exhibit, with German media referring to Greece as "Shuldenland" (debtor country) and Greeks largely seeing the move as a form of disaster capitalism that exploits Greece's predicament (largely attributed to German-backed European Union austerity measures) while the Germans hold "colonial attitudes" (Smith 2017; Donadio 2017; "Connoisseurs or Colonists?" 2017).

In two different entries, Preciado, one of the curators for the exhibit, examines the controversy (Preciado 2019, 38). In the first, published on April 7, 2017, and before documenta 14 takes place, he describes that the show, with its roots in post-WWII German cultural resurgence and its artists taking inspiration from Greek financial disaster, symbolizes the end of Western epistemological categorizations that precedes the collapse of democracy and insists that documenta 14 must be a space where artists experiment with new identities that reject national and gender categories (Preciado 2019, 268–73).[7] He then follows this analysis with an entry on June 23, 2017, that reflects on a debate about whether or not the move indicates that Europe is becoming more like the Global South. Refuting this claim, Preciado (2020) explains that "The South is not a place, but rather the effect of the relationships between power, knowledge, and space. Colonial modernity is inventing a geography and a chronology: the South is primitive and past. The North is progress and future" and this relationship produces the South as a site of capitalist extraction while the North becomes "the museum, the archive, the bank" (232, 233).[8] Preciado concludes that every place has a South—or a place that is designated for extraction—because capitalist economies demand borders. The South as a set place does not exist as a stable location, and indeed, there are sites of wealth and exploitation within the Global North and Global South (2019, 291). The documenta 14 controversy displays the harm of stagnant categories that demand an unequal balance of power and proves that Europe can no longer isolate itself from the impacts of its capitalist ventures. Preciado's discussion destabilizes this hegemonic relationship by drawing attention to the way in which these categories are constructed to marginalize and abuse.

The current crises Preciado records and the questions he raises about the stability of geographic and national definitions for his readers uncover the current threats democracies face and the fact that we are in a period of global transition. Notably, Achille Mbembe (2019), influenced by Frantz Fanon, writes that contemporary periods of violence and catastrophe, in which migrants flee their countries to avoid environmental devastation and/or state violence, unveil that democracies are not failing per se, but that the power dynamics that make democracies possible are being exposed (23–27). He writes that, "No democracy exists without its double, without its colony—little matter the name and the structure. The colony is not external to democracy and is not necessarily located outside its walls. Democracy bears the colony within it, just as colonialism bears democracy, often in the guise of a mask" (27). Integral to democracy is that this mask remains intact, as "the great fear of democracies is that this violence, latent on the interior and exteriorized in the colonies and other third places, suddenly resurfaces, and then threatens the idea that the political order was created out of itself (instituted all at once and once and for all)" (27). Thus, the current period of catastrophes Preciado catalogues is the fracturing of borders that separate powerful democracies from their colonies: in the migration crisis, the colonized "doubles" are revealed to the European people in democratic nations like France. As Nay and Steinbock (2021) write:

> [The] [r]efugee crises that manifest in forced detention, death, and destruction
> are materializations of the effects of climate change, the industrial revolution,
> proxy wars, and late-stage capitalism. The enforcement of the borders of nation
> and body is one-sided, as the leakages of Europe's ongoing colonial project seep
> into marginalized peoples and states alike. In short, Europe's crises are being
> brought to its own door despite efforts to contain them elsewhere. (146)

As we see with Europe's calamities, the distinction between the Global North
and Global South is muddied: Europe can no longer separate its economies
and politics from the colonial ties that made the production of Europe—and
its democracies—possible. The migration crisis thus challenges the binary
thinking that is so central to Western thought and shows how dichotomous
categories influence other aspects of Western societies. Preciado, as a trans*
feminist theorist, provides a needed perspective of these global emergencies
that he links to gender and sexual identities.

This period, Preciado underlines, is one of necessary revolution and one
that can be tied to our bodily subjectivities. Scholars such as María Lugones
(2008) argue that modern heteropatriarchal racial, gender, and sexual identities are products of colonization and capitalism (1–4). Likewise, John
D'Emilio (1992) explains that the development of capitalist economies made
gay and lesbian identities possible, displaying the interconnection between
economies and sexual identities (5–9). In Preciado's work, *Testo Junkie*
(2008), he posits that late-stage capitalism has further altered sexual and gendered subjectivities to invent "technogenders" ("technogenres") (105–15).
Thus, *An Apartment on Uranus* builds on the theme that our economic and
political conditions shape our gender and sexual expressions. In the essays,
readers understand that Preciado sees his bodily existence as the manifestation of our current global political economy that is produced by Western
epistemologies. However, as he documents that the faltering of democracies
dependent on capitalism and colonialism allow for revolutionary thinking, his
body also becomes a site of radical possibility. He states that, "My existence
as a trans man constitutes at once the acme of the sexual *ancien regime* and
the beginning of its collapse, the climax of its normative progression and the
signal of a proliferation still to come" (Preciado 2020, 30).[9] Thus, Preciado
posits the theory of his body, his experiences in the margins and disidentify-
ing with categorization, while traversing the globe and writing about crises
as a method for rethinking our ties to nation, gender, borders, and binaries.

THE MOBILE TRANS* SUBJECT: CREATING
REVOLUTIONARY ALLIANCES THROUGH ALLEGORY

Preciado uses his chronicles to form connections that disturb binary categorizations while also divulging how Western ideologies of nation and gender instigate violence for marginalized subjects and offers theories of transition and mobility to imagine new modes of being and relating to one another. Describing his legal transition while traveling to different countries, Preciado (2020) explains the questions he gets when presenting his passport because, taking testosterone, he does not resemble his pre-transition ID and concludes that, "In politico-legal terms, the status of the trans person is comparable to that of the migrant, the exile or the refugee. They all find themselves in a temporary process of suspension of their political condition" (173).[10] The comparison of trans* subjectivity to those of migrants is indeed common in French trans* narratives. As Todd W. Reeser (2013) explains, trans* texts often refer to trans* subjectivity with "nation-based discourses" and that the "necessity of representational movement means that transgender is closely linked to the immigrant" in French narratives of transition (4, 7). Relating himself to migrants throughout his chronicles, Preciado exposes how national discourses of gender and immigration produce his subjectivity as a trans* subject and this vantage point allows him to make meaningful comparisons to other socially, legally, and politically minoritized subjects.

Relating to marginalized subjects, Preciado seeks to, as Mohanty (2002) says, "look upward" and make transnational networks between peoples, animals, and machines that are based on "common differences" (511, 518). This is necessary, Mohanty explains, because "colonized peoples must know themselves and the colonizer. This particular marginalized location makes the politics of knowledge and the power investments that go along with it visible so that we can then engage in work to transform the use and abuse of power" (511). As a trans* subject who refuses established definitions and also traverses around the world, never staying in the same bed for more than a couple nights at a time, Preciado aligns himself with migrants and animals to emphasize the relationship between his unfixed identity and his nomadic position and to create transnational, human/animal community (Preciado 2019, 200–201). From his local position of dispossession, Preciado makes comparisons to exhibit how minoritized individuals are subjected to similar global oppressive systems. For example, in pieces such as "Strays" ("Le peuple des errants"), Preciado (2019) equates the wandering dogs that dominate Istanbul's streets to the migrants seeking refuge on their way to Europe to underscore the cruelty migrants (and dogs) experience (153). Explaining that, in 1910, 50,000 stray dogs were captured and then abandoned on the Turkish island of Sivriada to fuel Istanbul's modernization, Preciado compares the million and a half refugees that pass through Istanbul, often delayed there on the journey to Europe, to stray dogs to evoke the way the current global economic and political systems cause displacement (152–53). He describes that, in trekking through Istanbul, the human undergoes a metamorphosis, writing, "the refugee loses any identity as a political citizen, in his transit from Asia to Europe, and is transformed into a stray dog" and that living beings—whether human or dog—are global citizens that are subjected to dislocating policies (Preciado 2020, 126).[11] Critiquing the nationalism that keeps migrants in dangerous environments and their citizenship in limbo, Preciado stresses to the French audience of *Libération,* as well as more mainstream francophone and anglophone readers, that we need to rethink how nations and economies perpetuate systemic violence against the most marginalized.

Preciado's analogies throughout the collection accentuate the necessity of reimagining how our societies are organized into hegemonic power structures and, through comparisons, sees his trans* identity as a site in which this revolution can take place. Metaphors abound: trans* bodies are compared to houses, trans* lives are linked to Catalonia's struggle, and humans are animals (Preciado 2019, 227–30; 119–22; 152–54). Preciado's purpose for detailing such relationships highlights the need for radical change and underlines that we are in a period of transition on individual levels as well as in the global arena. Likening human skin to phone screens and predicting that, in the future, technocapitalism will produce screens on our skin (2019, 252), he writes that "We are all in a metamorphosis, but only a few of us (the ones who have been marked as monsters, the ones whose own subjectivity and bodies were publicly pointed out as fields for experimentation and material proofs of mutation) realize it" (2020, 205).[12] Because Preciado is a trans*man who initially bootlegs testosterone and must submit to administrative systems to change his legal identity, he understands what it is to be marked as "Other" by dominant ideals and the pressure to adhere to normative identities (whether it be as a gender or a citizen) which allows him to form alliances with other subjects who are marginalized by heteropatriarchal capitalist societies. At the horizon of this changing world, Preciado sees nonnormativity and mobility as methods to imagine more liberating ways of being and to establish community between marginalized groups. As a trans* figure in the media, his unique perspective on these emergencies and the call for revolution provide important perspectives that encourage transnational solidarity.

Writing between borders, communicating in different languages, shifting identities as needed to overcome administrative barriers, Preciado shows the promise of mobility as a way to disavow nationalist ideologies, heteronormative logics, capitalist economies and to inspire solidarity. In Preciado's view, his embodiment as a trans* subject necessitates that he rejects rigid categorizations and occupies an identity that resists any stable gender or national affiliation. Equating the trans* subject to the struggle for Catalonia's independence, he writes that, "Becoming trans, like becoming independent, means that one must above all always resign from nationhood and gender identity . . . Renounce laws based on body, blood and soil. National identity and gender identity must be neither foundation nor goal" (Preciado 2020, 103).[13] Abdicating gender, sexual, and national categories to adopt a multifarious, unfixed identity permits people to reject investments in oppressive categories and become agents of revolutionary change. Readers see this particularly when Preciado discusses his bodily changes, such as when his voice deepens due to his self-administered testosterone (2019, 160). Discussing the effects of his new voice, he evokes Gayatri Spivak and posits that disavowing his previous voice permits him to discard the subjectivity assigned to him as well as the ontological processes that make established subjectivities possible and thus becomes a way to let the subaltern, or dispossessed, speak (160). Assuming an identity that repudiates prescribed notions of gender and nationality, Preciado inhabits, as Tija Uhlig describes in her border-crossing performance, a gender that is unsettled, fluid, and that "refus[es] the unity of the whole, and the monstrosity of familiarity and estrangement at the same time" (Uhlig 2021, 225). Indeed, his gender is one that "can't be an identity, as it is part of the monstrous destabilization of identity and difference" that disturbs preconceived ideas of gender and nation (225). This kind of disidentification Preciado proposes (and that he demonstrates in earlier texts such as *Testo Junkie* and *Countersexual Manifesto*) is, according to José Esteban Muñoz (1999), a survival strategy for minoritarian subjects who do not (or do not desire) to conform to normative ideals of identity and citizenship (4–5). Disidentification, however, as Muñoz (1999) explains, is not always a satisfactory strategy, and, at times, minoritarian subjects, such as Preciado, neglect the positionalities of other marginalized subjects, particularly those who experience multiple intersecting oppressions (8). Because he is a popular intellectual voice in the media, it is necessary to consider how Preciado's theorizations are inhibited by his own Western positionality that ultimately curtails his revolutionary calls for transnational solidarity.

THE PROBLEM OF METAPHOR: MOBILITY AND THE LIMITS OF TRANSNATIONAL SOLIDARITY

Preciado's essays articulate the importance of reimagining the way Western societies depend on harmful binary categorizations, but his work also discloses his position as a white Western marginal subject, who, even though he disavows Western epistemologies, nevertheless participates in them. As Aren

Z. Aizura (2018) emphasizes, mobility—how one moves across borders and how one crafts a fluid identity that rejects stable definitions—necessitates that an individual can transcend race and class backgrounds and depends on capitalist, Western notions of identity and mobility (17). Furthermore, Jasbir Puar (2017) critiques Preciado's exaltation of nonnormative identity as revolutionary because, as she argues, having a mobile, nonnormative subjectivity is still only available to the most privileged of marginalized subjects and can be particularly useful to white transmen such as Preciado who embodies what Puar calls "trans exceptionalism" (45). Trans exceptionalism is not about, "passing as gender normative; it is also about inhabiting an exceptional trans body . . . A new transnormative citizen is predicated not on passing but on 'piecing,' galvanized through mobility, transformation, regeneration, flexibility, and the creative concocting of the body" (Puar 2017, 45). We see Preciado's Western positionality as a transnormative citizen in the metaphors he employs in his efforts to make transnational alliances. For example, in an entry titled, "Our Bison" ("Nos bisons"), Preciado (2019) discusses how, in the nineteenth century, the American military, led by Colonel Sheridan, killed the American West's bison in an effort to eradicate Indigenous people. He compares this genocide to the restrictions transmen experience when accessing testosterone in many European countries (278–79). As he explains, pharmaceutical companies make testosterone prohibitively expensive unless government health care supplements the cost; yet, to receive this through national health care in Europe, a trans* subject must be diagnosed and recognized by the state, which forces trans* individuals to be pathologized and to meet the state's requirements of what a trans* subject should be (279–81).

Testosterone, Preciado claims, is the trans* subject's bison and it is regulated through neoliberal capitalist markets that create new forms of life to generate profit. Thus, he concludes, "We will not make one more bison fall. We will leap onto the last horse that remains to us and we will gallop away" (2020, 226).[14] For Preciado, the neoliberal government control over trans* identities necessitates that trans* individuals must flee the system and not participate within it. While the analogy of bison to testosterone promotes Preciado's conclusion and allows for the theorization of an idealized way to escape systems of regulation, it ignores that this is not a viable path for most marginalized trans* individuals. As Puar (2017) notes, "piecing" identity or accessing medical resources and technology while rejecting state interference, as Preciado does when he catalogues his own experience of bootlegging testosterone in *Testo Junkie*, is more accessible to white Western transmen because they can more easily partake in capitalist economies (46). Moreover, this metaphor—which attempts to align the European trans* subject with American Indigenous people—disregards the critical difference that the bison were slaughtered to directly kill Indigenous people and denies the reality of ongoing attacks against them, their sovereignty, and the ways their material conditions limit their ability to counter state oppression today. The bison metaphor is especially interesting, since, at the time Preciado published the original article in *Libération* (May 17, 2017), the Dakota Access Pipeline (DAPL) protests at the Standing Rock Indian Reservation in South Dakota were underway—and were covered in *Le Monde* and *Libération*—from August 2016 until February 2017 (Hersher 2017; *Le Monde* avec AFP 2016; Massiot 2016). The protests called for the end of a pipeline that would threaten the tribe's water supply and disrupt tribal burial grounds and other important cultural sites (Hersher 2017; Zambelich and Alexandra 2016). Capitalist, colonial economic and political systems continue to directly threaten Indigenous lives by targeting water resources, and Preciado's comparison neglects the genocidal history and continuation of harm these communities experience, further exposing his Western perspective.

Additionally, we understand Preciado's positionality through his references to slaves and migrants that he uses to build alliances. Throughout the work he envisions his positionality as that of a slave, or, as previously discussed, similar to that of migrants and exiles (Preciado 2019, 173; 115; 213–14). While Preciado's goal for such equivalencies is to underline the connection between oppressive state and economic systems, by making such parallels, Preciado echoes French feminists, such as Monique Wittig and members of the *Mouvement de libération des femmes*, who equated women to serfs or slaves (Vergès 2020, 89–90).[15] These comparisons, as Françoise Vergès (2020) explains, neglect France's (and Europe's) history of colonization and participation in the slave trade (89–90). Likewise, Preciado's analogies, in their equation of the white Western trans* subject with African slaves, Indigenous people, and migrants, obfuscates the material reality, marginalization, and violence these populations have experienced at the hands of Western ideologies and political-economic pursuits. Preciado's envisioning for revolutionary change that depends on the destruction of binary thinking is thus limited by his analogies. Importantly, as Miranda Joseph (2002) observes about analogy, it "works to incorporate all sorts of subjects as equivalent but not equal producers and consumers" and, ironically, perpetuates binary thinking (273). Even as Preciado attempts to establish alliances between different marginalized subjects' struggles across the globe, his metaphoric rhetoric that prizes disidentification and liminality disregards the way in which race, nation, and geographic location impact one's ability to access mobility and possess fluidity.

The material privilege Preciado has due to his status as a white Western subject, which makes his mobility possible, is made evident through the very trans*/migrant allegory he utilizes to rouse transnational solidarity. While this metaphor allows him to make transnational, border-crossing associations discussed previously, it also reveals the way his privileged position separates him from most migrants and refugees. The book that Preciado writes to document his traversing across the globe (and, indeed, his column in *Libération*) attests to his ability to pass through most screenings, indicating his privileged position. Even if he is limited by his trans* identity, he can compensate for this marginalization through his whiteness and his European Union citizenship. Toby Beauchamp (2019) explicates in *Going Stealth* that the surveillance systems that emerge in airports and borders post-9/11 identify gender deviance as cause for scrutiny, but, trans* people who are "able to comply with dominant standards of appearance and behavior (themselves grounded in ideals of whiteness, U.S. citizenship, able-bodiedness, and compulsory heterosexuality), may be legible to surveillance mechanisms not as transgender but as properly gendered and thus nonthreatening" (7). Although Beauchamp is speaking specifically about the United States, he underlines how surveillance has been developed to screen those who do not appear to belong to a nation. Preciado, as a white, European, transmasculine person of class privilege, is deemed normative through these administrative processes in ways that Brown and Black migrants and asylum-seekers are not. Preciado's—and other white trans* European or American citizens'—navigation of borders is vastly different from a cis or trans* undocumented migrant from the Global South, as the protest at documenta 14, in which an activist group, LGBTQIA+ Refugees Welcome, stole an art piece to give attention to trans* migrants, highlights (Voon 2017). Coupling these experiences, while underlining the way the heteronormative state harms marginalized people, equates these positionalities without acknowledging the more severe consequences for those who are not white or citizens of Western nations. Importantly, Preciado's use of these metaphors in the French media perpetuates the erasure of the specific oppressions that Black and Brown migrants and asylum-seekers undergo in this catastrophic period.

CONCLUSION

An Apartment on Uranus provides critical arguments about the way in which contemporary crises of the West are due to hegemonic categorizations that produce inequality and instigate violence for Others in our late-stage capitalist economy and are much needed critiques. Yet, his insistence that disidentificatory or mobile identities are ways to disturb these categorizations is limited in its revolutionary capacity and his analogies illustrate his positionality as a Western marginal subject who nonetheless participates in capitalist and colonial thinking. Preciado's influence as a respected trans*feminist philosopher in the French media is integral to showing the way global economic and political systems oppress, but the material conditions of the most marginalized must be further underscored to depict how these experiences contrast to Preciado's Western, privileged trans* perspective. This type of analysis is much needed, as, in an investigation released in October 2021, *Lighthouse Reports* uncovered that migrants and asylum-seekers continue to face extreme violence, "unlawful pushbacks," and deportations at the hands of EU countries such as Greece, Poland, and Spain (*Amnesty International* 2021). Media coverage and discussion of these humanitarian crises and the relationship to gender and sexual politics is vital during simultaneous global catastrophes. Assessing Preciado's work during the COVID-19 pandemic, which has unveiled systemic inequalities across the globe, it is imperative to understand the limitations of mobility—and that it is not available, nor desirable, nor revolutionary for many people—as we consider ways to imagine more liberating identities and transnational feminist movements.

NOTES

1. I use trans* to refer to Preciado's identity as in his writings he cultivates an identity and politics that Jack Halberstam refers to as trans*, in which one refutes a gender identity that "situate[s] transition in relation to a destination, a final form, a specific shape, or an established configuration of desire and identity . . . [it] holds off the certainty of diagnosis . . . and makes trans* people the authors of their own categorizations" (Halberstam 2018, 2). I apply the term throughout the essay for consistency.

2. Since the mid-2000s, anti-gender campaigns, or demonstrations against progressive policies that include women's and LGBTQIA+ rights, have emerged in Europe. For a comprehensive discussion on the rise of these movements, see Roman Kuhar and David Paternotte's edited collection, *Anti-Gender Campaigns in Europe: Mobilizing Against Equality* (2017).

3. The English quotes of Preciado's text come from the 2020 translation, *An Apartment on Uranus*. I use this translation to provide English quotes throughout the essay. The original French text reads: "Il a inventé un nouveau langage et une nouvelle scène de l'énonciation. Dans chaque mot d'Ulrichs s'adressant depuis Uranus aux juristes munichois, résonne la violence produite par l'épistémologie binaire de l'Occident" (Preciado 2019, 24).

4. The original French text reads: "Comment pouvez-vous, comment pouvons-nous organiser tout un système de visibilité, de représentation, de concession de souveraineté et de reconnaissance politique selon de telles catégories? Croyez-vous vraiment que vous êtes homme ou femme, que nous sommes homosexuels ou hétérosexuels, intersexués ou transsexuels? Ces distinctions vous inquiètent-elles? . . . Si vous sentez un tremblement gagner votre gorge en entendant l'un de ces mots, ne le faites pas taire. C'est la multiplicité du cosmos qui tente de traverser votre poitrine" (Preciado 2019, 26–27).

5. Although Spade focuses on American legal procedures and the US context, his explanation of the way nations administer identity can be applied to a European context, emphasized by Preciado's own discussion of the legal processes he must participate in to change his identity (Preciado 2019, 223–26).

6. Following this condemnation, France lifted the barrier, and trans* people are no longer required to seek medical treatment before changing their legal identity. However, trans* individuals are still hesitant to go through the legal barriers to change gender status in France (*Le Monde* 2018).

7. Importantly, an activist group, LGBTQIA+ Refugees Welcome, angered by what they saw at the exploitive, performative themes of migration, resistance, and trans rights in the exhibition, stole an art piece—Roger Bernant's "Philosopher's Stone"—in protest, explaining that "stones can't talk, but we can" (Voon 2017; Nay and Steinbock 2021, 147).

8. The original French text reads: "Le Sud n'est pas un lieu, mais plutôt l'effet de relations entre pouvoir, connaissance et espace. La modernité coloniale invente une géographie et une chronologie: le Sud est primitif et passé. Le Nord est progrès et futur" and "le musée, l'archive, la banque" (Preciado 2019, 290).

9. The original French text reads: "Mon existence en tant qu'homme trans constitue en même temps le point culminant de l'ancien régime sexuel et le début de son effondrement, le climax de sa progression normative et l'annonce d'une prolifèration à venir" (Preciado 2019, 29).

10. The original French text reads: "En termes politico-légaux, le statut de la personne trans est comparable à celui du migrant, de l'exilé et du réfugié. Ils se retrouvent tous dans un processus temporaire de suspension de leur condition politique" (Preciado 2019, 214).

11. The original French text reads: "le réfugié perd toute condition de citoyen politique, dans son transit de l'Asie vers l'Europe, transformé en chien vagabond" (Preciado 2019, 153).

12. The original French text reads: "Nous sommes tous en mutation mais nous ne sommes que quelques-uns (ceux qui ont été marqués en tant que monstres, ceux dont la subjectivité propre et les corps ont été publiquement signalés comme camps d'expérimentation et preuves matérielles de la mutation) à nous en rendre compte" (Preciado 2019, 254).

13. The original French reads: "Devenir trans, comme devenir indépendant, signifie qu'il faut surtout et toujours démissionner de la nation et du genre . . . Renoncer au corps, au sang et au sol en tant que lois. L'identité nationale et l'identité de genre ne peuvent être ni fondement ni téléologie" (Preciado 2019, 121–22).

14. The original French reads: "Nous ne ferons pas tomber un seul bison de plus. Nous sauterons sur le dernier cheval qui nous reste et nous partirons en fuyant" (Preciado 2019, 282).

15. See Wittig's (1992) *The Straight Mind* for an example (34).

REFERENCES

Aizura, Aren Z. 2018. *Mobile Subjects: Transnational Imaginaries of Gender Reassignment*. Durham, NC: Duke University Press.

Amnesty International. 2021. "EU: New Evidence of Systematic Unlawful Pushbacks and Violence at Borders," October 6, 2021. www.amnesty.org/en/latest/news/2021 /10/eu-new-evidence-of-systematic-unlawful-pushbacks-and-violence-at-borders/.

Beauchamp, Toby. 2019. *Going Stealth*. Durham, NC: Duke University Press.

Burns, Katelyn. 2019. "The Rise of the Anti-Trans 'Radical' Feminists, Explained." *Vox*, September 5, 2019. www.vox.com/identities/2019/9/5/20840101/terfs-radical -feminists-gender-critical.

Committee on Equality and Non-Discrimination. 2021. "Combating Rising Hate Against LGBTI People in Europe." Doc. 15121. Parliamentary Assembly, Council of Europe. assembly.coe.int/LifeRay/EGA/Pdf/TextesProvisoires/2021/20210921-RisingHateLGBTI-EN.pdf.

"Connoisseurs or Colonists?: Documenta's Controversial Stay in Athens." 2017. *The Economist*, April 6, 2017. www.economist.com/books-and-arts/2017/04/06/documentas-controversial-stay-in-athens.

Corrêa, Sonia, David Paternotte, and Roman Kuhar. 2018. "The Globalisation of Anti-Gender Campaigns: Transnational Anti-Gender Movements in Europe and Latin America Create Unlikely Alliances." *International Politics and Society*, May. www.ips-journal.eu/topics/democracy-and-society/the-globalisation-of-anti -gender-campaigns-2761/.

D'Emilio, John. 1992. *Making Trouble: Essays on Gay History, Politics, and the University*. New York, NY: Routledge.

Documenta. n.d. "documenta gGmbH." Accessed October 19, 2021. www.documenta .de/en/about#16_documenta_ggmbh.

Donadio, Rachel. 2017. "German Art Exhibition Documenta Expands into Athens." *The New York Times*, April 5, 2017. www.nytimes.com/2017/04/05/arts/design/ documenta-german-exhibition-greek-crisis.html.

Dryef, Zineb. 2021. "Paul B. Preciado, La Révolution Du Genre." *Le Monde*, June 25, 2021. www.lemonde.fr/m-le-mag/article/2021/06/25/paul-b-preciado-par-dela -le-genre_6085594_4500055.html.

Giami, Alain, and Emmanuelle Beaubatie. 2014. "Gender Identification and Sex Reassignment Surgery in the Trans Population: A Survey Study in France." *Archives of Sexual Behavior* 43: 1491–1501.

Halberstam, Jack. 2018. *Trans*: A Quick and Quirky Account of Gender Variability*. Oakland, CA: University of California Press.

Hersher, Rebecca. 2017. "Key Moments in the Dakota Access Pipeline Fight." *National Public Radio*, February 22, 2017. www.npr.org/sections/thetwo-way/2017 /02/22/514988040/key-moments-in-the-dakota-access-pipeline-fight.

Joseph, Miranda. 2002. "Analogy and Complicity: Women's Studies, Lesbian/Gay Studies, and Capitalism." In *Women's Studies on Its Own: A Next Wave Reader in Institutional Change*, edited by Robyn Wiegman, 267–92. Durham, NC: Duke University Press.

Krishnakumar, Priya. 2021. "This Record-Breaking Year for Anti-Transgender Legislation Would Affect Minors the Most." *CNN*, April 15, 2021. www.cnn.com /2021/04/15/politics/anti-transgender-legislation-2021/index.html.

Le Monde. 2018. "Trans, Surmonter Les Obstacles Pour Vivre. Une Rencontre Du Monde Festival." October 22, 2018. www.lemonde.fr/festival/video/2018 /10/22/trans-surmonter-les-obstacles-pour-vivre-une-rencontre-du-monde-festival _5372752_4415198.html.

Le Monde avec AFP. 2016. "Le Gouvernement Américain Gèle Le Chantier de l'oléoduc de La Discorde." *Le Monde*, September 10, 2016. www.lemonde.fr /ameriques/article/2016/09/10/le-gouvernement-americain-gele-le-chantier-de-l -oleoduc-de-la-discorde_4995456_3222.html.

Le Monde avec AFP. 2017. "La CEDH Condamne La France Pour Les Obligations Imposées Aux Transgenres Pour Changer d'état Civil." *Le Monde*, April 6, 2017. www.lemonde.fr/societe/article/2017/04/06/la-cedh-condamne-la-france -pour-les-obligations-imposees-aux-transgenres-pour-changer-d-etat-civil _5106895_3224.html.

Liano, Thomas. 2020. "Un Appartement Sur Uranus Par Paul B. Preciado (Review)." *French Studies* 74 (1): 144–45.

Lugones, María. 2008. "The Coloniality of Gender." *Worlds & Knowledges Otherwise*, Spring: 1–17.

Massiot, Aude. 2016. "Dans Le Dakota, Le Mouvement Antipipeline Violemment Réprimé." *Libération*, November 3, 2016. www.liberation.fr/planete/2016/11/03/ dans-le-dakota-le-mouvement-antipipeline-violemment-reprime_1525924/.

Mbembe, Achille. 2019. *Necropolitics*. Durham, NC: Duke University Press.

Mohanty, Chandra Talpade. 2002. "'Under Western Eyes' Revisited: Feminist Solidarity Through Anticapitalist Struggles." *Signs* 28 (2): 499–535.

Muñoz, José Esteban. 1999. *Disidentifications: Queers of Color and the Performance of Politics*. Cultural Studies of the Americas 2. Minneapolis, MN: University of Minnesota Press.

Nay, Yv E., and Eliza Steinbock. 2021. "Critical Trans Studies in and beyond Europe: Histories, Methods, and Institutions." *TSQ: Transgender Studies Quarterly* 8 (2): 145–57.

Paternotte, David, and Roman Kuhar, eds. 2018. *Anti-Gender Campaigns in Europe: Mobilizing Against Equality*. New York, NY: Rowman & Littlefield.

Preciado, Paul B. 2000. *Manifeste Contra-Sexuel*. Paris: Balland.

Preciado, Paul B. 2008. *Testo Junkie: Sexe, Drogue et Biopolitique*. Paris: Grasset.

Preciado, Paul B. 2019. *Un Appartement Sur Uranus: Chrnoiques de La Traversee*. Paris: Grasset.

Preciado, Paul B. 2020. *An Apartment on Uranus: Chronicles of the Crossing*. Translated by Charlotte Mandell. Boston: Semiotext(e).

Puar, Jasbir. 2017. *The Right to Maim: Deblity, Capacity, Disability*. Durham, NC: Duke University Press.

Reeser, Todd W. 2013. "TransFrance." *L'Espirit Créateur* 53 (1): 4–14.

Smith, Helena. 2017. "'Crapumenta!' . . . Anger in Athens as the Blue Lambs of Documenta Hit Town." *The Gaurdian*, May 14, 2017. www.theguardian.com/artanddesign/2017/may/14/documenta-14-athens-german-art-extravaganza

Somerville, Siobhan B. 2000. *Queering the Color Line: Race and the Invention of Homosexuality in American Culture*. Durham: Duke University Press.

Spade, Dean. 2015. *Normal Life: Administrative Violence, Critical Transpolitics, and the Limits of Law*. Durham, NC: Duke University Press.

Tsaggari, Alexia. 2018. "Unsafe Haven: Life and Death for LGBTQ Refugees." *BalkanInsight*, January 23, 2018. balkaninsight.com/2018/01/23/unsafe-haven-life-and-death-for-lgbt-refugees-12-14-2017/

Uhlig, Tija. 2021. "Failing Gender, Failing the West: The Monstrous (Un)Becoming of a Genderqueer Clown in a Post-Soviet Borderland." *TSQ: Transgender Studies Quarterly* 8 (2): 223–37.

Vergès, Françoise. 2020. *The Wombs of Women: Race, Capital, Feminism*. Translated by Kaiama L Glover. Durham, NC: Duke University Press.

Voon, Claire. 2017. "LGBTQ Refugee Rights Group Steals Artwork from Documenta in Athens." *Hyperallergic*, June 1, 2017. hyperallergic.com/382407/lgbtq-refugee-rights-group-steals-artwork-from-documenta-in-athens/

Wittig, Monique. 1992. *The Straight Mind and Other Essays*. Boston, MA: Beacon Press.

Zambelich, Ariel, and Cassi Alexandra. 2016. "In Their Own Words: The 'Water Protectors' of Standing Rock." *National Public Radio*, December 11, 2016. www.npr.org/sections/thetwo-way/2017/02/22/514988040/key-moments-in-the-dakota-access-pipeline-fight

Chapter 3

Multiple Bodies

The Digital and the Physical in Arthur Cahn's Les Vacances du petit Renard *(2018)*

Brian J. Troth

Its signature sound file—a synthesized succession of ascending notes—might cause a few heads to turn if enough people in the room recognize it. The same sound was indispensable for a TikTok trend that made the rounds on the app in early 2021: users played the sound to capture their significant other's reaction. That unique tone is none other than the sound bite that Grindr uses to notify its users of a new message. A downloadable app that bills itself as the "world's largest social networking app for gay, bi, trans, and queer people," Grindr has made its staying power a non-negotiable aspect of dating in the twenty-first century, despite a staggering 77 percent of users being "unhappy" to use it (Naselli 2019, 76). Though Grindr is not without its faults, it can be celebrated that the app has democratized access to queer spaces by removing them from the confines of the brick-and-mortar world. It has also given us reason to reexamine and therefore refine our definition of the human body.

For my contribution to this volume on trans identities in French media, I am taking the prefix *trans*-at its most literal meaning of being "on the other side" or "crossing" to analyze the type of body-switching that is central to Arthur Cahn's *Les Vacances du petit Renard* (2018). Susan Stryker defines transgender as the "movement across a socially imposed boundary away from an unchosen starting place" (Stryker 2008, 1). The protagonist of *Les Vacances du petit Renard* uses Grindr to create *multiple* bodies and navigate his sexual identity by constructing several unique online profiles. While Paul, the protagonist, is not transgender or transsexual, he does use Grindr to cross a boundary that has been imposed upon him: because of his age, he cannot interact with his crush in the body he was born in.

My reading of *Les Vacances du petit Renard* will highlight passages where Paul uses one or more digital identities to circumvent the limitations of his physical body. His physical body is too young for a dating app and Hervé (Paul's crush and Paul's aunt's friend) would recognize him. To that end, I will be revisiting my previous scholarship on Deleuze and Guattari's theory of the *corps sans organes* (the body without organs) in tandem with Judith Butler's foundational texts on gender performativity to demonstrate one modern way in which queer people are able to curate their identities. In so doing, I will show that Grindr and similar dating apps reveal the variability and fluidity of the human body. That is, the body comes in many forms and one need not confine themselves to one.

PERFORMING THE SELF

Judith Butler's *Gender Trouble* (1990) remains an applicable foundational text in the field of gender studies. In it, Butler seeks to convince her reader that the creation of gender is a series of performances. This phenomenon, referred to as gender performativity, allows us to establish that inasmuch as all gender is a performance, there is no such thing as a pure, innate gender. Gender is more than a social construct: it is a cooperative project of creation. She suggests that gender is the external projection of an internal core (Butler 1990, 185). Indeed, her entire conceptualization of the human body depends on her reader accepting that the boundaries of the body are politically constructed.

Butler pushes the limits of her own idea of gender performativity by looking at the phenomenon of drag as a manner of mocking the standard gender binary (185). Take the example of the world-famous drag queen, RuPaul. As host of the successful reality show *RuPaul's Drag Race*, RuPaul appears both in and out of drag and reportedly has no pronoun preference. Out of drag, RuPaul presents as conventionally masculine, providing information about the episode's challenge and giving feedback as drag queens prepare. In drag, RuPaul dons beautiful gowns, tall wigs, and critiques the contestants' performance. By so fluidly passing between bodies, RuPaul is able to deconstruct the illusion of gender, putting it on display on national television: RuPaul's biological sex really has no impact on the gender that is being presented.

Certainly, this same example could serve to support the importance of the body's materiality, which Butler elaborated in *Bodies That Matter* (1993). The body's materiality is best defined as how it interacts with the world around it, or how the world around it judges the value of the body. So much of the heterosexual hegemony depends on the materiality of the body: if a body is sexed as male, then it is treated as a masculine-gendered body. If the body's sex is what qualifies a body for cultural intelligibility, as Butler argues, then the drag queen is able to perturb that order by mocking it. Yet a lot of that mocking is able to occur precisely because the queens manipulate a physical body into looking certain ways. The body's materiality is dressed up, altered, and re-presented to the audience which must then see the body in a new way.

What happens, then, when the body is made up of matter that isn't physical at all? This is a question that we can seek to answer in today's connected world, where the creation of digital avatars and online profiles has become commonplace. It may be easy to dismiss digital creations as being less real than the physical bodies that they are supposed to represent. Yet it is far more fruitful to consider that these digital creations allow users to liberate themselves from their physical body, create bodies that correspond to their wants and needs, and proliferate existences quicker than ever before.

Grindr is one example of the plane on which this process of body creation is made possible. Grindr is a downloadable app for smartphones. Founded in 2009, it had grown to more than 10 million users by 2015, its website claiming that it is the largest social networking app for gay, bi, trans, and queer people. When users download the app and create their profile, they are encouraged to add photos to garner attention. They *may* include brief biographies in their profiles yet most of the categories of profile creation pertain to physical characteristics: age, height, weight, body type (toned, average, large, muscular, slim, stocky), and ethnicity. Users may also indicate their preferred role in sex and choose to self-identify in a "tribe." These tribes, of which there are currently (in December 2020) thirteen options, do include some personality-driven modifiers. Yet here as well the user is pushed to further refine their physicality. One might join the "Bear" tribe if they are larger, hairier men, the "Otters" (the Bears's average-build cousins), or the "Twinks," where one finds thinner men usually lacking body hair. The list goes on.

Indeed, Grindr's entire user interface blurs the distinction between social networking app and body creator: the profiles that make up the grid of users do their absolute best to recreate, represent, and re-present the physical body that made them. Grindr is not the only option out there for men who have sex with men (MSM): Hornet, Jack'd, Scruff, and others make up this group of apps that function in more or less the same way. Apps exist, of course, for straight people too, but the *modus operandi* is often different. Emily Witt, in her book *Future Sex* compares the different models and how different audiences require different mechanisms for the apps' success. She writes that:

> The founders of Manhunt, which transitions from a phone chat line to a website in 2001 and became one of the most popular early dating sites for gay men,

quickly recognized that in the world of men interested in meeting men, what job the person had or where he went to college were secondary questions. Sexual attraction and explicitly sexual communication tended to come first. (Witt 2016, 26)

It is clear, then, that the success of apps that came after Manhunt (such as Grindr) assumed that sexual attraction—that is, physical attraction—was the currency of its sexual market. It follows then that Grindr et al. would capitalize on this by frontloading physicality and making it the app's most salient feature.

CREATING A CYBERSELF

Grindr plays an important role in Arthur Cahn's *Les Vacances du petit Renard* (2018). The "little fox" refers to young Paul Renard, the book's titular protagonist. In *Les Vacances du petit Renard*, Paul is a 14-year-old gay adolescent boy who leaves Paris for a family vacation in the South of France. Paul is like many boys his age: he is on the cusp of adulthood and navigating his sexuality. Two events set the plot into motion: Paul meets Hervé, his aunt's 45-year-old best friend, and Paul's parents give him an iPhone for his 14th birthday, which he uses to watch pornography and download Grindr.

From the beginning of the text, Cahn emphasizes Paul and Hervé's bodies. The author introduces other minor characters in the first few pages (Paul's sister, his parents, his aunt Maude), but only Paul and Hervé are described in a way that the reader knows what they look like. Paul "is 13 years old, almost 14, has brown curly hair, dull skin, and is a little puffy. That's him, Paul Renard" (9).[1] As for Hervé, he has white hairs around his temples, dark and thick eyebrows, and skin that shines with "a beige glow" (13).

Time and time again, Paul reveals himself to be obsessed with the pursuit of the physical. He moves quickly from scrolling through Tumblr to watching pornography on his phone. Cahn writes of:

Bare-chested men on parade. They whip their penises—usually huge—out of their sweatpants or their boxers, they wear undershirts, sleeveless ones, or overalls. And they all have a beard and body hair, lots of body hair and some excess weight or sometimes some muscles. Some of them show off tattoos, one in particular which comes up a lot: a bear's paw print. (35)

This description of the men that Paul watches in his pornographies recalls the same type of language employed by Grindr as users create their profiles. The reader learns that the actors are hairy and what type of body they have. The final sentence, in which Paul reveals that he often sees a bear paw print tattoo, recalls the tribes of Grindr: the bear paw is a symbol of the Bear community, appearing notably on Bear pride flags.

At the same time that Paul is using his phone to escape the ennui of his summer vacation, Paul also finds himself falling in love with Hervé. While going downstairs so that he may masturbate in the privacy of his bedroom, Paul sees Hervé and Maude sunbathing in the yard. Hervé is "in a small blue shirt, his sleeves rolled up; his arms come out of his sleeves and cross behind the nape of his neck; his head is resting between his hands. His hair is impeccably combed" (36). Paul stops moving, watches Hervé sunbathe, and unbuttons his pants to masturbate to thoughts of Hervé's mouth, Hervé's hands rubbing Paul's thigh under the table, and to Hervé's penis being revealed at the dinner table (36–37). Cahn's description of Hervé deconstructs the whole man into his constituent body parts. On one hand, it again reinforces the primacy of the body in the very body-oriented activity that is sex. On the other hand, it also foreshadows Paul's later fabrication of a body that he will present to Hervé on Grindr.

As summer continues, Paul finds himself increasingly bored and spending more time on his phone. One night, when everyone is asleep, he opens the App Store in order to download some games to distract himself. Instead, he finds himself typing the word *Grindr* into the search box. He downloads it, ignoring the warning that it is meant for users who are at least 18 years old. Though he feels some anxiety over it, he justifies the download to himself as being just like his videos games and no different than lying about his age in order to watch pornography.

Paul's first steps into the world of Grindr are familiar to anyone who has ever used it or a similar app. In order to participate in this world, Paul must create an account. He arbitrarily chooses the age of 19 and is then able to look through all of the profiles, potentially sending any of them a message. Paul has made the first move toward creating and eventually curating a cyberself-hood. One's cyberself, argued Dennis Waskul in *Self-Games and Body Play*, has all the essential elements of any other self (2003, 43). Waskul goes on to stake the claim that because of the disembodied nature of the internet, "one must literally write oneself into existence" (42). The process of writing oneself into existence is an ongoing task, with the self constantly being presented and negotiated through communication (44). This then becomes another type of performativity, which as Butler reminds us, allows for both gender and sex to be perceived either through the repeated act of the "performer" or through the types of interactions others have with the "performer."[2]

For Waskul, the most important part of one's performance is the screen name. In the absence of other social cues, "screen names function as a kind of substitute" (41). For all his focus on the written word, it's easy to wonder what role—if any—the body will take. Waskul's book is about online chat rooms and cybersex, though. Thus, the body cannot be left out of the equation since sex is by its definition a body-oriented activity. Rather, Waskul posits that in the absence of a body, one needs merely to evoke one in order to participate in cybersex (73). He writes that:

> Sex is an act that requires, or is at least dependent upon, physical bodies . . . yet, in cyberspace, there can be no physical body or fixed material entity that represents the person. Nonetheless, cybersex does not escape claims of the flesh. (89)

It is obvious that differences between sex and cybersex and bodies and cyberbodies present an enigma that cannot be resolved without reconceptualizing bodies and sex altogether. Grindr further reveals lacunae in Waskul's theory that sex can be achieved by writing the body into existence (this theory being perhaps only applicable to the very specific reality of cybersex in chat rooms of the internet's earlier days).

First, it should be noted that cybersex is not the goal of Grindr. Whether or not users are successful in their endeavors, the digital bodies that they use are designed to entice fellow users to engage in physical sex in the physical world. Witt recalls that "Grindr introduced the theory that one could look at a picture of someone's abdomen and soon be having sex with a neighbor, and the theory became a question" (27).

Second, it is hardly conceivable that the screen name could take precedence in a space such as Grindr, precisely because the interactions that begin in this digital space are designed to be carried over into the physical space. Grindr attempts to assure that interactions materialize in the physical world by emphasizing physicality. Paul gets a taste of this the first time he scrolls through his Grindr app:

> A ton of square portraits appears. Each one or nearly each one has a photo of a man, often a face, sometimes a muscular torso, or a closeup of some underwear; empty profiles are rarer. (Cahn, 79)

The use of certain screen names do communicate important information such as penis size or sexual positions, yet this passage shows that the most important seems to be the representation of a physical human body.

Witt wrote that the body was "not a secondary entity," noting that "until the bodies were introduced, seduction was only provisional" (Witt 2016, 21). I would go even further to suggest that on Grindr, the body is a non-negotiable requirement for participation in this world. Paul discovers this the hard way when his lack of digital body shuts him out of this world. The young protagonist is swiping through profiles one night when he comes across Hervé,

11 kilometers away, with a photo of him against a gray brick wall. He sends Hervé a 'salut' ('hi') from an empty profile (that is, one that does not have a photo). The message is simple, of course, but nonetheless Paul's mind rests on that 'salut' as he goes about his day running errands with his mom. When Hervé responds, Paul wastes no time in seeing what he has to say:

> He has a message from RV.[3]
>
> To his *hi*, Hervé has responded: photo? Then a second message: *Are you really 19?*
>
> He doesn't have a photo to send him. Should he respond? He answers: *yes*.
>
> He waits, sitting on the toilet, both hands on the phone, all of his attention directed to the screen.
>
> Outside, it has stopped raining. The birds still aren't singing, though.
>
> *Sorry, without a photo, this is over, especially if you're so young. Happy hunting.*
> Cold shower. (98)

Thus, the protagonist will soon realize that in order to engage with Hervé, he will need a body. However, the reader knows that Paul cannot use his *own* body. For this reason, Paul will need to evoke and then breathe life into bodies that are not his own. Like a digital Dr. Frankenstein, Paul will craft different bodies and then take them on as characters, performing these multiple roles in order to communicate with Hervé. In total, Paul will create three new profiles "to figure out RV" (101).

DIGITAL FRANKENSTEIN IN THE LAB

Paul's first attempt at creating a cyberself that does not in fact correspond to his physical self is rather incomplete. Paul notes that he creates a new profile mostly as a way of multiplying his chances. He does not take the time to curate his profile with details such as his age or his body type. This time, however, he does add a photo of stacks of hay as an avatar. Though clearly not meant to represent a body, the photo of the bales already humanizes Paul's profile over one that is completely blank. That is, in order for a photo to be taken, a physical person must be present in that location. Even if we do not see the person, we generally trust that there was someone on the other side of the lens. Yet the incomplete nature of this profile is perhaps why it is ultimately unsuccessful. Paul does not see Hervé connected and will not interact with him until the character is further developed. In the meantime, Paul is interrupted by Arnaud, the son of a local gardener who is also gay and with whom Paul is pushed to become friends while in the South.

Later, Paul returns to his phone to find Hervé is now connected. Paul must decide who he wants to be and which body he would like to perform on Grindr. He begins the process of creating his first fully-realized digital body by conducting 'research' in a Facebook group for gay men in Québec:

> He clicks on a few profiles. Whom would he like to be? Could he be? Not this man who's starting to go bald. Not this man with the sickly complexion, nor the one posing as a drag queen. But why not Maxime Ménard? Brown-haired, brown-eyed, skin a bit fair, he doesn't look his own age, he must be between 28 and 34. He's slender, certainly taller than him, with a long and very thin face. He scrolls through the photos and finds Maxime very appealing. His smile is always crooked; when he shows himself shirtless—because he has put photos of him at the beach online, he is smooth and his body is skinny yet sculpted, *longitudinal*. (107)

Cahn's language here relies heavily on visual imagery, painting a picture of Maxime Ménard. We don't know anything about his character or personality, but that was never part of Grindr's model. The questions that Cahn poses (whom would he like to be? Could he be?) indicate that Paul is not merely borrowing Maxime. He is becoming Maxime, *performing* as if he were actually Maxime. Paul tells Hervé that his name is Marc, that he is 17 years old, and that he has not had a chance to experience his homosexuality. "Marc" and Hervé communicate often and get to know each other through their conversations.

Paul uses Marc to get closer to Hervé. Through a combination of their conversations and stalking his Facebook, Paul learns intimate, non-sexual details about Hervé:

> Now he knows: his favorite color is purple. His favorite dessert is baba. His dad died three years ago. His ex is allergic to pretty much everything that is a joy to eat. He likes Philippe Katerine. He kept his teddy bear until the sixth grade. One day, he thought that he had seen a ghost. (163)

Likely, Hervé would not have divulged this information to Paul. Or, if he would, the situation would have to have been quite different. However, because Paul is performing the character of Marc, Hervé treats the character as someone in whom he can confide and share these personal details.

Paul later creates another, final alias through which he is able to communicate with Hervé. This body, named Mekamek (a play on words on the homophonic 'man on man'), serves a very different purpose:

> He picks up his phone again. Hervé is online. He decides to create a new profile. Now that he has a small collection of photos, he can dress up new identities if

he chooses. He selects a brown-haired man who is Hervé's age. Fit and hairy. He calls him Mekamek. He says *hi* to RV. Then he adds:

— Horny?

— A little, especially when I see that torso.

— What d'ya like?

— Everything you want.

— Top? Bottom?

— Usually bottom, I like to suck too. Are you hung?

He sends a photo of a penis. (169)

The conversation continues. Hervé asks if Mekamek can host. Paul is of course obliged to deny Hervé. Hervé laughs it off, says "next time," and sends a photo of his butt in the air. Paul sighs and turns off his phone.

Unlike the act of performing Marc, this passage shows that Mekamek's connection to Hervé is much more sexual. This sexuality is explicit, even if it does ultimately fail to produce a physical encounter in the physical world. Paul, who appears to be amassing a collection of photos that will allow him to take on any body that he chooses, is demonstrating just how easily he can cross from body to body, according to his needs. In one form, Paul is able to get Hervé to "se livre[r],"[4] and when conversation slows down, "il revêt [le masque] d'un autre, Mekamek ou une nouvelle invention" (175).[5]

Yet if I have employed Mary Shelley's Dr. Frankenstein as a metaphor for how we might understand Paul's creative process, then I should also recall the ethical concerns that are deeply imbued in this popular monster narrative. Is it wrong to take something from someone else, even if they aren't using it? Should someone play God, even if that is possible? Paul's collection of new inventions illustrates the awesome power that the internet enjoys in the creation of bodies. Waskul speaks of the internet 'disembodying' social interaction or "dislocating" our selfhood from our bodies (2003, 3, 45). The argument *can* be made that Grindr is the tool through which Paul is dissociating his selfhood from his body, yet it misses the fact that Paul is not merely disembodied. He's *liberated* from his body and presented with the opportunity to *multiply* bodies.

With this particular type of body creation, a new question is raised: can we consider these to be bodies at all? Of course, Paul's body is "real," and Maxime's body is equally "real," but are they still real when they navigate a digital space? One indicator that the answer may be "yes" can be found in Julian Dibbell's "A Rape in Cyberspace," in which the author recounts a digital rape that took place in a text-based virtual world called LambdaMOO. One user manipulated the program to force other characters to perform textual sexual acts. The rape in cyberspace is an early indication that if digital bodies are real, we have to ask ourselves if the digital bodies can, should, or do respect the rules that we've come to expect of physical bodies.

In "Hookups," I argued that digital bodies are twenty-first-century iterations of the *corps sans organes* or the body without organs, a concept that is developed in Deleuze and Guattari's *L'Anti-Oedipe* (Troth 2021). Deleuze and Guattari posit that capitalist society is imbued with binaries, not the least of which is the "productive" and its complement the "non-productive." "The whole body without organs is non-productive, sterile, non-produced, non-consumable," they write of the *Corps sans Organes* (Deleuze and Guattari 1972, 19). I think that most people would agree that dating profiles aren't quite the same as the physical body that they (are supposed to) represent. Yet the profiles on Grindr are hardly non-consumable. Rather, it is no harder to scroll through profiles to see what looks good on the sexual market than it is to do one's shopping online.

Oftentimes, we already treat these digital bodies as if they were physical ones precisely because these digital bodies represent potential. We choose to believe that the person behind the screen is the person being re-presented *on* the screen. Without trusting that belief, the entire model of *any* dating app would fail. That is because:

> The body without organs is an egg: it is crossed by axes and thresholds; by latitudes, longitudes, geodesics, it is crossed by gradients that mark what it can become and its journeys, the destinations of the thing that is developing inside. (Deleuze and Guattari 1972, 28)

An egg has no value by itself, and yet we assign it value based on what it could potentially become. The bodies that Paul performs throughout *Les Vacances du petit Renard* are not representative of the body that he actually inhabits. Yet Hervé does not realize that. Hervé has no reason not to believe in the potential that these digital bodies are "real," that they "really" represent who they are supposed to be, and that the interactions can someday become 'more real.'

WHAT IS REAL?

Paul's body-crossing comes with moral shortcomings. In a 2019 *Têtu* article entitled "Ces 10 profils qu'on aimerait ne plus voir sur Grindr," ("The ten profiles we no longer want to find on Grindr") the second entry is the *usurpateur d'identité* (the *identity thief*):

> We've all crossed him at least once, no question. It's a matter of that profile that uses someone else's photo. He tries to pass for a person who perfectly meets beauty standards (that is, well-defined muscles and a face like a Hugo Boss model). (Ques 2016, para. 3)

It is unclear whether Paul regrets his behavior, but he nonetheless recognizes that he is, as we might say in English, catfishing Hervé with his multiple bodies:

> He's in his room. They've left. He creates a new profile. The last profile. *Hung Dom.* He waits. He waits. Outside, on the window frame, a spider is also spinning its web. Hervé gets online. (182)

The use of the adverb "also" draws a parallel between Paul and a spider awaiting its prey. Paul seemingly cannot help himself. Hervé has become a life-sustaining force for him, even if their connection is built on deception. That deception, though, does not mean that the connection isn't real.

Our society is obsessed with the real, with the truth. We seek true love, fact over fiction, a real man, a post-university job in the real world, and so forth. "The thing with real is that once you've experienced it, there's no going back" (McCaffrey 2016, 24). But *what* exactly does it mean to be real? In McCaffrey's article, the line between real and unreal seems to be drawn at technology: "for Hayles, the human body is irreplaceable and technology can only be incorporated into it and human life practices" (24). It seems that as soon as the bodies or the experiences are not physical, their veracity is called into question.

All three of Cahn's gay characters question what it means to be "real" on Grindr at one point or another, and to varying degrees. Hervé asks Paul's first profile if he's really 19; he cannot believe that Marc is only 17. Ironically, it is because Paul is performing the role of Marc too maturely. Paul asks himself:

> What's the meaning of all these little lives, these little stories behind these little vignettes that show heads, torsos, and sometimes something else, a landscape, a drawing, or nothing, are they lying too? Are they inventing themselves? Is this man who calls himself *Very Hung Masc* really 35 years old like he's written, or much older like his photos suggest? Is he really masculine and very hung? (101)

None seem to be more skeptical of Grindr's *realness* than Arnaud, Paul's friend and the son of a local gardener. Arnaud complains that Grindr doesn't produce the types of connections that he would prefer to make with men. He laments:

> You won't find anything beautiful [. . .] It's completely different to meet some-one because he is a part of your world in one way or another. You might tell me that being in the same region is something in common. But I prefer to meet someone because we went to the same concert, because we have friends in com-mon or a job in the same field, rather than because he was less than 800 meters away and we were horny at the same time. (105)

Arnaud's cynicism lies in his refusal to believe that connections on Grindr are genuine or meaningful. For him, simply being geographically close to someone and aroused at the same time is less worthy than having the same musical tastes or common friends. It is a common trope that we hear repeated elsewhere in our lives: we are told to put ourselves out there to find true love, we are told to go outside instead of spending time on our phones.

I would argue, though, that Arnaud is being too critical of Grindr. I *cannot* argue that Paul wasn't deceptive in his use of Grindr, but the line between real and unreal is much blurrier than McCaffrey or Arnaud would like to see it. The following are all true within the world of *Les Vacances du petit Renard*: Paul is a real person, Hervé is a real person, Maxime (the man whose photos are being re-presented as Marc) is a real person in Canada, the conversations are real, the details that Paul learns about Hervé are real. If *all* of these are true statements, do we really believe that Paul's deception can dismantle all that we know to be real?

So what happens when Paul decides to use his *own* body for an interaction with Hervé? His time in the South coming to an end, Paul arranges to have a blindfolded, anonymous hookup with Hervé. When Paul arrives and finds Hervé at the ready, the narrator describes Hervé as "more than real, his body naked, almost naked, even more naked than naked" (184). The impossibility of being more real than real, more naked than naked, forces us to wonder: at what point was Hervé at his most authentically real? At what point was he at his most authentically naked?

These unanswered questions serve to highlight ways in which the division between real and unreal, between genuine and cosmetic is not as stark as we may have once thought. Paul enters Hervé's bedroom, where the latter is blindfolded and waiting:

> When he enters the bedroom, he's there, he's really there, on all fours on the bed, well not exactly, he's resting on his forearms, his butt lifted, raised, spilling

out from his jockstrap like an invitation. When he enters the bedroom, he's there, it's like in a dream, or no, it's actually the opposite, it's like everything before was never anything but a dream [. . .] Like in movies. He's in a movie. He woke up. It's as if he opened his eyes for the first time and of course you have to get used to seeing, to understand perspectives, colors, it all gets so murky, everything is flat: the wall the bed the ass the hair. (184–85)

Cahn's long sentences here serve to create tension and to build suspense. Everything from Paul's summer has been leading up to this moment; the conversations between his constructed identities and Hervé have led to a culminating moment in which all that has been digital can become physical. The reader can feel Paul's excitement and his anticipation as he walks into the room and is confronted by that for which he has longed the entirety of his summer vacation in the South.

Cahn's repeated use of the word "like" introduces several metaphors to describe how Paul is interpreting this moment. The metaphors establish a dichotomy between what is real and what is unreal. At first, Paul thinks that seeing Hervé spread out before him is "like a dream," that is, that what is happening in front of him is only a figment of his imagination. Paul changes his mind and determines that this moment is not a dream, but that everything that has led up to it was only a dream. In that case, then every conversation and interaction with Hervé has become less real in Paul's eyes.

The narrator compares this moment to a video, presumably like the pornographic videos that Paul watches on his phone. We know that Paul attaches real meaning to this type of sexually-explicit content. Earlier in the novel, when he is masturbating to Hervé sunbathing in the lawn, Paul feels guilt over it: "in addition to the distress he should be feeling, he should also be ashamed for having implicated him in his pornographic dream without his permission" (37). Imagined events have real consequences for Paul, just as his appropriation of other bodies has led to this episode in Hervé's bedroom.

McCaffrey has argued that the virtual world is an excess of representation, meaning that its entire existence is dependent on its ability to recreate the real without *being* real. The virtual, he says, is always undermined by a return to the real and once one goes "real," you can never go back to a virtual world that is void of feelings. Paul certainly seems to be overwhelmed by an excess of stimuli that he didn't experience when he was on Grindr. His eyes opening as if for the first time, Paul is struggling to understand what he is seeing. Cahn ends the above passage with a series of nouns yet doesn't use any punctuation to separate them. The effect is that we can almost hear Paul's heart race, put ourselves in his position, and come close to understanding how he feels.

Standing before Hervé's more-than-naked body, Paul is unable to control his emotions. The return to the real is indeed accompanied by a burst of feelings that Paul had avoided through his virtual interactions with Hervé. Cahn writes:

> He realizes that he is going to cry, that it's too much, too strong, too sad, too beautiful, too ugly, too much, too much, too much, and the other rocks back and forth below, not understanding anything about what is happening on the surface of his skin which is too soft, too beautiful, too, too, too, too, and so suddenly he lets go. (186)

And so, it becomes somewhat clearer what Cahn meant when he described Hervé's body as more than real, more than naked. Paul, at one point, spoke Hervé's name aloud. He enjoys it because it is real and he likes feeling Hervé's name on his tongue. Yet there comes a point where real becomes more than real and what Cahn actually means is that it is *too* real. For Paul, the "real" world is too overpowering. His access to it is not as controlled as his access to the digital world and the young boy simply cannot handle it. A series of runaway "too's" is like a train that cannot be stopped. The young protagonist bursts into tears, runs away, and hopes that the abandoned Hervé does not think to go to the window in order to watch him escape.

ESCAPING REALITY . . . AGAIN

It is the end of summer and Paul must return to Paris. Only his sister takes notice that he is crying in the backseat of the family car:

> Anyway, he's going to uninstall Grindr. It doesn't make sense anymore. When he's in Paris, he won't feel like knowing that his baker or his neighbor is looking to suck now. He doesn't want that, or to go to highway rest stop parking lots. He'll have to wait for Hervé. Or another Hervé. He dreams about a man, he will dream while waiting. (187–88)

Throughout the entire book, the reader is not truly privy to Paul's "real world." That is, Paul is temporarily displaced from his normal life, presumably characterized by long days at school and the hustle of the Parisian landscape. His return to Paris is difficult partially because it means leaving Hervé. He wonders how Marc will explain his absence, or surmises that Hervé may realize that Marc's silence and Paul's return to Paris are more than simultaneous coincidences. Yet Paul's return to Paris is also hard because it is a return to the real, and the reader knows that Paul cannot handle that.

And so Paul will dream. He will seek refuge in a world and in a body that are not his own because it is what he must do in order to self-preserve. This essay began by defining *trans* as that which crosses a border and moves away from an unchosen starting point. Paul, despite his youth, is acutely aware of the power that digital body-building has for him. He writes that "nothing can define him, or little can. His body. But not his name. When he speaks to Hervé, he is lying, yet he is more himself than he normally is" (Cahn 2018, 122). Though Paul is not a trans-individual in the way we may think, he benefits from the body-crossing that marked his summer in the South. It may have been morally ambiguous, but one cannot deny that it served Paul a purpose. It protected his true identity, gave him access to a world that would have otherwise been forbidden to him, and allowed him to live out—in some form—an adolescent love story.

Emily Witt writes:

> To experience sexuality was to have a body that pursued a feeling, a dot in the distance toward which it must move. We wanted to follow the body into a more progressive future, to think there might be some intuition to rely upon, but the number of people any one life contained was finite. (Witt 2016, 202)

The same is *not* true of Paul. Paul does not have one body: he has multiple bodies and found a way to create an infinite supply of them. Paul's use of Grindr pushes the theories of gender performativity and the body without organs to new levels. Paul, as I have shown, is not confined to one body. Thus, he does not merely *experience* sexuality and corporality, Paul accrues them. The real world is a fine place, but Paul would prefer to live elsewhere.

NOTES

1. All translations, unless otherwise noted, are my own.
2. Judith Butler, "Introduction," in *Bodies that Matter*.
3. In French, the letters RV are pronounced homophonically to the name Hervé.
4. "to open up."
5. He puts on another mask, Mekamek's or a new creation.

REFERENCES

Butler, Judith. 1993. *Bodies That Matter: On The Discursive Limits of "Sex."* New York: Routledge.

Butler, Judith. 1990. *Gender Trouble: Feminism and The Subversion of Identity*. New York: Routledge, 1990.

Cahn, Arthur. 2018. *Les Vacances du petit Renard*. Paris: Seuil.

Deleuze, Gilles, and Félix Guattari. 1972. *L'Anti-Œdipe*. Paris: Minuit.

Dibbell, Julian. 2005. Reprint. "A Rape in Cyberspace." In *The Village Voice* (December 1993). www.villagevoice.com/2005/10/18/a-rape-in-cyberspace/

McCaffrey, Enda. 2016. "Towards an Ethics of Distance: Representation, Free Production and Virtuality." *Australian Journal of French Studies* 53: 23–38.

Naselli, Adrien. 2019. "Faut-il brÛler Grindr?" *Têtu* (Summer 2019): 74–79.

Ques, Florian. 2016. "Ces 10 profils qu'on aimerait ne plus voir sur Grindr." *Têtu* (October 2016). tetu.com/2019/10/06/ces-10-profils-quon-aimerait-ne-plus-voir-sur-grindr/

Stryker, Susan. 2008. *Transgender History.* Berkeley: Seal Press.

Troth, Brian. "Hookups: Social Networking and Digital Bodies in Twenty-First-Century France." In *Queer(y)ing Bodily Norms in Francophone Culture,* edited by Polly Galis, Antonia Wimbush and Maria Tomlinson, 29–45. New York: Peter Lang.

Waskul, Dennis D. 2003. *Self-Games and Body Play: Personhood in Online Chat and Cybersex.* New York: Peter Lang.

Witt, Emily. 2016. *Future Sex.* New York: Farrar, Straus and Giroux.

Chapter 4

Dubbing *Transparent* (2014–2019)

A "Ballsy" Translation?

Justine Huet

The titular "ballsy"—"couillue" in French—is what Sarah Pfefferman calls her parent who just came out as transgender to the family in the French version of the Amazon series *Transparent*. While the translation choice for the adjective "brave" in the original version (OV) may sound odd, or possibly humorous, at least to some viewers, the French translation quickly devolves into a problematic portrayal of characters who are gender non-conforming. The French version's take on transgender identity can be disheartening considering how innovative and thought-provoking a series *Transparent* was, declared as a "transgender tipping point" (Steinmetz) and "the transgender wave in the media" (Espineira 2018, 30) in the United States. Despite some issues raised by the transgender community,[1] *Transparent* was not only both a critical and commercial success for Amazon in the United States, but also groundbreaking insofar as the series features the first mature transgender lead character on television.

In France, *Transparent* airs in its French dubbed and subtitled version;[2] in the former, each character's voice is replaced with a corresponding foreign-language audio track provided by a voice actor. While the belief that dubbing and, by extension, translation, is a simple transfer of meaning between languages has long been debunked, dubbing has the dubious distinction of originating in fascist regimes of the 1940s (Danan 1991, 610), which we will revisit later on. In light of its origins, it comes as little surprise that dubbing is often criticized for its "domesticating" approach (Venuti 1995, 20), understood as the suppression of the original version's "foreignness," and its manipulation, if not outright censorship, of controversial content. If we understand dubbing as both a process and a product anchored in a target[3] language culture whose sociocultural and linguistic norms inevitably condition the translation of the audiovisual text, what version of *Transparent* are French viewers watching? To what extent does the French dubbing of transgender characters and discourse in *Transparent* reflect the lived experience of the French transgender community?

In order to answer these questions, we will examine the terminological inconsistencies in the French version (FV) of *Transparent* as well as its failure to grasp trans identity. At times the FV critiques trans identity—compounded with misgendering—by assuming that it is a choice rather than the expression of one's self, while, at other times, it is infused with a more inclusive and pedagogical intent aiming at educating the French audience about the transgender community and other queer and trans identities. The FV's inconsistencies is evidence of the lack of understanding of trans identity from the translation team, which affects the characterization of the main cast.

We will briefly observe to what extent the sociocultural, political and audiovisual contexts influence the series' message and function. We will then determine the role of translation in (re)creating and (re)presenting trans identity and trans voices in the media, with keeping this key question in mind: if "translation is . . . 'speaking for someone else'. . . " (Robinson 2019, xi), who speaks for trans characters in the French version? The final and last section of the article will attempt to answer this question through a close investigation of the French dubbing of *Transparent*.

WORLDS APART: THE AMERICAN AND FRENCH SOCIOCULTURAL AND POLITICAL CONTEXTS

The audience is first introduced to *Transparent*'s main character, Mort(on) Pfefferman,[4] a Jewish, (apparently) cisgender and heterosexual man who comes out as transgender to his family. Pfefferman's true identity is that of Maura, a woman. While we would expect Maura's relationships to become strained and for her[5] to face resistance and even rejection from Sarah, Ali and Josh, her three children, and Shelly, her ex-wife, Maura's coming out sets them free; the family embarks on a journey of self-discovery and an exploration of past trauma. As a result, the family unit becomes closer, with the notable exception of Maura's transphobic sister, Bryna.

Transparent is first and foremost a story about family relationships and love. The series is partly an autobiographical family affair; Joey Soloway, the show's creator, based it on their own lived experience. Their parent came out as trans at the age of 75 in 2011, three years prior to the series premiere; Soloway co-wrote the series with their sister and subsequently came out as non-binary, like Ali, one of Maura's children. Inspired by the lived experience of gender expansive identities, Soloway lends a distinctive softness to the cinematography and treats trans bodies with reverence. In a refreshing and welcoming take on trans bodies, that are often hypersexualized, fetishized and meant to be "looked at" by a heterosexual cisgender male audience (Espineira 2016, 326), the camera caresses Maura's body without ever objectifying her.

QUEER[6] IN AMERICA: BETWEEN RECOGNITION AND ERASURE OF THE TRANSGENDER COMMUNITY

Maura's family embraces her trans identity not only with humor but, first and foremost, with indefectible and unconditional love. Maura's community is also depicted as, for the most part, accepting and tolerant of her. While a history of the American transgender community would be beyond the scope of the article—and our expertise—a few key events are necessary in order to fully grasp the "lineage" of *Transparent* and its impact on American culture. Various opposing forces have shaped the fate of the transgender community which seems to be going down a similar path as the 1960s Black Civil Rights movement, insofar as it is a struggle for recognition and equality often met with political rejection, especially under Trump's presidency—the last two seasons aired during his administration.

The fight for recognition and acceptance of trans and gender non-conforming identities coincides with the birth of departments of Women's and Gender Studies, and queer studies in the United States following the import of so-called "French Theory" in the 1970s and 1980s. The recycling of theories of sexual identities and gender proposed by French scholars such as Michel Foucault, Luce Irigaray, Gilles Deleuze, Jacques Derrida and Hélène Cixous, to name but a few, allowed American scholars to start questioning the essentialist approach to gender as a natural extension of sex assigned at birth. In that regard, Michel Foucault's *History of Sexuality* (1978) is a fundamental work in the deconstructionist theories of sexuality and gender in which the French thinker challenges discourses around both normative and non-normative sexualities. Jacques Derrida's questioning of the logic of binary oppositions at the center of Western thinking and its relationship to language also has had a lasting impact on the deconstruction of binary thinking.[7] The work of these scholars led to the birth of queer theory in the 1980s and 1990s. The application of the word "queer" was the reappropriation of what was a slur at a time when American health officials and political authorities linked AIDS to gay men—AIDS was then known as GRID, gay-related immune deficiency—and transsexualism[8] was still labelled as a gender identity disorder by the *American Psychiatric Association* (Meyerowitz 2002, 255). Since the 1990s, organizations fighting for trans people's rights and acting in favor of the community's interests have multiplied. Transgender advocacy groups, such as the now-defunct *GenderPAC*—the first national transgender advocacy group –founded by scholar Riki Anne Wilchins in 1995, fight against any form of discrimination associated with gender and other oppressions: race, sex, social class, age, etc.[9] On the legislative front, a number of states include transgender people in non-discrimination laws.

The 2000s bore witness to trans activism with the inclusion of the "T" in the LGBT umbrella. On the legal front, however, numerous states still demand sex affirmation surgery to acquire new identity papers and, to this day, there is still no comprehensive non-discrimination law that includes gender identity at the federal level of government. Discriminations endure and are legally sanctioned in different American states, the most infamous and mediatized one being discrimination based on gender identity in public accommodations, that is, the prohibition of transgender people from accessing public bathrooms that correspond with their gender identity. Or, as recently as December 2017, the American administration under Trump banned the word "transgender" from documents used in the elaboration of the budget from the *Centers for Disease Control and Prevention*.[10]

In contrast, in the contemporary United States, academic departments of Gender and Women's Studies are now commonplace and many researchers on trans identity are actively disseminating their work, including Sandy Stone in her milestone work "The Empire Strikes Back: The Posttranssexual Manifesto" (1989), Kate Bornstein, Riki Anne Wilchins, Judith Butler and Susan Stryker.[11] Cultural and intersectionality studies have taken a firm hold in American academic circles and allow scholars to make sense of and investigate the marginalization of communities at the intersection of race, class, religion and gender.

Besides academic circles, one of the most significant contributors to the visibility and acceptance of the transgender community is undoubtedly the entertainment industry. Since the 2010s, trans personalities such as Chaz Bono, Laverne Cox and MJ Rodriguez have become public icons and beacons of hope for the transgender communities whose lives are increasingly, and positively, featured in popular TV series—*Transparent, Orange is the New Black, Vida, Pose* and *Euphoria* to name a few.

THE QUEER THREAT TO THE FRENCH REPUBLIC:
A MITIGATION STORY

It would be fair to assume that, since "French theory" has been revolutionary in the rethinking of gender identities, the French intelligentsia would have been forerunners in studying the intersection between queer theory, cultural studies and interdisciplinary studies. This is not the case, however, and by the 1970s, French poststructural scholars gradually disappeared from the center stage. In fact, " . . . Europe had seen little formal transgender activism between the heyday of the sexual liberation movements and the early 1990s" (Stryker 2006, 5). As a telling example of the lack of interest from French intellectuals in deconstructing gender, Judith Butler's *Gender Trouble*, published in 1990, did not have a French translation until 2005, which coincides with a renewed but cautious interest for cultural studies within French academic circles, and who, until then, had shown little to no interest in—even outright scorn and rejection of—the Anglocentric cultural studies theories and their perceived "ghettoization" as threats to the French republican[12] identity (Bourcier 2005, 393). Indeed, "queer theory" is considered a direct threat to the French universalism narrative according to Bruno Perreau (2016):

> Queer theory argues that identification and deidentification work in tandem. The theory therefore runs afoul of how belonging exclusively to the nation is posed as a condition of citizenship in France, both in public discourse and in law. In the French republic, 'communitarianism,' acknowledging a basic loyalty to a given community (whether ethnic, religious, cultural, or sexual), is viewed as a democracy-corrupting illness. Across almost the entire political spectrum, from far left to far right . . . France is described as living under the constant threat of disintegration as a result of the effect of communitarianism. (145)

Eric Fassin, a French sociologist, succinctly explains the rejection of intersectionality and cultural studies in academic circles: "In France, . . . feminism did not take hold at universities at the end of the 1970s. The structure of the French University neither knew how, nor wanted, to make room for feminists who were doomed then to either marginalization or conversion. There have been very few feminist careers until very recently. As a consequence, France does not have a developed field of study that would be comparable to the one found in the United States"[13] (17). The "ghettoization spectre"[14] (18) effectively scared off any scholar interested in rethinking marginalized identities, benefiting a binary and essentialist system where communitarianism is incompatible with an idealized republican universalism. The expression and production of minority knowledge were interpreted as threats to Republican universalism: "The republican discourse enables the rejection of feminism and, more broadly, challenges to sexualities, while capitalizing on anti-Americanism. Indeed, they claim, on one hand, it would be opening up the door to American-style communitarianism, and, on the other hand, it would undermine the separation between the public and private spheres, just like it is supposedly happening on the other side of the Atlantic"[15] (18). Todd Reeser also points at the ubiquitous nature of the nation-state in France where " . . . transgender subjects are frequently defined through nation-based discourses, institutions, and state-sanctioned forms of power, including especially the arduous process related to changing one's *état civil*" (4).

The pseudo "natural" identity pushed by the French republican discourse is at the center of Sam/Marie-Hélène Bourcier's works, one of the very few French researchers bringing cultural studies to the hermetic French academic realm. A few contemporary French scholars are now acknowledging and harnessing the power and richness of cultural studies and exploring how they can contribute to understanding the multiplicity, or unreliability, of identity. In addition to Sam/Marie-Hélène Bourcier, whom we will discuss later in our analysis of *Transparent*, one such scholar is Karine Espineira, a French sociologist who specializes in the media representation of trans identity in France through an intersectional lens and is the founder of the now-defunct *L'Observatoire des transidentités*. In their works, Espineira surveys the visibility of the French trans community and traces it back to the 1960s–1970s, a time when " . . . 'to break out of isolation even at the cost of being marginalized' describes the context surrounding the birth of the first organizations"[16] (Espineira 2015a, 89). In the 1980s and 1990s, the mediatization of trans identity coincided with the creation of new organizations whose goal is "to welcome and support" trans people (89).[17] French militancy in both academic circle and in the streets is virtually non-existent, at least in the way it was being done in the United States at the time, and it will not be until 1993 for "discourses and demands related to the state of the trans community, and within medical protocols, to evolve and become more assertive" (90).[18] The 1990s militant turn was reflected at the legislative level in France with the possibility of changing one's sex on identity documents, provided the change is supported by medical or surgical procedures, including sterilization. This obligation was only abrogated in 2018, ten years after the French government announced that trans identity will no longer be considered a psychiatric illness.

These advances were made possible with "[t]he 2000s [trans] organization boom in France" (Espineira 2015a, 90)[19] and facilitated by the Internet and social networks enabling trans associations to occupy "public space as a political space" (91).[20] Despite legal progress, in France, between 2016 and 2017, the number of violent incidents against transgender people has increased by 53 percent, as reported by *SOS homophobie*—physical threats, aggressions, insults, and slurs targeting mostly trans youth (Calvès 2019).

While the media has contributed significantly to the visibility of the trans community in the United States, this is not quite the case in France, according to Karine Espineira and Maude-Yeuse Thomas (2014): " . . . a 'televisual transsexualism' starts taking shape during those years [from the beginnings of mediatization to the 1970s] and buttresses the maintenance of gender hierarchy. The staging of *something acceptable and consensual to be seen* comes from a dominant sociocultural and heterocentric model of representation" (para. 3)[21] or again "media discourses constantly produce and reproduce a naturalist and essentialist binarism" (para. 17).[22] Trans people shown in the French media—mainly documentaries and talk shows—are only acceptable as long as they "pass" and follow heterocentric gender norms. Whether this gender essentialism is at work in the translation of *Transparent* remains to be determined.

BEING TRANS IN TRANSLATION

"By translation, we understand all the negotiations, intrigues, calculations, acts of persuasion and violence, that to which an actor or a force takes, or causes to be conferred on itself, authority to speak or act on behalf of another actor or force . . ." (Callon and Latour as cited in Robinson 2019, xvii). If language is ideologically layered (Spurling 2014, 203), and if a translation can never be a neutral transfer of meaning, this overtly negative definition from Callon and Latour seems fitting. As a transcultural and mediated practice that can be disruptive, dissident and transgressive (Spurling 2014, 202), translation operates within "contact zones," those "social spaces where cultures meet, clash, and grapple with each other, often in contexts of highly asymmetrical relations of power, such as colonialism, slavery, or their aftermaths as they are lived out in many parts of the world today" (Pratt 1991, 34). If "translation . . . is 'speaking for someone else' . . . " (Robinson 2019, xi), who speaks for transgender characters in *Transparent* and what do they actually say?

In dubbing, target language actors speak for the original version actors. Dubbing, to put it as succinctly as possible, is to replace the original dialogue with voices recorded in the target language and to synchronize them (lip-synch) to perfect the illusion that the characters speak, in our case, French. Dubbing has to be as undetectable (or invisible) as possible in order to "pass"[23] for the original version. France is one of the main countries that favor dubbing over subtitling—Spain, Italy and Germany are other dubbing European countries. This nationalistic technique (Danan 1991, 610) dates back to WWII and was designed to minimize the influence of American culture and language and to ensure the future of a national language in the service of social cohesion in France. In other words, the goal was, through a "domesticating" process (Venuti 1995, 20), to suppress the voice of the Other and minimize any forms of otherness to turn the product into a recognizable and acceptable Same. Prime for manipulation and censorship, dubbing has its fans and detractors, mistakes and censorship often eliciting ridicule such as the French version of the movie *Dumbbells*, briefly available on *Netflix*, crowned "the worst French dubbing ever" (Turcan 2016). Where does manipulation occur, then? Because of the complex nature of dubbing, every step can lead to varying degrees of manipulation.[24]

When it comes to translating transgender characters, little research has been conducted. In "Translating Gender on Screen Across languages: The Case of *Transamerica*," Alessandra De Marco (2017) conducts a linguistic analysis of the Italian dubbing of the American film *Transamerica* and notes that "the main difference between the SL [source language] and the TL [target language] which emerges from an analysis of the film's dialogue is the opposition between the grammatically gendered nature of the TL and the grammatically neuter SL. Such a difference profoundly affects the AVT [audiovisual translation] in relation to adjectives, copular verbs, verb tenses which in the TL require a gender agreement with the person they refer to" (124).

Szymon Misiek (2020) draws a similar conclusion in his article "Misgendered in Translation?: Genderqueerness in Polish Translations of English-language Television Series" in which he analyzes the Polish translation of non-binary characters' speech and the consequences on their characterization in *Degrassi: Next Class*, *Billions* and *She-Ra and the Princesses of Power*. The author concludes that the heavily gendered Polish language "erase[s] the non-binary characters' identities" (179) through systematic misgendering—feminine forms being privileged in some instances while masculine forms prevail in others. We would then assume and expect a similar observation for French, another grammatically gendered language.

DUBBING *TRANSPARENT*: THE TRIALS OF THE TRANSGENDER COMMUNITY IN FRENCH SOCIETY AND LANGUAGE

Transparent is the visual presentation of " . . . the contrary subjective identities of transsexuals, the sartorial practices of transvestites and the gender inversion of butches and queens [that] all work to confound simplistic notions of material determinism, and mirror-style representation practices, in relation to questions of gender" (Stryker 2006, 9). The show introduces its audience to an array of non-normative identities—cross-dressers, so-called butch and femme lesbians, non-binary characters, drag queens, transsexuals as well as subversive imbroglios in the storylines. Issues of race, class, rape and the Israeli-Palestinian conflict are all seamlessly part of a show that goes far beyond the impact of one trans person's coming out story.

THE DOOM AND GLOOM OF
BEING TRANS IN FRENCH

Maura comes out to her three children in the series premiere while still dressed in men's clothing:

> MAURA: *There's a big change going on*, and . . . oh God, I love you kids, I love you kids, I love you kids, I love you kids.

> MAURA: *Il va y avoir du changement dans nos vies* et je . . . oh Seigneur! Je vous aime. Je vous aime tellement. Je vous aime tellement. Je vous aime tellement.

(Season 1, episode 1; *emphasis added*)

The FV reproduces a dominant model in discourses surrounding a trans coming out narrative where "family and socio-professional consequences are always discussed" (Espineira 2015b, 59)[25] in the early media coverage of trans identity in France. While the OV uses implicit language ("there's a big change going on"), the FV inserts the possessive "nos vies" ("our lives"), effectively displacing the impact Maura's coming out will have; this is no longer an intimately lived-in experience of one person and, instead, it will have an impact on the entire family. While this might be a subtle and benign manipulation of the subtext, as the series progresses, season 4 provides blatant examples of a translation placing the emphasis on the suffering a trans person's coming out inflicts on others.

In season 4, the family goes on a pilgrimage to Israel to reconnect with their Jewish heritage. While lost in the desert, Maura has hallucinations of herself as a transgender youth. Young Maura asks older Maura:

> YOUNG MAURA: Do you remember when you thought if you weren't trans *you wouldn't hurt anymore*?

> YOUNG MAURA: Tu te souviens de l'époque où tu pensais que si tu n'étais pas trans *tu ne ferais plus souffrir personne*?

(Season 4, episode 8; *emphasis added*)

The VF shifts the emotional impact living one's true gender identity can have. While it affects the person making their coming out in the OV, it makes others suffer in the FV ("you would not make anybody suffer anymore"). The VF insists on the negative impact the existence of a trans family member has on others.

In the VF, the entire society is in fact more hostile to trans people. In one particularly revelatory scene, Maura is shopping for clothes and is verbally attacked by a cisgender client who is with her daughter:

CUSTOMER: I'm calling security because there are young women in here that *you* are traumatizing.

CUSTOMER: Je vais appeler la sécurité parce que la présence de *ce dégénéré* traumatise ces jeunes filles.

(Season 4, episode 4; *emphasis added*)

While the customer is transphobic in the OV, the pronoun "you" becomes a vicious "ce dégénéré" ("this degenerate"), which perpetuates the belief that trans women are mentally ill or are sexual predators. Even worse, this hateful name-calling appears to be internalized by Maura herself, shortly after the incident, in a self-loathing that is not present in the OV. After leaving her Pacific Palisades mansion to her daughter Sarah and her girlfriend to go live with Davina, her transgender friend, Maura goes for dinner at Sarah's. Davina is in disbelief when she enters the mansion Maura has left behind. However, Maura warns her that this neighborhood is not a safe haven for trans people:

MAURA: They would *chase our kind out with a stick.*

MAURA: Ils *s'amuseraient à lapider les dégénérés* comme nous.

(Season 1, episode 6; *emphasis added*)

Maura not only refers to herself and trans people as degenerates but the FV also switches "chase with a stick" to a more violent "they would enjoy stoning degenerates like us": the act of naming oneself by Maura is revelatory of a problematic internalized self-identity in the FV. The violence of the imagery in the FV surpasses the OV and paints a grim picture of the broader society depicted in *Transparent*.[26]

Not only is the society depicted as more violent toward trans women but it is also far cruder and sexually explicit in the FV. The FV tends to sexualize trans people—Espineira (2016) drew a similar conclusion in her studies of the French media depiction of trans people. The FV resorts to crude language when Maura is attending a transgender support group. Valerie, one of the participants, recounts an encounter with a man:

VALERIE: As a trans woman, I appreciate that you want me because I'm trans, I'm good with that. What's inappropriate is asking me things like, are you *fully functional*?

VALERIE: En tant que trans, ça m'pose aucun problème qu'un mec me désire parce que j'suis transgenre. C'que j'ai pas du tout apprécié, c'est quand il a voulu savoir si *mon garage à bites était fonctionnel.*

(Season 2, episode 3; *emphasis added*)

The euphemistic "fully functional" becomes a more explicit and coarser "dick garage" in the FV, which incidentally focuses on male genitalia, a tendency the FV displays as we have seen previously with the titular "ballsy." The French language is a grammatically gendered one, and the FV emphasizes this aspect to buttress the intolerance of some characters and the tolerance of others; it arguably becomes one of the characteristics of the FV.

THE DUAL AND OPPOSING PURPOSE OF RESORTING TO GENDERED LANGUAGE: DENYING AND AFFIRMING TRANS IDENTITY

If doubts about the reluctance to adopt a more gender-inclusive vocabulary in France exist, a look at the debate surrounding inclusive writing—non-sexist writing including epicene wording—should put those doubts to rest. Faced with growing calls for inclusive writing, the *Académie française* (2017)—the linguistic authority overruling the norms of the French language in France—went so far as to declare that the French language was in "péril mortel" ("mortal danger") because of it. The debate around inclusive writing concluded with its ban from schools by the French Education Minister in 2021. Needless to say, much remains to be done for an inclusive French language and, more than ever, this governmental decision confirms that language is "ideologically layered" (Spurling 2014, 203).

Since inclusive writing is not sanctioned by official authorities in France and since dubbing studios tend to adhere to official linguistic norms in place, the translation team uses gendered language to its advantage to play on the performativity of gender. Susan Stryker's take on gender performativity deserves to be quoted at length:

To say that gender is a performative act is to say that it does not need a material referent to be meaningful, is directed at others in an attempt to communicate, is not subject to falsification or verification, and is accomplished by 'doing' something rather than 'being' something . . . The biologically sexed body guarantees nothing; it is necessarily there, a ground for the act of speaking, but it has no deterministic relationship to performative gender. *A woman, performatively speaking, is one who says she is—and then who does what woman does.* (10; *emphasis added*)

Maura refers to herself as a woman—and presents as one—and the FV plays with the performativity of gender through its use of gendered language to shore up the transphobia of some characters and the tolerance and acceptance of others.

Bryna, Maura's sister, is the only family member who is not accepting of Maura for who she is and is unrelenting in her verbal abuse and misgendering. When Maura expresses her desire to visit her mother to Bryna, her sister lashes out at her:

> BRYNA: I forbid you Mort. You let that woman get off this planet *without knowing about this.*

> BRYNA: Je te l'interdis Mort. Laisse cette femme quitter cette planète *sans lui imposer cette vision d'horreur.*

> (Season 2, episode 1; *emphasis added*)

The OV remains implicit ("without knowing about this") whereas the FV is explicit and vicious ("without imposing this horrific vision on her"): Bryna's transphobia is more pronounced in the FV. In addition to her refusal to use Maura's proper name in both versions, Bryna repeatedly misgenders her in the FV:

> BRYNA: You're so *ungrateful.*

> BRYNA: T'es pas *reconnaissant.*

> (Season 3, episode 1; *emphasis added*)

The FV uses the masculine form of adjectives to underscore Bryna's transphobia throughout the course of the series. What is more troubling, however, is, while Bryna finally seems to accept Maura's true identity in the fourth season, she sees it as a hereditary illness *à la* Zola:

> BRYNA: It's like dyslexia. You're born with it; you can't help it.

> BRYNA: C'est comme la dyslexie. On naît avec, *c'est héréditaire*, on n'y peut rien.

> (Season 4, episode 9; *emphasis added*)

Conversely, the use of a gendered language in the French dubbing emphasizes the tolerance of some parts of Maura's community. When Dean Carl runs into Maura after her coming out, he compliments her both in the OV, "you look great," and in the FV, in which he uses the feminine adjective "radieuse" ("radiant") (season 2, episode 1). A similar translation trope applies to Shelly,

Maura's ex-wife, who is the first one of her relatives to acknowledge her identity as a woman. The French dubbed Shelly consistently uses the feminine form of adjectives:

(1a) SHELLY: I hope you feel *beautiful*. You are *beautiful*

SHELLY: J'espère que tu t'sens *belle* parce que *t'es la plus belle personne que je connaisse.*

(Season 2, episode 1; *emphasis added*)

(1b) SHELLY: *We* had some good times.

SHELLY: *Toutes* les deux on a eu de bons moments.

(Season 2, episode 2; *emphasis added*)

Additionally, the FV is hyperbolic and accentuates Shelly's acceptance of Maura with the use of the superlative "you're the most beautiful person I know" (1a).

"BALLSY" HUMOR AND PUNS AS A WAY TO STRENGTHEN BINARISM

The FV also heavily relies on puns and humor through the use of a gendered and binary language, which would indicate that a certain 'normalization' of trans identity by the translators might be at work. Additionally, the use of a type of humor relying on binary oppositions arguably makes Maura's identity more acceptable to the audience.

When Maura and her friend Mark arrive at a cross-dressing retreat, Maura excitedly notices the first attendees wearing dresses:

MAURA: Excuse us, *we're new*.

MAURA: Excusez-nous on vient d'arriver, vite *on tombe le pantalon.*

(Season 1, episode 8; *emphasis added*)

In the FV, the expression "let's lose the pants" reproduces a form of gender essentialism (Espineira and Thomas 2014, 18) where women would traditionally wear dresses and men pants. The FV previously used the same trope in season 1, episode 6 in which Maura moves to a residence where several trans people live together. Two residents are having a conversation and one of them cheekily tells the other: "Anybody can be your kind of man." In the FV, the character declares: "Tout c'qui porte un pantalon est ton type d'homme" ("everything that wears pants is your type of man") in a reversal of the infamous sexist saying "tout ce qui porte une jupe" ("everything that wears a skirt"), which once again reproduces essentialistic patterns.

The FV's language also plays on human anatomy as suggested in the title of this article. When Tammy is discussing her parent's coming out with her girlfriend, she calls her "brave" in the OV which becomes a crass "couillue" ("ballsy") (season 1, episode 2) in the FV. This is not a one-off attempt at this type of humor since Vicky, Maura's girlfriend in season 2, tells her that she is "cool" in the OV, which inexplicably becomes "couillue" (season 2, episode 9) in the FV. These different translation decisions indicate an attempt at humor targeted at the French audience. The FV seems resolutely focused on corporality and, more particularly, male genitalia.

In an episode where Maura, Sarah and Ali decide to attend the Michigan Womyn's Music Festival (Michfest) where trans women are excluded—only "womyn-born-womyn" are allowed, which is a direct reference to trans-exclusionary feminism[27]—Maura, who has not undergone a sex reassignment surgery due to health issue, sharply bites back at the attendees:

MAURA: *This woman* is leaving this *feminist fuckhole*.

MAURA: *La femme avec des burnes* quittte ce putain de *ghetto féministe*.

(Season 2, episode 9; *emphasis added*)

Not only does Maura refer to herself as having "burnes" ("balls") but, more importantly, the "feminist fuckhole" in the OV becomes a telling "ghetto" in the FV. The dubbing seems to allude to the fear of communitarianism and ghettoization within French society, which echoes Sam/Marie-Hélène Bourcier's take on the ideology of French universalism in *Sexpolitiques* (2005):

French universalism is a particularism that refuses to say its name. But it's increasingly difficult to deny it. This is the reason why we have been witnessing for the past four or five years a real backlash with the emergence of literary works against communitarianism, be it from the political right or left ends. This backlash is bent on blaming tribes and other 'ghetto' fans for particularism: American-style feminists, Jews, gays . . . [t]he conspicuous, visible ones . . . , those supporters of identity politics who are deemed guilty just so the politics of French identity enforced by the republic will remain hidden. (393)[28]

The rejection of communities and other visible minority groups with different claims and objectives is at the core of French universalism and the French version of Maura apparently subscribes to this discourse. French Maura wants to "pass" for a woman-born-woman, thus becoming invisible within a French society whose motto is "liberté, égalité, fraternité," three values that are thought to be universal and, according to French nationalism, citizens are equal regardless of race, gender, religion and culture. This ideology effectively shrugs off the reality of what is meant by "French citizen," namely a white, cisgender, heterosexual man. The translation choice in this particular scene is not benign and more inconsistencies seem to reinforce the republican discourse at work in the FV.

DID YOU SAY TRANS, TRANSGENRE, OR TRANSSEXUELLE? ISSUES IN TERMINOLOGY

The FV struggles with appropriate terminology and shows increasing inconsistencies that deeply affect the characterization of the main cast. Chief among those is the interchangeable use of "transsexuelle," "trans" and "transgenre," sometimes in the same scene. Very briefly, we understand that "[t]ransgender is for the most part a vernacular term developed within gender communities to account for the cross-identification experiences of people who may not accept all of the protocols and strictures of transsexuality . . . The term transgender in this context refuses the stability that the term transsexual may offer to some folks, and it embraces more hybrid possibilities for embodiment and identification" (Halberstam 2005, 53–54). Or again, "[t]his broad umbrella term becomes an even broader umbrella when it is abbreviated to 'trans'" (Robinson 2019, xi). Both contemporary French and American trans communities widely use "transgender/transgenre," "trans" and refer to "trans identity/identities" as opposed to "transsexuelle/transsexual" and "transsexualisme/transsexualism," the latter pair now considered stigmatizing and pathologizing (Espineira 2018, para. 21).[29]

Sarah is the worst offender when it comes to referring to her parent's identity:

(2a) SARAH: *Outing a trans person*, it's like an act of *violence*.

SARAH: Pour *un transsexuel, sortir du placard*, c'est un acte de *grande* violence.

(Season 1, episode 4; *emphasis added*)

(2b) SARAH: Anyway, I say this because I have a *trans parent.*

SARAH: Je dis ça parce que j'ai moi-même un *père transsexuel.*

(Season 3, episode 1; *emphasis added*)

In the OV, the act of outing a trans person against their will, a real-life occurrence, is violent. The FV, however, reverses the situation and, not only, does

Sarah declare that to out oneself is an act of "great" violence (2a) (hyperbolic adjective) toward others, but she also refers to her parent as a "transsexual father" (2b). This translation choice is difficult to explain since the OV is a callback to the title of the show and could have easily been translated by "parent trans." While Sarah's inexplicable denial of her trans parent's identity is inconsistent with her use of the feminine forms to refer to Maura throughout the series, the terminological confusion affects Sarah throughout the series. Additionally, French Sarah also seems to point out, once again, the negative impact a trans person's coming out has on their relatives. The denial of trans identity is not Sarah's prerogative and other characters go down a similar path, like Ali in season 2, episode 3:

> ALI: I'm just here 'cause *my parent* is *giving a lecture* at the conference.
>
> ALI: J'accompagne *ma, mon père* qui *participe* à la conférence. (*emphasis added*)

The FV clearly indicates a shift in discourse and characterization. While, in the OV, Ali calls Maura her "parent," in the FV, Ali is hesitant and even confused about her parent's identity and mumbles her explanation using the feminine form of "my" immediately followed by the masculine one and juxtaposed to "père" ("father"). To add insult to injury, Maura, who is an accomplished scholar giving a lecture, becomes a mere "participant" at a conference in the FV.

Additionally, throughout the show, the FV favors "transsexuelle" over the broad umbrella term "trans," which came into use in the 1990s and was popularized in the early 2000s. When Shelly muses "I might be *trans*," her French counterpart wonders whether she might be "*transsexuelle*" (season 4, episode 9; *emphasis added*); Vicky welcomes Maura's presence at the lesbian festival with "I believe that *transwomen* have every right to be here" but, in FV, she tells her "J'estime qu'on ne devrait pas bannir les *transexuelles*" (season 2, episode 9; *emphasis added*). Leslie, one of the festival attendees, does not want "*transwomen* around" or, in the FV, "des *femmes transsexuelles*" (*emphasis added*). What is more troubling is that Maura refers to herself as "transsexuelle" when she finds out that she cannot undergo a gender reassignment due to health issues:

> (3a) MAURA: *I've already transitioned*, I'm *trans*, I'm just . . . *me*.
>
> MAURA: Ça ne m'empêche pas d'être *transsexuelle*. C'est mon . . . *destin*.
>
> (3b) MAURA: Some days *you don't know who was gonna show up*.
>
> MAURA: On se réveille certains jours et *on se sent plus homme que femme*.

(3c) MAURA: Honey, I should have taken you out to lunch and *we should have talked* but I didn't do that. And I'm sorry about the Mort and the Maura and the he and the she. I'm just a person and you're just a person. And here we are.

MAURA: J'aurais dû vous parler de ma *trans identité* autour d'un déjeuner mais je ne l'ai pas fait. Et je suis désolée pour Mort qui devient Maura et il qui devient elle. *C'est déstabilisant* mais je suis avant tout une personne tout comme vous.

(Season 1, episode 6; *emphasis added*)

These few examples give us a glimpse into the profound alteration of Maura's characterization in the FV. Indeed, the FV is more critical and fatalistic than the OV. While American Maura has transitioned and has asserted her identity, her French counterpart is "transsexual" (3a) and in the process of becoming because it is her "destiny/fate" (3a); the FV denies her agency. American Maura also rejects the norms and limits of gender when she recalls her life before her coming out; the use of "who was gonna show up" (3b) and "I'm just me" (3a) clearly indicates that her identity "embraces more hybrid possibilities for embodiment and identification" (Halberstam 2005, 53–54) unlike the binarism present in the FV ("you feel more like a man than a woman" 3b) that, once again, insists on the "destabilizing" (3c) effects of her coming out on her family. The FV is also more explicit and normative when referring to her "trans identity" (3c): her identity becomes a feeling, rather than a being, in the FV and is thought in terms of a "man vs woman" binarism ("you feel more man than woman"). In the FV, Maura is struggling with her identity unlike her American counterpart who has embraced a fluid identity.

Trans Identity as a Choice

However, where the FV is more troubling and inconsistent is with the depiction of trans identity as a choice. When discussing Maura's coming out, Sarah states:

SARAH: He's *trans*.

SARAH: Il *est devenu* trans

(Season 1, episode 5; *emphasis added*)

While in both versions Sarah seems to be grappling with her parent's identity at the beginning of the show and uses the wrong pronoun "he," she still acknowledges Maura's trans identity as always being there but unrealized whereas, in the FV, Maura "became" trans. The French dubbing doubles down on the trope of choice in the next episode:

SARAH: He really . . . *he is* a girl.

SARAH: *Il a décidé* d'être une fille, c'est une fille, c'est tout.

(Season 1, episode 6; *emphasis added*)

The French dubbing unequivocally talks about a "decision" rather than a repressed, always present, identity. Maura herself appears to be questioning her trans identity when coming out to Josh, her son:

MAURA: Did they talk about what's going on with me?

MAURA: Est-ce qu'elles t'ont parlé de moi, *de mes choix de vie*?

(Season 1, episode 6; *emphasis added*)

The FV uses the transphobic trope that being trans is a "lifestyle choice."

However, it would be disingenuous to blame the translation team without acknowledging its resolutely didactic approach to non-normative identities. The French dubbing seems to echo the target audience's questionings—a mostly cisgender heterosexual audience. Indeed, when discussing *Transparent* and *Orange is the New Black,* Caél Keegan (2016) contends that these mainstream series "'teach' transgender to liberal cisgender audiences through universalist metaphors or through pedagogical forms of affect" (606).

A Didactic Approach to Transgender Identities

With gender studies, cultural studies and intersectionality being largely unknown in academic, and especially, non-academic circles, and the very recent visibility of transgender and non-normative identities in France, the French version of *Transparent* fumbles its way through "educating" its audience about the array of non-normative gender identities. When Ali meets Baxter, a gender studies professor, they explain to her:

BAXTER: I was born with, quote-unquote, ambiguous genitalia. And *I'm one of those.*

BAXTER: Je suis né.e avec des organes génitaux anatomiquement ambigus. *J'fais partie des intergenres intersexes.*

(Season 3, episode 1; *emphasis added*)

While the OV is implicit, the FV opts for a more explicit translation to educate its audience about "intergender intersex people."

The same explicitation technique is used when Sarah tries to explain Ali's non-binary coming out:

SARAH: She's a *they*. Like *non-binary, androgynous*. She's *gonna be a they*.

SARAH: Ali est *il/elle*. *Elle ne s'enferme pas dans un genre, les bigenres, les anti-binaires, androgynes.* On est en présence d'un *chevauchement d'identités de genres*.

(Season 4, episode 9; *emphasis added*)

The translation becomes more explicit with Sarah's explanation, "she does not confine herself to one gender," and culminates in "an overlap of gender identities." While the FV could have used the pronoun "iel"—a combination of "il" and "elle" in inclusive writing equivalent to the English pronoun "they"—it includes further explanation for an audience unfamiliar with the array of non-conforming identities and also reflects Sarah's awkward grasp of gender identity throughout the series.

CONCLUSION

While representations of trans identity in the media have positively evolved in the United States, French society remains unfamiliar and resistant to non-normative identities. A cursory survey of Facebook comments on articles about non-conforming gender identity, as well as the rise in transphobic attacks in France, would quickly dampen any depiction of a seemingly more inclusive French society. The lack of understanding of identities that do not fit the ideology of French universalism, effectively making the nation-state colour and gender-blind and shutting down any debate around the very nature of the "French citizen," is clear in the French translation of *Transparent*. Translators are not living in a vacuum and their sociocultural and political surroundings inevitably inform their decisions in their work. There is no doubt that the French version of the series is marred by serious inconsistencies in its depiction of trans identity and that the translation team struggles with appropriate terminology. One of the consequences is the alteration of the characterization of the main cast: Maura is less at ease with her trans identity;

Sarah, her daughter, is struggling with naming her parent; and, through the French universalism at work in the dubbing process, the broader French society is more hostile to Maura than the American one. On the flip side, the FV becomes a voice for questions that the French viewing public might have and for which trans identity is still "new" and misunderstood. It exposes the French audience to a lexis and non-conforming gender identities that are largely unknown, and, in that regard, the translation deserves some praise. An analysis of the reception of *Transparent* in France, focused on the unfamiliar terminology and the array of non-normative identities, would yield interesting results and tell us if this didactic approach has been beneficial to the trans human rights cause in France and whether the audience has developed, if not a better grasp of these identities, at least more acceptance and empathy.

NOTES

1. Namely the show's main focus on the response of Maura's mostly cisgender entourage to their coming out (Funk and Funk 2016, 70).

2. It aired on OSC channel (pay television network) before the launch of Prime Video in France. France is considered a "dubbing" country: free public television channels only offer the dubbed version of foreign programs. The French audience has also been more exposed to dubbing than subtitling. However, a comparative study of the subtitling and dubbing of the TV show might prove fruitful.

3. The culture for which the audiovisual product is translated.

4. The decision to write about *Transparent* has been complicated because of the accusation of sexual harassment against Jeffrey Tambor, the lead actor, by two trans actresses. *Transparent* has been a seminal series in opening up conversations about trans politics and television representation within broader society especially since all of the trans characters are played by trans actors and actresses, with the exception of Maura. Furthermore, "[a]s America's first TV series with an aging transgender protagonist, *Transparent*'s narrative focus and the show's success serve as evidence of the nation's social and political progress in recent decades. Transparent provides an exceptional perspective even among the increasing number of works about older LGBTQ persons produced since the 2010s" (Hess 2017, 15). *Transparent* was a forerunner in featuring marginalized voices and tackling broader contemporary societal questions and, as such, deserves more academic attention.

5. Maura identifies herself as a woman and we will be using the feminine form of adjectives and pronouns when referring to herself.

6. We understand "queer" as an umbrella term encompassing all trans and gender non-conforming identities.

7. In *De la grammatologie* (1967), Derrida questions the taken-for-granted stability of the relationship between the signifier and the signified and the overreliance on an immutable meaning. His work has had a lasting impact on the field of translation studies.

8. "Transsexualism" was the preferred term until the early 1990s when it was replaced by "transgender," a term that was considered less stigmatizing. In medical and media discourses, transsexualism refers to a person having undergone gender affirmation surgery while transgender people may or may have not undergone a surgery.

9. The National Center for Transgender Equality founded in 2003 by transgender activists continues the fight to this day.

10. Since Joe Biden became the President in 2020 the situation is once again evolving in a positive direction. As an example, the US State Department of Justice is now issuing a US passport with an X gender marker.

11. Susan Stryker founded the Trans Studies Research Cluster at the University of Arizona and one issue of *TSQ*, their academic online journal, is dedicated to the intersection of translation studies and issues in gender.

12. "Republican" is to be understood as "belonging to the French Republic." French republicanism is an ideology or discourse pertaining to civic virtue and assimilating to a singular culture, not to a political party.

13. Our translation of "En France . . . le féminisme ne s'est pas implanté dans les universités à l'issue des années 1970. La structure de l'Université française n'a pas su, ni voulu faire de place aux féministes, condamnées de ce fait à la marginalisation ou à la reconversion. Rares sont les carrières féministes, jusqu'aux toutes récentes années. En conséquence, la France n'a pas vu se développer de champ d'études comparable à celui rencontré aux États-Unis." All translations are ours, unless indicated otherwise. In "L'empire du genre: l'histoire politique ambiguë d'un outil conceptuel" (2008), Fassin highlights the lack of academic recognition for "les études féministes," an academic field scholars are deterred from entering if they want to thrive.

14. "Spectre de la ghettoïsation."

15. "La rhétorique républicaine permet donc de refuser le féminisme, et plus largement les questions sexuelles—tout en jouant de l'antiaméricanisme. En effet, d'un côté, ce serait ouvrir la porte au communautarisme à l'américaine, dit-on alors; et d'un autre, c'est ébranler la séparation entre le public et le privé, comme cela se produirait outre-Atlantique."

16. " . . . 'sortir de l'isolement même au prix de la marginalité' décrit le contexte de premières associations."

17. "l'accueil et le support."

18. " . . . les discours évoluent et les revendications deviennent affirmées quant à la condition des trans dans la société mais aussi au sein des protocoles médicaux de la prise en charge."

19. "L'explosion associative [trans] en France date des années 2000."

20. "L'investissement de l'espace public comme espace politique"

21. " . . . s'élabore au cours de ces années [origines de la médiatisation aux années 1970] un 'transsexualisme télévisuel'" qui contribue à maintenir un ordre des genres. Les mises en scène d'*un donné à voir acceptable et consensuel* résultent d'un modèle de représentation socioculturel hétérocentré dominant."

22. "Les discours médiatiques produisent et reproduisent constamment du genre dans le cadre d'une binarité naturaliste ou essentialiste."

23. In "Queer in Translation" (2017), Epstein and Gillett bring together translation studies and queer theories. The terminology they use—such as "visibility," "passing," and "binarism"—emphasizes the likeness of both disciplines and demonstrates how one field can inform the other.

24. 1. An American company or producer hires a dubbing company. 2. The dubbing company transcribes dialogue from the original film transcript and video. 3. The dubbing studio hires an adaptor who will translate the dialogue while the studio director will choose the actors to voice the characters. 4. The translated product is cut into short (15 to 60 seconds) extracts. The dialogue, translated by the adaptor, is then transcribed on a *bande rythmo*, a scrolling text at the bottom of the screen for voice actors to read and act out. 5. The film is recorded in studio. 6. The audio track goes through the mixing and post-editing stages.

Considering the complexity of the task, miscommunication can occur at any level and are difficult to determine.

We would also like to mention that this article is not designed to condemn audiovisual translators for their work. They face severe budget and time constraints to produce quality work. Additionally, the tepid and very recent interest for non-normative gender identities means that most translators are not well-versed in gender studies.

25. "Les conséquences familiales et socioprofessionnelles sont toujours abordées."

26. Whether these translation choices are reflective of the experience of the transgender community in France, who faces rejection and an archaic legislation that refuses to protect them, remains to be determined and an interview of the translation team might provide some insight.

27. The last edition of the festival took place in 2015.

28. "L'universalisme français est un particularisme qui ne s'affirme pas comme tel. Mais il devient de plus en plus difficile de le nier. Raison pour laquelle on assiste depuis quatre ou cinq ans à un véritable backlash avec l'émergence de toute une littérature anti communautariste, à droite comme à gauche, visant à faire porter le chapeau du particularisme aux tribus et autres adeptes du 'ghetto': les féministes à l'américaine, les juifs, les gais . . . Autant d'ostensibles, de visibles . . . Autant d'identitaires désignés coupables pour masquer la politique de l'identité française que mène la république."

29. In June 2010, the *SoFECT* (Société française d'études et de prise en charge de la transidentité/French society of trans identity studies and medical care) substituted "transsexualism" with "trans identity."

REFERENCES

Bourcier, Sam/Marie-Hélène. 2005. *Sexpolitiques: Queer zones 2*. Paris: La Fabrique.
Calvès, Maud. 2019. "Être trans: un combat du quotidien pour fuir les violences transphobes." *France Culture*. April 10, 2019. Accessed October 27, 2021. www .franceculture.fr/emissions/le-reportage-de-la-redaction/etre-transgenre-un-combat -du-quotidien-pour-fuir-les-violences-transphobes

Danan, Martine. 1991. "Dubbing as an Expression of Nationalism." *Meta* 36, no. 4: 606–614. doi.org/10.7202/002446ar.

"Déclaration de l'Académie Française Sur l'écriture Dite 'Inclusive.'" 2017. *Académie Française.* October 26, 2017. Accessed October 27, 2021. www .academie-francaise.fr/actualites/declaration-de-lacademie-francaise-sur-lecriture -dite-inclusive.

De Marco, Alessandra. 2013. "Translating Gender on Screen Across languages: The Case of *Transamerica.*" In *Bridging the Gap between Theory and Practice in Translation and Gender Studies*, edited by Eleonora Federici, and Vanesssa Leonardi, 122–32. Newcastle-upon-Tyne: Cambridge Scholars Publisher.

Derrida, Jacques. 1967. *De la grammatologie.* Paris: Minuit.

Epstein, B.J. 2017. "Introduction." In *Queer in Translation*, edited by B.J. Epstein and Robert Gillett, 1–7. London: Taylor & Francis Group.

Espineira, Karine. 2015a. "Le mouvement trans : un mouvement social communautaire?" *Chimères* 87, no. 385–94. doi.org/10.3917/chime.087.0085.

Espineira, Karine. 2015b. "Un exemple de glissement du lexique médiatique: le sujet trans dans les productions audiovisuelles." *Essais* 7: 47–63, doi 10.4000/ essais.6238

Espineira, Karine. 2016. "Transgender and Transsexual People's Sexuality in the Media." *Parallax* 22, no. 3 (July 2, 2016): 323–329. doi.org/10.1080/13534645.2 016.1201922.

Espineira, Karine. 2018. "Les corps *trans*: disciplinés, militants, esthétiques, subversifs." *Revue des sciences sociales*, no. 59 (October 23, 2018). doi.org/10.4000/ revss.701.

Espineira Karine, and Maude-Yeuse Thomas. 2014. "Les trans comme parias. Le traitement médiatique de la sexualité des personnes trans en France." *Genre, sexualité & Société*, no. 11 (July 1). doi.org/10.4000/gss.3126.

Fassin, Éric. 2006. "Le genre aux États-Unis et en France." *Agora débats/jeunesses* 41: 12–21. doi.org/10.3406/agora.2006.2280

Fassin, Éric. 2008. "L'empire du genre. L'histoire politique ambiguë d'un outil conceptuel. " *L'homme* 187–188 (January): 375–92. doi.org/10.4000/lhomme.29322

Foucault, Michel. 1978. *The History of Sexuality.* New York: Pantheon Books.

Funk, Steven, and Jaydi Funk. 2016. "An Analysis of Transparent through Dispossession." *Series—International Journal of TV Serial Narratives* 2, no. 1: 69–80. Accessed October 20, 2021. doi.org/10.6092/issn.2421-454X/6165

Halberstam, Judith Jack. 2005. *In a Queer Time and Place. Transgender Bodies, Subcultural Lives.* New York: New York University Press.

Hess, Linda M. 2017. "'My whole life I've been dressing up like a man': Negotiations of Queer Aging and Queer Temporality in the TV Series *Transparent.*" *European Journal of American Studies* 11, no. 3 (January 24, 2017). doi.org/10.4000/ ejas.11702.

Keegan, Cáel M. 2016. "Tongues without Bodies: The Wachowskis' *Sense8.*" *TSQ: Transgender Studies Quarterly* 3, no. 3–4 (November 1, 2016): 605–10. doi. org/10.1215/23289252-3545275.

Meyerowitz, Joanne. 2002. *How Sex Changed: A History of Transsexuality in the United States*. Cambridge, MA: Harvard University Press.

Misiek, Szymon. 2020. "Misgendered in Translation?: Genderqueerness in Polish Translations of English-language Television Series." *Anglica. An International Journal of English Studies*: 165–85.

Perreau, Bruno. 2016. *Queer Theory. The French Response*. Stanford: Stanford University Press.

Pratt, Mary-Louise. 1991. "Arts of the Contact Zone." *Profession*: 33–40. www.jstor.org/stable/25595469.

Reeser, Todd W. 2013. "'TransFrance.'" *L'Esprit Créateur* 53, no. 1: 4–14. doi.org/10.1353/esp.2013.0007.

Robinson, Douglas. 2019. *Transgender, Translation, Translingual Address*. London & New York: Bloomsbury Academic.

Spurling, William J. 2014. "The Gender and Queer Politics of Translation: New Approaches." *Comparative Literature Studies* 51, no. 2: 201–14. muse.jhu.edu/article/548822.

Steinmetz, Katy. 2014. "The Transgender Tipping Point." *Time*, May 29, 2014. time.com/135480/transgender-tipping-point/.

Stone, Sandy. 1987. "The *Empire* Strikes Back: A Posttranssexual Manifesto," *Sandy Stone.com*: 1–20. sandystone.com/empire-strikes-back.pdf.

Stryker, Susan. 2006. "(De)subjugated Knowledges: An Introduction to Transgender Studies." In *The Transgender Studies Reader*, edited by Susan Stryker and Stephen Whittle, 1–18. London & New York: Routledge.

Chapter 5

Trans(ing) the Rural

Metronormativity and Melancholia in Sébastien Lifshitz's Wild Side *(2004)*

R. Cole Cridlin

In a scene approximately halfway through Sébastien Lifshitz's 2004 film *Wild Side*, the film's transsexual[1] protagonist Stéphanie (Stéphanie Michelini)[2] is asked by the bisexual Beur hustler Djamel (Yasmine Belmadi) if she is unwell. Stéphanie confirms her lover's suspicion and explains that Djamel cannot help her simply "because" ("Parce que") and that she is merely tired ("J'suis juste fatiguée"), a fatigue that applies to her entire existence ("Mais c'est comme ça, j'suis la fatiguée"). Although a cursory moment in the broader narrative of *Wild Side*, what is notable about this scene is that the character dialogue is delivered in voiceover as the camera pans across the Parisian cityscape at night, a filmic gesture that invites the viewer to consider how Stéphanie's "fatigue" is just as much a product of her transgender subjectivity as it is a product of the physical landscape that she inhabits. To this end, this chapter proposes a reading of *Wild Side* that considers how the geography of the film's setting functions in tandem with its exploration of the protagonist's subjectivity as a transgender woman who returns to rural France where she provides care for her dying mother Dominique (Josiane Stoléru). In returning to her childhood village, Stéphanie is forced to contend with unresolved memories and experiences from her pre-urban life as well as her mother's attempts to understand her now-woman child. In this way, I argue that the rural setting of the film is not neutral, but rather serves an active, crucial role that allows Stéphanie to mediate her pre-and post-rural lives in a manner that ultimately produces a new, hybridized subjectivity for the character, one whose implications are alluded to by the film's open-ended final scene. I arrive at such a reading by considering *Wild Side*'s complicated narrative structure in relation to Jack Halberstam's concept of *metronormativity*, a theoretical approach that broadens the current ways in which the film has been considered by scholars by exploring Stéphanie's lingering attachments to rural France. A consideration of the film along these lines also promotes a reading of transgenderism in relation to what Lauren Berlant terms *cruel optimism* whereby Stéphanie's return to rural France allows her the opportunity to transform what I call her "rural melancholia" into a realized form of grief, which she is able to then incorporate into her own subjectivity and thereby establish new relationalities with the urban France she returns to at the end of the film.

As a film, *Wild Side* serves as an interesting object of study. A highly stylized film with spartan instances of dialogue, it presents a complex narrative composed of three distinct but interlaced plotlines: the "primary" narrative, which follows Stéphanie and her two lovers, Djamel and Mikhail (Édouard Nikitine), back to rural France to care for her dying mother; the "urban" narrative that recounts Stéphanie's life in Paris as a sex worker and her domestic arrangement with said lovers; and the "rural" narrative that is composed of flashbacks to Stéphanie's pre-urban youth as Pierre (Stéphanie's deadname). Woven together as they are over the course of the film, *Wild Side* steadfastly resists any easy categorization and instead offers a subtle and nuanced understanding of Stéphanie's life by way of her rejection of her rural past, the harsh realities of her urban life, and the slippery terrain of navigating these in her filmic present.

The complexity of this film has garnered it widespread acclaim, both within France and internationally; however, the intricacy of Lifshitz's narrative has gone undertreated by scholars.[3] What scholarly analyses do exist vary greatly in their theoretical approaches yet reflect the film's ability to offer commentary on the numerous cultural issues at work within its narrative. Todd Reeser has traced the manner in which the film employs temporality as well as Stéphanie's transsexual embodiment to arrive at what he names a "disruption of disruption" that destabilizes the notion of linear transsexuality (Reeser 2007, 159). Nick Rees-Roberts treats the film in both an article and book chapter to analyze the extent to which Stéphanie's urban and rural experiences are informed by underlying capitalist formations that arise from "the characters' shared alienation from the stability of secure employment" (Rees-Roberts 2007, 148). Denis Provencher analyses the film along with a suite of films featuring Maghrebi-French characters to trace how the characters of *Wild Side* come to terms "with their own childhoods, biological families, and points of origin" (Provencher 2007, 50). Damon R. Young studies the triangular romantic form of Stéphanie and her lovers as an alternative model to homonormative romantic coupling that "affirms an intimacy expounded not verbally but rather gesturally and graphically" (Young 2017, 208). More recently, Asuncion Aragon has called attention to the geography of the film functioning in tandem with Stéphanie's transsexual embodiment to understand how the two delineate the "resignification of affection [and embodiment] on the borders of heteronormativity and nationality" (Aragon 2020, 25). Finally, David Caron has taken up *Wild Side* in relation to the ideas of caring and waiting to "shed some light on the link between waiting and the unexpected" and finds meaning within the film by way of the care its main characters provide for Stéphanie's mother (Caron 2021, 23). In a more popular vein, the numerous reviews of the film that have appeared in newspapers and magazines offer synopses of the film notable for their repeatedly qualifying Stéphanie as a "pre-op" transsexual, a category of transsexuality ascribing an undue importance to the character's genitals that is not in keeping with the overall narrative of *Wild Side*. While Aragon's chapter does highlight the use of excavating meaning in *Wild Side* in the context of the film's geography, this chapter proposes a geographically-oriented reading that is set in consideration of the film's juxtaposition of the "rural" and "urban" elements of Stéphanie's life as well as the underlying metronormative narrative that these imply.

METRONORMATIVITY IN *WILD SIDE*

The concept of *metronormativity* is first coined by Jack Halberstam in *In a Queer Time & Place* to describe the compulsory rural-to-urban migration narrative that queer individuals follow for the sake of attaining cultural visibility and community-based legitimization. As an urban-terminal process, metronormativity grants a spatial (geographical) valence to the psychological process that is "coming out" (Halberstam 2005, 36). Notable about Halberstam's term is that it bears several key cultural implications in relation to how queer subjectivity is communicated and understood. First, metronormativity gives primacy to urban spaces, which become culturally coded as "queer" and construct rural spaces as inherently antagonistic to queer life. Further, the implicit narrative force that drives queer individuals to seek "new" lives in urban spaces constructs a "one-size-fits-all" storyline that does not promote tailored understandings of the various reasons that might cause an individual to feel compelled to leave rurality behind. Also implied by this narrative is the cultural assumption that "rural" and "urban" function as discrete and separate spaces that individuals *inhabit differently* or are somehow able to *leave behind entirely*.

This idea of separation can be found in the opening scenes of *Wild Side* as Stéphanie's body is "separated" into its various parts—male penis, female breasts, painted nails—by a series of cut shots, a gesture that both fragments and announces her transsexual body to the viewer. These anatomical shots are accompanied by the song "I Fell in Love with a Dead Boy," whose lyrics effectively recast Stéphanie's body for the viewer as a *transgender* body through its titular evocations of "a dead boy." This separation takes on a different meaning when the scene shifts to reveal Stéphanie in a room full of transgender women who listen to the song as it is performed by Anohni, lead singer of Antony and the Johnsons. As the camera shifts back and forth between the singer and Stéphanie, the song's refrain of "Are you a boy or a girl?" seems to be posed directly to the protagonist, whose only response is offered by way of silent tears. Here, Stéphanie's tears indicate an implied psychic "separation" by virtue of her inability to answer Anohni's question and introduce the psychological aspects of transgenderism as a working concept in the background of the film. As the scene shifts once more, the song is replaced with the sound of passing cars and Stéphanie is surrounded by a different group of transwomen, sex workers who lure passing men by flashing their bodies. When considered in relation to metronormativity, these opening scenes can also be read as a "separation" between the realities of Stéphanie's Parisian life and the overly optimistic promise of what she expected.

Indeed, the harshness of these urban realities are underlined in the film when Stéphanie's mind flashes back to moments from her childhood. But these retrospective moments also serve the function of demonstrating a crucial aspect of the film that has not been thoroughly treated, which is the fact that, even though she has moved to Paris, Stéphanie maintains a relationship with rural France. This "rural relationship" is important in the film because it challenges the facile popular reading of Stéphanie's transsexual body as "pre-op"[4] along the lines of what Nicole Seymour calls "medicalized transsexualism," which is the rendering of "the body [into] a commodity to be obtained from 'authorized' sources, [and that] also exacerbates the sense that the trans person does not own hir own body, whether pre-operative, post-operative, or somewhere in between" (Seymour 2013, 44). Instead, the film's exploration of Stéphanie's (re)connection with and (re)inhabiting of rural space in her mother's dying days highlights the film's preoccupation with Stéphanie's transgender subjectivity and how she perceives herself in ways that are not necessarily tied to her physical body. In other words, the film's rural setting provides insights into who Stéphanie is as a *person* in ways that her urban life cannot afford her since her life in Paris is based upon being seen as an *object*.

One key way in which the rural landscape performs this function is by drawing upon the affective force that is inherent in rural spaces. Karl Schoonover and Rosalind Galt identify this force in queer cinema where "pastoral landscapes are not mere temporary escapes from oppressive national cultures" but rather "rural environments [that] nourish transformation [by] queerly upsetting" the human-nature binary (Schoonover and Galt 2016, 246). Although the evocation of the "pastoral" mode here by Schoonover and Galt indicates films that take part in the literary and artistic tradition that stretches back to Antiquity and the works of Theocritus and Virgil, the term itself provides a unique window into considering how Stéphanie's subjectivity might be contextualized in relation to the rural space of the film. While pastoral idylls and imagery often call upon the figures of shepherds and field workers living in harmony with the natural world, in contemporary film pastoral landscapes can signal an individual's (dis)connection with the world. For urban individuals, these pastoral spaces are often seen as "perfect" or "ideal" and so at odds with urban spaces that they produce a melancholic longing for a (re)connection with the perfection of the natural world.

Wild Side diverges sharply from the pastoral and instead presents a more realistic image of rural Northern France, which is to say by way of images that are set against gloomy skies and that showcase buildings in various states of decay. When taken at face value, these images might indicate the realist bent of the film as well as its preoccupation with a narrative that is likewise invested in a realistic plotline; however, the manner in which rural space is treated in Lifshitz's film also consolidates Stéphanie's relationship with her childhood village. A portion of this may be understood in relation to her metronormative life, which precludes her from being able to return. Halberstam notes that "[i]n reality, many queers from rural or small towns move to the city out of necessity, and then yearn to leave the urban area and return to their small towns" but fail to do so because of various social and cultural pressures (Halberstam 2005, 37). In *Wild Side* there is a sequence of cut shots that capture various buildings (e.g., a defunct factory, a fallen roof, an empty school) around the town that are notably devoid of people, a moment that simultaneously presents the *un*-pastoral nature of the rural setting while also suggesting that this is a place that refuses Stéphanie any possibility of return. In essence, the external forces alluded to by Halberstam as preventing ex-rural queer individuals from returning to rural lives are exerted by the rural landscape itself.

Even though returning to live permanently in rural France might be an impossibility for Stéphanie, she nevertheless returns to take care of her dying mother and takes part in a short-lived (re)connection with rural space in the film that reconfigures how she understands herself. Further, as demonstrated by the film's flashback sequences, it is revealed that Stéphanie has always maintained a connection with her rural past by way of the unresolved memories she carries from her youth. These connections, while at odds with metronormative life, ultimately illustrate the extent to which Stéphanie's life has been caught "in between": between rural and urban France, between being a boy child and a woman. In this way, *Wild Side* demonstrates that Stéphanie's life as a transgender woman who lives in Paris has actually been a melancholic life since she has been unable to move past her rural childhood and into a fully-urban adulthood. It is only by virtue of the rural setting that the film nourishes the transformation of this melancholia into instances of tangible loss (via interpersonal interactions with her mother and a childhood love) that are able to be realized, grieved, and then incorporated into a newly-hybridized subjectivity.

Melancholic Metronormativity

In *The Psychic Life of Power*, Judith Butler argues that compulsory heterosexuality transforms gender itself into a melancholic condition. Moreover, in *Precarious Life*, she expands on this notion of melancholia to arrive at what she calls a "grievable life" by analyzing the ways in which the recognition of grief is realized and hierarchized in ways that "seem to follow from our being socially constituted bodies, attached to others, at risk of violence by virtue of that exposure" (Butler 2006a, 20). Because compulsory heterosexuality obfuscates homosexuality, the former is deemed more "real" while the latter becomes rendered socially uniterable and thus "un-grievable."

To this end, homosexuality takes the form of a "loss" that is enforced through "a set of culturally prevalent prohibitions" that render it so (Butler 2006b, 139). Consequently, she writes, "we might expect a culturally prevalent form of melancholia, one which signals the internalization of the ungrieved homosexual cathexis" (Ibid., 139). In the case of Lifshitz's film, Butler's ideas can be considered in terms of Stéphanie's transgender life as well as her urban life, both of which reveal themselves to be melancholic forms of existence.

Taking up Stéphanie's (trans)gender identity and reframing it in accordance with the geographical forces to which it is subject under metronormativity, it becomes clear that, for Stéphanie, Butler's "compulsory heterosexuality" might also be named "compulsory urbanity" when thinking along these lines. Indeed, while she does not set her article in these precise terms, in "Get Thee to a Big City," Kath Weston contends that the compulsive forces of sexuality and geography have always functioned in tandem through "a symbolics of urban/rural relations [which] locates [queer] subjects in the city while putting their presence in the countryside under erasure" (Weston 1995, 262). While she raises the idea of metronormativity, Weston's sociological article does not invest itself solidly in the idea as I do here; however, it is productive as it articulates that the hierarchy of geography also factors into what constitutes a "grievable life." Thus, the primacy of urban spaces in social discourse establishes rural spaces as sites of melancholia that are defined by what they lack. With relation to queer metronormativity, rurality is melancholic precisely because it is perceived as hostile to queer existence and thus "devoid" of any symbolic meaning. In one's movement toward an urban center, the queer subject leaves behind their rural past to "attain" an (urban) identity; however, the price of this movement is the inability to be able to incorporate past rural experiences at the risk of being seen as "the country bumpkin, naïve and uninformed" (Ibid., 264).

This incorporation is capable only through the process of mourning, which, returning to Butler, is a process "of accept[ing] that by the loss one undergoes one will be changed, possibly for ever [*sic*]" (Butler 2006a, 21). This process is reliant upon the psychoanalytic distinction between mourning and melancholia as outlined by Sigmund Freud in his 1915 essay "Mourning and Melancholia." To him, both refer to the reactions a subject undergoes following the loss of a beloved object that result in "grave departures from the normal attitude to life"; however, the two differ significantly in the attachments they allow the subject to make (Freud 1957, 243).

Whereas mourning is a terminally-focused process that "we rely on in its being overcome after a certain lapse of time" and after which the ego "becomes free and uninhibited again" to attach itself to a new object, melancholia becomes a suspended state in which the ego refuses to let go of what it has lost (Ibid., 244–45). Instead, the melancholic refusal of transfer results in the internalization of that which has been lost. While melancholia takes many forms, one of its most notable examples is rooted in the realm of how one considers what has been lost: memory.

In *Wild Side*, memory takes the shape of Stéphanie's flashbacks to her youth in Northern France and are representative of her melancholic attachment to her childhood. While this chapter will explore to a greater extent what precisely Stéphanie has "lost" in her movement away from her home and Paris, the motif of the childhood flashbacks signal Stéphanie's ongoing attachment to rural France that extend past her gender identity. These include sequences in which Lifshitz reveals her attachment to her family (in a dinner scene), her local culture (Carnival), and the landscape itself (Stéphanie as a child playing in a planted field). Given these attachments, it becomes evident in *Wild Side* that queer melancholia is not limited to specific aspects of a subject's sexual identity, but rather encompasses personal identity as it is rooted in geography.

For the subject, this internalization is an attempt at preservation, although this, too, bears the consequence of an unconscious ego-identification. Because of this, melancholia might be considered as a hybrid state that "borrows some of its features from mourning, and others from the processes of regression from narcissistic object-choice to narcissism" (Ibid., 250).

Additionally, Freud notes that melancholy is able to produce in the subject feelings of pain and self-hostility that result in "an extraordinary diminution of [one's] self-regard, and impoverishment of [one's] ego on a grand scale. In mourning, it is the world which has become poor and empty; in melancholia it is the ego itself" (Ibid., 246).

To return us to a discussion of how melancholia factors in relation to metronormativity, it is important to signal the function of rurality in the overall narrative. As a progress narrative, metronormativity functions on the preconceived belief that "the city represents a beacon of tolerance and [queer] community [while] the country [is] a locus of persecution and [queer] absence" (Weston 1995, 262). Therefore, metronormativity gives little to no credence to a subject's pre-urban life. Rather, it is something left behind or, in other words, something that one must "lose" in order "to be." But this is an idealized form of loss because it functions upon the presupposition that queer individuals are able to categorically situate their identities into discrete "pre-urban" and "post-urban" moments. Stéphanie's flashbacks to her youth belie this claim and reveal metronormativity itself to be an inherently melancholic position that places the individual in a state of suspended melancholia for their (potential) inability to incorporate their rural experiences into their post-urban queer lives since the rural is assumed to be absent of queer significance.

As is made clear in *Wild Side*, this inherent melancholia of the metronormative narrative has a compounded impact when it interacts with other identity categories such as "gender, age, [. . .] class, [and] race [that can] also constitute boundaries that separated [the] self from the [hegemonic queer] imaginary" (Ibid., 272). In the case of Stéphanie, this absence functions at two levels. At the level of sexuality, Stéphanie's flashbacks are devoid of any romantic attachment. In fact, the only flashbacks that treat any emotional ties that could be read as even potentially "romantic" are those that express filial (being embraced by her father), fraternal (sharing a hammock with her sister), and courtly (pledging fealty to her sister in an imaginary knighting ceremony) affection. But more important than this is the fact that Stéphanie herself is absent from her rural past. Having run away at the age of 15, Pierre did not exist in Northern France as Stéphanie, a fact made evident early in the film when the camera captures various still shots of the rural school Stéphanie attended while the voice over of a teacher calls roll, identifying her with "Pierre." Thus, Stéphanie's return to rural France as a post-rural transgender woman can be read in relation to Freud's third form of melancholia since her metronormative migration to Paris allows her the ability to identify aspects of her life she has left behind (e.g., her family, her past as "Pierre") but her subsequent return reveals that she has been unable to incorporate the true impact of these losses.

This failure to consciously recognize the impacts of loss recalls Butler's notion of "grievable lives" wherein only those losses that are deemed to be socially "real" are able to be mourned. Considering the metronormative narrative retrospectively rather than as a *fait accompli* implicitly begs the question of how rural experiences factor into and shape a subject's post-rural identity. Indeed, *Wild Side* illustrates just how crucial it is to consider the capacity of pre-urban moments to resonate with a person even after they have moved to an urban center. The film, which begins *in media res* with Stéphanie living in Paris, implies that the metronormative narrative has been achieved; however, this proves to be far from the case.

As demonstrated by her return to rural Northern France, Stéphanie's departure from her childhood home and her subsequent life in Paris may have given her the means to attain a culturally "legitimate" (read: urban) transgender identity; however, it has failed to give her what she needs to be happy there: closure by way of the integration of her pre-urban experiences into her post-rural identity. To set this in theoretical terms, rural France is a lost object that Stéphanie has been unsuccessful in fully letting go of so that she can be "uninhibited and free" to create attachments to her now-urban home. As the film's flashback sequences demonstrate, her life in Paris has forced her to occupy a state of suspended melancholia that bars her from being able to mourn the childhood, family, and land she left behind.

This melancholia is due just as much to Stéphanie's life experiences in the film as it is to the function of rurality in the queer imagination. A site from which queer individuals must necessarily flee in order to arrive at social validity, this failure to give credence to rural spaces and experiences also removes the possibility of the individual to fully process and let go of their past. Instead, as is the case with Stéphanie, it bears implications for the post-rural transgender individual that affect not only their subjectivity, but also their affective relationships with the environment.

Metronormativity in Retrospect

As a narrative, metronormative migrations to the city only ascribe a one-sided validity to the queer subject in urban space. Synonymous as they are to cultural notions of visibility and community, cities are ascribed as the only place where queer subjectivity can be *validated*.[5] One implication of such a coding of urban spaces is that rural spaces, as previously mentioned, become coded as backwards. But more than this, such an ascription renders these spaces "devoid" of any cultural meaning other than as something *from which* the queer individual must flee. To this end, then, the rural holds no value in and of itself. It is only after having moved to the city that the queer subject is able to process their lived experiences in rural settings; however, these moments of reflection are from an inherently skewed vantagepoint since their processing takes place in a retrospective manner, geographically removed from where these moments actually took place.

In this way, metronormativity forces the rural to become a site of rupture that is intrinsically antithetical to the post-rural, now-urban subject, effectively rendering it a place from which an individual becomes detached and thus unable to adequately mourn and incorporate into their post-rural subjectivity. This failure to recognize the importance that rurality has contributed to the now-urban individual's queer life, in turn, reworks rurality so that it takes on a melancholic nature all its own. This is perhaps best evidenced by the terminality of the narrative itself, which refuses to recognize the possibility of a metronormative "homecoming" back to rural places.

While one series of flashbacks used in *Wild Side* reflects the urban experiences of Stéphanie and her lovers, the second, more visually-arresting series relates memories of Stéphanie's youth in the French countryside. Occurring as they do before Stéphanie has moved to Paris (or ostensibly self-identified as transgender), these flashbacks are useful for considering the ways in which the film constructs French rurality and rural life. Though all of these flashbacks set themselves against rural landscapes, they nevertheless highlight critical aspects of rural existence from which Stéphanie may have wished to flee, including poverty, schoolyard violence, and isolation. The extent to which one might argue these retrospective moments are informed by metronormativity cannot be adequately assessed; however, they can all be read as imbuing the landscape for the post-urban queer subject with a sense of loss: the loss of financial security, the loss of personal security, the loss of community security.

This sense of loss also bears a figurative meaning for Stéphanie. In an early flashback scene, Pierre is called in from playing in a field by her mother. He walks into the family home only to be told by her that his father and sister Caroline will not be coming home ("Ton père et Caroline, on ne les verra plus"). Though the film never explains the manner in which they have died, their loss is a significant one for Pierre, who goes even so far as to pray at his local church that he be allowed to take his sister's place. The importance of both father and sister is bolstered by the fact that they are reoccurring characters in Pierre's other flashbacks and, unlike the aforementioned flashbacks that treat the gritty truths of rural France, these are all laden with large degrees of filial and fraternal affection.

Regardless of how one might be tempted to analyze these retrospective sequences, they contextualize Stéphanie in relation to rural space as she returns to take care of her mother. The most obvious of the forces communicated by the flashbacks in *Wild Side* are those of time and distance. In a scene approximately halfway through *Wild Side*, Stéphanie washes her mother's hair when her mother suddenly announces that she would like to know more about her daughter's life ("Tu voudrais que je te pose des questions sur ta vie?") in Paris; however, this proves not to be the case. Rather than taking the form of a question, Dominique's next words are a declarative apologia for not having reached out to her daughter ("Si j'ai jamais appelé, c'est . . . c'est parce que je pensais que c'était mieux comme ça . . . que tu vis . . . que c'était mieux . . . tu préférais pas savoir"). She then goes on to describe how difficult it has been living alone with neither her husband nor her daughter (Caroline) and with Stéphanie living in Paris. Stéphanie's response is only that it was difficult for everyone ("C'était dur pour tout le monde"). The scene concludes with Stéphanie washing the suds from her mother's hair as the latter assures herself that her daughter has a life for herself in Paris ("Et tu as ta vie, toi").

Although brief, this scene bears several key implications of metronormativity that Halberstam fails to account for in his model. Here, Dominique's words prove just as important as those of her daughter because they offer the "flip side" of the metronormative narrative, namely that the queer cultural significance placed on urban centers is understood by both queers and non-queers alike, a significance that (at least for Dominique) legitimates her decision not to reach out to Stéphanie, whose separation from her family is made distinct from the "separation" of her father and sister, both of whom have died. Instead of using "sans" to describe Stéphanie's relation to home as she does with the other two family members (" . . . sans ton père, sans Caroline . . ."), Dominique names the distance between the two women as having been exclusively geographical (" . . . et toi à Paris").

An optimistic reading of this might claim that her mother situates their separation in geographical terms to suggest the possibility of a reconnection; however, the notion of a purely geographical barrier between the two women is belied by the suggestion that this "separation" operates at psychological (" . . . tu préférais pas savoir") and social (" . . . que tu vis . . . ") levels in addition to the most easily recognizable geographical one. Instead, her mother's words imply that the cost of the metronormative narrative for the family (or what remains of it) is the affective (and effective) silence left in the wake of Stéphanie's flight from home. Stéphanie's acknowledgement that she, too, has felt the pain brought about by this (named here as a "difficulty" with which she has had to contend) acknowledges the existence of a problematic relationality to her rural past. In sum, Stéphanie's difficulties are as much the product of her metronormative migration as they are the melancholic conditions under which she left Northern France.

"Rural Melancholia" and Recuperative Landscapes

Stéphanie's return to her childhood home is captured in *Wild Side* via a sequence that captures the rural road and forlorn rural landscapes that lead from the hospital to the farmhouse where her mother lives. As two men in white jackets install Dominique inside the home, Stéphanie and Mikhail set about preparing the house. It isn't until later in the film that Djamel joins the couple but, unlike their life in Paris where the three share everything, Stéphanie makes it clear that he won't be allowed to share the same bed with them lest her mother ask questions.

But Dominique does ask questions. Many, in fact. The most notable of these are about Stéphanie's relationship with Mikhail (which occurs prior to the arrival of Djamel to the family home), to which Stéphanie gives curt albeit quasi-truthful answers. These tentative efforts to know more about her daughter's Parisian life reveals Dominique's optimistic desire to get to know more about Stéphanie. As Laurent Berlant notes, "[a]ll attachments are optimistic. When we talk about an object of desire, we are really talking about a cluster of promises we want someone or something to make to us and make possible for us" (Berlant 2012, 23). In this case, the cluster of promises sought is (for Dominique) a (re)connection with her lost son Pierre and (for Stéphanie) a connection between a heretofore unknown (transgender) daughter and her mother.

Moreover, the interactions between mother and daughter hold notes of what Berlant terms *cruel optimism*, a specific type of optimistic attachment in which that something desired "is actually an obstacle to [one's] flourishing" (Ibid., 1). Although these interactions in *Wild Side* are not intentionally cruel as much as they are the confused attempts of a mother to reconcile herself with Stéphanie's past as Pierre as well as her daughter's subsequent return home as a post-urban transgender woman, they nevertheless produce, for both women, a "force that moves [each] out of [her]self and into the world in order to bring closer the satisfying *something* that [she] cannot generate on [her] own but sense in the wake of a person, a way of life, an object, project, concept or scene" (Ibid., 1–2). What is notable about this passage from Berlant is how Lifshitz's film uses Dominique's death (or rather, her imminent death) as the affective force that pushes the mother to reconcile with her daughter in addition to the practical hospice care that Stéphanie provides.

So, given the presence of cruel optimism that saturates the rural scenes of *Wild Side*, the question then becomes one of determining the degree to which Stéphanie's melancholic subjectivity is reliant upon these cruelly optimistic exchanges. One entry point for such a consideration is to be found in the manner in which the mother's comments and questions interact with Stéphanie's transsexual narrative. Jay Prosser notes that, "[f]or the transsexual, passing is becoming, a step toward home, a relief and a release: it aligns inner gender identity with social identity; one is 'taken' in the world for who one feels one-self to be" (Prosser 1998, 184). Dominique's repeatedly calling Stéphanie by her deadname can be read as ruptures of this step forward, which, in turn, cast Stéphanie back to the doldrums of melancholia.[6] Further, Prosser's evocation of "a step toward home" can be read ironically since Stéphanie's movement in the film literally forces her to take a backward step in going to take care of her mother. Further, the concept of *home* itself proves to be a fraught topic in the film. Indeed, the film toys with this notion and reveals:

> That there is no place *like* home—home is where we long to belong; there is no place better than home—conveys the value of realness and belonging. [. . .] That there is *no place* like home, however—home doesn't exist; there is no place that is home—recognizes that home is, on some level, always a place we make up, that belonging is ultimately mythic—for all of us perhaps unreachable without some act of sweet imagination. (Ibid., 205)

Depicted as she is between her Parisian "home" that she shares with Mikhail and Djamel and the childhood "home" she resumes from her youth, *Wild Side* inherently calls into question the category of "home" as a stable and linear concept that follows along the same lines as the way in which Stéphanie's mother treats her daughter's transgender identity.[7]

Although Dominique serves as the trigger for the majority of cruelly optimistic scenes in *Wild Side*, the cruel optimism exhibited in the film is not limited exclusively to her character. Indeed, Stéphanie herself seems to act as a catalyst for cruel optimism to rear its ugly head. This happens on the heels of the moments when Stéphanie enters a flashback sequence to her youth. For example, when Stéphanie enters the local church shortly after her return, she mistakes a nun for her long-dead sister, even going so far as to call out to the woman using Caroline's name. This filmic moment stands in stark contrast to the filmic reality in which Stéphanie must surely remember her sister has passed, thus implying that Stéphanie "leans toward promises contained within the present" rural landscape of her youth (Berlant 2012, 24). While the flashback sequences in *Wild Side* offer no clear-cut answer to this question, her interactions with landscapes, people, and memories in these spaces reveal an investment in her reconciliation with her past in order to move forward with her life.

In her theorization of the term, Berlant makes clear that *cruel optimism* is different from *melancholia* when she explains:

> I described "cruel optimism" as a relation of attachment to compromised conditions of possibility whose realization is discovered either to be *im*possible, sheer

fantasy, or *too* possible, and toxic [. . .] because whatever the *content* of the attachment is, the continuity of its form provides something of the continuity of the subject's sense of what it means to keep on living on and to look forward to being in the world. This phrase points to a condition different from that of melancholia, which is enacted in the subject's desire to temporize an experience of the loss of an object/scene with which she has invested her ego continuity. (Ibid., 24)

If, as Berlant claims, cruel optimism is relegated to the realm of possibility whereas melancholia is limited to a temporally-incorporated moment, then *Wild Side* calls attention to an untreated area in her conceptualization of cruel optimism: that of transgenderism as both a mental and bodily process reliant upon psychic and physical self-crafting. Although I do not seek to undermine the terminological distinctions Berlant makes between "cruel optimism" and "melancholia," I do contend that the distinction between the two is not as clear-cut as she suggests. Instead, I offer the argument that it is possible to conceive of melancholia as a particular form of cruel optimism since the loss incorporation that a subject's ego undergoes is not always a singular temporal moment. Instead, this incorporation can be constant and continually suspended until the loss is recognized for what it is and able to be adequately mourned. *Wild Side*'s treatment of Stéphanie's melancholia, which arises from her attachment to her rural past, reveals how, in fact, she experiences what I would term a "rural melancholia," which is brought about by these unresolved rural attachments. Indeed, by naming her melancholia in this manner, we are able to assess not only the geographical implications of Stéphanie's melancholia, but also how rurality works to shape the melancholia that she also experiences by way of her transgender identity.

Returning to the earlier discussion of mourning and melancholia as outlined by Freud and Butler, if we are to take melancholia as "a loss [that] is refused" and thus internalized, then "the internalization of loss is part of the mechanism of its refusal" (Butler 2006b, 134). At this point, the object lost "can no longer exist in the external world" and its "internalization will be a way to disavow the loss, to keep it at bay, to stay or postpone the recognition and suffering of loss" (Ibid., 134). In this way then, Berlant's notion of *optimism* can be read as a method by which the self is able to postpone the recognition/suffering of the loss. In other words, the loss (to whatever degree it is "recognized") is always deferred because of the optimistic belief in an imaginary set of promises that may be able to reveal that the loss was never really a "loss" at all.

To this effect, the rural landscape in *Wild Side* becomes a recuperative setting against which Stéphanie is forced to reconcile the optimistic beliefs that she has carried with her through her childhood memories. By returning to rural France as a post-rural transgender woman, the protagonist is able "to return to the scene of fantasy that enables [her] to expect that *this* time, nearness to *this* thing will help [her] world become different in just the right way" (Berlant 2012, 2). Stéphanie's disillusionment throughout the film transposes rural France from a site of reconciliation to one of pragmatic being. Her forays through the empty post-industrialist town mirror the stark poverty demonstrated in flashback sequences. The world is revealed for what it is: a physical site of connection mediated by the people inhabiting it.

Reading the interactions Stéphanie shares with her mother in *Wild Side* through the lens of Berlant, Dominique's home becomes a tense battleground where Stéphanie is forced not only into the role of (healthcare) provider, but also into one where she must constantly reassert her own subjectivity as a transgender woman. In addition to revealing the illusory and thereby cruel optimism of believing her mother will accept her, the home becomes a site of tension that proves productive for allowing Stéphanie the space to formulate a new subjectivity: a rural, post-urban transgender subjectivity.

In these moments when Stéphanie is forced to grapple with her own subjectivity, she is simultaneously divested of the nostalgic perceptions of her youth that she carries with her. In what might be considered an all too stark reading of these moments in the film, Stéphanie realizes that the home she has left behind as Pierre is one to which she can never fully return to as herself. In this way, the flashbacks collapse upon themselves and become relegated to the territory of nostalgia, or illusory memory. This proves crucial, though, for tying Berlant together with Freud and Butler since these moments of tension are also moments when the cruelly optimistic hopes to which Stéphanie has held are also broken down.

With these optimistic attachments raised and subsequently uprooted only to be replaced by tension, cruel optimism reveals itself in *Wild Side*. While one might argue that these moments are removed from mourning and melancholic processes because they do not have stakes in Stéphanie's subjectivity, I contend that they reveal cruel optimism as an inherent precursor to melancholic revelation. In these moments, the hopes, beliefs, and desires about her return to Northern France reveal themselves to the protagonist as nothing but dreams and wishes. They become devoid of any real substance and force her to acknowledge the true state of her childhood home in contrast to the idyllic picture she has made of it in her memories.

CHILDHOOD LOVE AND
COMPLICATING SUBJECTIVITY

Having divested herself of the illusion of a happy homecoming and Dominique's immediate and unconditional acceptance of her, Stéphanie is now free to sever her cruelly optimistic notions and to engage differently with the rural landscape. Recalling the aforementioned montage of still shots of village buildings, Stéphanie is now able to see her childhood village as it is. Since she is no longer defined by these nostalgic flashbacks, she can bear witness to the abject poverty experienced by many in the northern regions of France. Among the buildings shown is one of an out of operation factory, recalling at once the failed industrial project of the building as well as serving as a reminder of the stark difference between the rural space and the industry of Paris.

But the French rural and urban aren't as separate as one might think. In a later scene, Stéphanie is shown walking into a suburban subdivision. Although it is not situated contextually against either the old houses of the village or Dominique's farmhouse, the fact that Stéphanie is walking indicates that it is at some proximity that allows her this method of transportation. As the camera captures the uniformity of the cookie-cutter houses, one recalls the uniformity of the *banlieue* apartment complex where Stéphanie and her lovers live in Paris. And it is to the front door of one of these houses that Stéphanie ventures. Two young boys are shown playing in the front garden as Stéphanie begins speaking with a man at the garden gate. It is quickly revealed that Stéphanie knows this man and that his name is Nicolas; however, when asked if he recognizes her, he responds in the negative. Stéphanie tells him to "think for a bit" ("cherche un peu") but when he again answers that he doesn't know her, she announces herself using her deadname ("C'est moi, Pierre").

What is remarkable about the beginning of this sequence is that it represents the only time in the film where Stéphanie willingly assumes her pre-transgender name. Perhaps only to hasten Nicolas' identification of her, Stéphanie's choice here is reminiscent of what Prosser would call an autobiographical act. Inasmuch as gender and genre mirror one another, "[a]utobiography, like the transsexual's first look in the mirror, breaks apart the subject into the self reflected upon and the self that reflects; autobiography, like transsexuality, instantiates (or reveals) a difference in the subject" (Prosser 1998, 102). Only this moment in *Wild Side* has no physical mirror. Rather, Nicolas serves the function of the mirror by holding the image of Stéphanie before him against his memories of the young Pierre.

The camera then cuts to the pair walking through a forest while conversing as the same two children run and play ahead of them, oblivious of the adult conversation. As the pair talks, it is revealed that 17 years span between now and the last time Stéphanie and Nicolas have seen one another. So, too, is it revealed that Pierre ran away from the village at the age of 15, although the reason for this is left unmentioned. In that time, Stéphanie has made a life for herself in Paris and Nicolas has lived in Brussels for five years. As with Stéphanie, he also felt the familial demand to return home; however, unlike her, who returned willingly ("à cause de [sa] famille"), his return is forced upon him because he had no other option ("pas de choix"). This pressure can be interpreted as the demand to live a heteronormative life close to home since Stéphanie then turns her attention to the man's two children, one of whom has been named Pierre in honor of Stéphanie.

As the two continue to catch up on their lives, Nicolas reveals that he is happy that Stéphanie has come home ("Je suis content que tu sois là") and that, even though she has returned to the village much changed, he doesn't think that she has changed all that much ("C'est bizarre, en fait. T'as pas tellement changé."). He goes on to explain that she still seems to be like Pierre ("Je veux dire que j'ai l'impression que c'est toi encore"), to which Stéphanie, in a second moment of identification with Pierre, responds that she is still the same ("Mais, c'est moi").

It is in this scene that *Wild Side* treats the affective "pull" of metronormativity in the rural sphere that works to legitimize Stéphanie's identity for Nicolas as they walk through the woods.[8] This legitimization can be said to take place at the level of a "second skin." In her ability to seamlessly acknowledge her past as Pierre in the present ("C'est moi, Pierre") as well as her acknowledgement that her current identity doesn't erase who she was ("Mais c'est moi"), Stéphanie creates a "story [that weaves] around [her] body in order that [her] body may be 'read'" (Ibid., 101). In the case of Nicolas, the story that weaves Stéphanie's stories together is his desire for her and, while the presence of his children and move back home might be read as his following a heteronormative trajectory, he acknowledges they two are linked by what Prosser calls the *home narrative*, which in the context of *Wild Side* creates an interesting social space that allows for the characters to "negotiate the real differences between [their life] trajectories at the same time as [they both] widen [their understanding of] transgender" (Ibid., 205).

In addition to this moment creating a narrative that both she and Nicolas can understand, his unconditional acceptance of her transgender embodiment alongside his commentary of how she still reminds him of Pierre echoes Nicole Seymour's notion of "organic transgenderism" that she describes in *Strange Natures*. Unlike a medicalized view of transgenderism that looks to the body to legitimate identity, she argues that rural spaces are able to cultivate an alternative model wherein one's transition can be viewed as "a phenom-enon that is at least partly natural" (Seymour 2013, 36). Seymour contends:

> Organic transgenderism [. . .] involves the treatment of gender transitioning as a biological phenomenon on the same order as puberty; and obviation of the medico-technological complex and its commodification of the body, in favor of "homegrown" and psychic solutions to bodily problems; the characterization of self-knowledge as equal, if not superior, to medical knowledge; and a focus on individual will as transformative. (Ibid., 36)

Surrounded as they are by the natural landscape, Stéphanie's trans body seems just as natural to the pair as the trees that surround them. And, rather than questioning or commenting upon how Stéphanie has changed from Pierre, Nicolas binds her pre-transition self with her current embodiment. As the scene concludes, Nicolas turns his questions to Stéphanie's love life and discovers that she is in a relationship and happy. When Stéphanie turns the tables to ask why he wants to know, Nicolas quickly backpedals and assures her that he was just curious, to which Stéphanie asks him if he really thought she would love him her entire life. But whether Nicolas would love Pierre or Stéphanie is never asked and instead the rural landscape functions as a pseudo-palimpsest upon which Stéphanie (re)inscribes herself.

CONCLUSION: "GOOD" GRIEF

In the wake of Dominique's death, Stéphanie's reason for remaining in rural France comes to an end. It is at this moment in the film that a tacit question arises: With no ailing family member to care for, will Stéphanie and her lovers continue to reside in Northern France or will they return to Paris? It is a question that *Wild Side* anticipates and answers as the film cuts to reveal Stéphanie standing before a cardboard box of photographs. As she picks up, rips, and discards the old pictures on the floor around her, Mikhail enters the room and, picking up a picture, says he wants to keep a photo of Pierre. Stéphanie shows her dissent by roughly pulling the photograph from Mikhail's hand and ripping it in half as she has done with the others.

Her refusal to keep any photograph from her youth stands in stark contrast to her earlier interaction with Nicolas where she seemingly had no problem identifying herself with Pierre and acknowledged that he still exists within her. The difference between these two filmic moments is revealed as Djamel enters the room through the doorway and, holding a lamp in each hand, asks if she wants to bring them back with them to Paris. Her response is curt but tell-ing: she wants nothing from the house and they will take nothing with them when they leave. While it may be a small thing, her refusal to bring back a single photograph from her youth or to allow her lover to do so is representative of how Stéphanie now incorporates Pierre into her own identity formation. Namely, his existence in her life narrative is restrained both temporally (flashbacks) and geographically (Northern France).

Unlike Nicolas who shared a boyhood with him, Pierre is entirely unknown to her lovers. And for her to bring back (or to allow Mikhail to bring back) photographic evidence of Stéphanie from her pre-urban life might threaten her urban existence by undermining her subjectivity as she would have herself known upon her return to the city. Instead, Pierre becomes neutralized by being relegated to both the past and to rural Northern France where he now exists as nothing but a memory. As the camera switches to a series of cut shots that capture the walls of Stéphanie's childhood home, now devoid of any adornment or reminder that the house had previously been occupied. The house itself, too, belongs only to memory.

Although she may have wished not to carry anything with her, the final scenes of *Wild Side* when Stéphanie and her lovers are aboard a Paris-bound train reveal the futility of that wish. Captured in close-up, Stéphanie cries alone while locked in a bathroom on the train, revealing one thing she has carried back with her, even if against her will: her grief.

Coming on the heels of her mother's death, the grief that Stéphanie expresses at the end of *Wild Side* is crucial. Indeed, it singularly affords her the ability to move past her melancholic condition while also granting her a new relationality to rural France (both the one she experienced as a child and the one she shared with her lovers/mother). As the film ends, the Paris-bound train carries Stéphanie and her sleeping lovers back to the urban city they call home. The train is likewise carrying Stéphanie to a new existence, one that incorporates what she has both lost and found in rural France as well as the newfound emotional intimacy she has attained with her lovers. Bound as she was to the rural melancholia she experienced for 17 years, Stéphanie now returns to Paris with a subjectivity that has integrated her rural past and toward a new future subjectivity we can't yet even imagine.

NOTES

1. I use the word "transsexual" here rather than "transgender" in keeping with the manner in which director Sébastien Lifshitz has described the character of Stéphanie in interviews conducted around the time of the film's initial release. More recently, he has begun to use the term "transgender" (*transgenre*) to describe her when referencing the film. For the purposes of this chapter, my argument is invested in the psychic and interpersonal implications of Stéphanie's sexual subjectivity and

I have accordingly chosen to set my claims in relation to her transgender identity. In instances where my argument delves into specific corporal implications that are rooted Stéphanie's embodiment (or experience by way of embodiment) rather than her gender identity, I employ the term "transsexual" before linking these back to the concept of transgender subjectivity.

2. It is worth mentioning that Stéphanie Michelini's role in *Wild Side* marked her debut as an actress and won her the Prix Michel-Simon (for Best Actress) in 2004. Further, her presence in the film as a transgender individual playing a transgender character is worthy of note since the majority of transgender characters still tend to be played by cisgender actors.

3. *Wild Side* won a Teddy Award for best feature film at the 2004 Berlin International Film Festival as well as the Special Jury Award at the Gijón International Film Festival (where it was also nominated for the Grand Prix Asturias). Within the United States, the film won the Grand Jury Award at the L.A. Outfest (2004) as well as the New Director's Showcase Award at the 2004 Seattle International Film Festival.

4. For example, see Stephen Holden's June 10, 2005 article "Visions of a Dangerous and Beautiful World" (*The New York Times*).

5. The word "validated" here implies that the subject is capable of both *seeing* and *being seen* as queer in a context that also sets itself against the backdrop of an assumed space of protection (in the case of urbanity, this takes the forms of anonymity and community).

6. In an effort to do justice to the character of Dominique, I do feel a certain level of pardon should be given to Dominique throughout her "cruel" scenes with her daughter. She is, after all, a dying woman just returned from the hospital and struggling with not only her health, but also the newness of her now-daughter.

7. This reading of "home" can be expanded to consider the end of the film when Dominique's house (now ostensibly Stéphanie's through inheritance) is left in an unknown state—was it sold or just abandoned? Likewise, the trio's return to Paris leaves open the question of not only the *what* but the *where* of their new romantic formation—will they inhabit the same apartment or do they now have means to move elsewhere, possibly closer/farther from the city center.

8. Indeed, it is significant that this portion of the sequence featuring Stéphanie and Nicolas takes place as the characters walk through this forested area, especially given that the scene first begins in a (sub)urban setting. As if taking a cue from the natural beauty of their surroundings, the verbal exchange and intimacy of their conversation draws attention to the "naturalness" of their being able to (re)connect upon Stéphanie's return to rural France and, by extension, to the constructed nature of gender that informs their discussion.

REFERENCES

Aragon, Asuncion. 2020. "Queering Spaces and Borders Resignifying a Third Space in Angelina Maccarone's *Fremde Haut (Unveiled)* (2005) and Sébastien Lifshitz's *Wild Side* (2004)." In *Gender, Sexuality and Identities of the Borderland*, edited by Suzanne Clisby, 15–28. New York: Routledge.

Berlant, Lauren. 2012. *Cruel Optimism*. Durham: Duke University Press.

Butler, Judith. 2006a. *Precarious Life*. London: Verso.

Butler, Judith. 2006b. *The Psychic Life of Power*. Stanford: Stanford University Press.

Caron, David. 2021. "Queer Relationality and the Dying Mother: Waiting and Caring in Sébastien Lifshitz's *Wild Side* and Jacques Nolot's *L'arrière-pays*." *L'Esprit Créateur* 61, no. 1: 13–25.

Freud, Sigmund. 1957. "Melancholia and Mourning." In *The Standard Edition of the Complete Psychological Works of Sigmund Freud. Vol. 14. (1914–1916)*, edited and translated by James Strachey, 243–58. London: Hogarth Press.

Halberstam, Jack. 2005. *In a Queer Time & Place*. New York: New York University Press.

Lifshitz, Sébastien. 2004. *Wild Side*. Ad Vitam Distribution and Peccadillo Pictures Ltd.

Prosser, Jay. 1998. *Second Skins*. New York: Columbia University Press.

Provencher, Denis. 2007. "Maghrebi-French Sexual Citizens: *In* and *Out* on the Big Screen." *Cineaste* 33, no. 1 (Winter 2007): 47–51.

Reeser, Todd W. 2007. "Transsexuality and the Disruption of Time in Sébastien Lifshitz's *Wild Side*." *Studies in French Cinema* 7, no. 2: 157–68.

Rees-Roberts, Nick. 2007. "Down and Out: Immigrant Poverty and Queer Sexuality in Sébastien Lifshitz's *Wild Side* (2004)." *Studies in French Cinema* 7, no. 2: 143–55.

Schoonover, Karl, and Rosalind Galt. 2016. *Queer Cinema in the World*. Durham: Duke University Press.

Seymour, Nicole. 2013. *Strange Natures*. Urbana: University of Illinois Press.

Weston, Kath. 1995. "Get Thee to a Big City." *GlQ* 2, no. 3: 253–77.

Young, Damon R. 2017. "Queer Love." In *Gender: Love*, edited by Jennifer Nash, 197–210. Farmington Hills: Macmillan.

Chapter 6

Transfeminine Embodiment in the Films of Sébastien Lifshitz and Lukas Dhont

Laurel Iber

In recent years, trans narratives have grown increasingly popular in French and Francophone cinema.[1] While this is likely due, in part, to shifting cultural attitudes toward transness and its broader social acceptance, it is also worth contemplating why the moving image lends itself so readily to trans representation. In a sense, trans identity constitutes a perfect cinematic subject, given the visual and temporal dimensions intrinsic to transition and transformation. Central to these stories is a fundamental tension between interiority and exteriority, and past and present, where their discontinuity is a major source of conflict, posing a set of existential problems and representational challenges.

Concentrating specifically on Sébastien Lifshitz's *Bambi* (2013) and *Petite Fille* (2020), as well as Lukas Dhont's *Girl* (2018), this essay examines the cinematic staging of transfeminine embodiment through the lens of three seemingly oppositional yet paradoxically fluid couplings: invisibility/hypervisibility, reality/fiction, and lived identity/performance, which overlap and intersect in complex and interesting ways. Vacillation between these poles—which mimics unsteady positioning within the gender binary—is inherent to these trans narratives and their filmic translations. *Bambi* offers a window onto the life of the eponymous entertainer and early trans icon, otherwise known as Marie-Pierre Pruvot, who later discreetly transitioned to teaching in public education. *Petite fille* chronicles seven-year-old Sasha Kovac's daily struggles for the right to be herself at school, in her ballet classes, and within her community. *Girl* is the tale of adolescent ballerina Lara, who must simultaneously contend with puberty and the rigors of a competitive dance conservatory.

While all the films present distinct visions of trans femininity, the three antipodal pairs surface in similar manners. First, each of the main characters alternatively experiences being unseen and excessively scrutinized, primarily by virtue of their nonconformity to binary gender within norm-enforcing institutions. Second, the boundary separating reality from fiction in these films is more porous than one might assume. Lifshitz's documentaries employ cinematic techniques more traditionally associated with fiction, whereas Dhont's film, though partially a fabrication, was inspired by the true story of Belgian dancer Nora Monsecour. Third, all these works throw into relief the precarious relationship between lived identity and gender performance. The link between performativity and the figuration of trans bodies is especially salient within the context of highly codified and overtly gendered art forms such as classical ballet and drag cabaret, where the constructedness of gender and the power of illusion are brought sharply into focus.

While the films share certain commonalities, they diverge in their handling of temporality. Most basically, each protagonist is captured at a different life stage: Sasha is a child, Lara a teenager, and Bambi a mature adult. More significantly, Lifshitz's and Dhont's films represent opposite impulses in their approach to their subjects' pasts, which goes beyond the distinction between documentary and fiction. Though *Petite fille* covers a period of one year and *Bambi* many decades, both offer long temporal arcs. Lifshitz grounds his subjects within a historical continuity, highlighting visual evidence of an existence prior to when we meet them on screen. By contrast, in *Girl*, we join Lara just before her conservatory audition and follow her from thereon. There is no evocation of her childhood or how she comes to an awareness of being female; everything is taken as given. We see no flashbacks of her as a small child, nor are there family portraits hanging on the wall, home movies, or photo albums. In fact, there is a double elision of the archive, where the background for Lara's character and Monsecour are strategically effaced.

Both directors developed close ties to their subjects, and both deal with trans stories from cis queer male perspectives, yet their works have been received very differently. One is compelled to ask why Lifshitz escaped the criticism Dhont endured. To attribute the public's polarized reactions to the genres of their films would be an oversimplification. Lifshitz's *Wild Side* (2004), a fictional drama about a trans sex-worker (played by trans actress Stéphanie Michelini), was hardly the lightning rod that *Girl* was. One must also consider the transparency of trans contributors' inclusion, distribution, cinematography, and narrative. Pruvot and Kovac unambiguously participated, whereas Monsecour avoided the limelight, letting cis actor Victor Polster stand in for her. *Girl* had a wider and higher-profile release, reaching international mainstream audiences. Lifshitz's camera maintains a polite distance from his subjects, whereas Dhont's encroaches on the actor's personal space. Dhont foregrounds the body itself in terrain that is extremely fraught, while Lifshitz's documentaries address other, non-corporeal aspects of transness. All these elements have affected popular opinions of the films. Together these works shed light on thorny debates concerning the politics of trans representation. Additionally, they demonstrate how cinema can be an ideal medium for representing the plasticity of trans experiences, well-suited for nuancing and enhancing trans representation, but under certain conditions, can be construed as threatening the image of a vulnerable group, even when endorsed by a trans consultant.

LIFSHITZ, THE ARCHIVE, AND THE FICTION OF THE REAL

When Lifshitz met Pruvot at Chéries-Chéris (Paris's international LGBT film festival), he knew immediately that he wanted to transpose her story to film (Lifshitz and Pruvot 2014). His initial plan was to include her in *Les Invisibles*, the project he was working on at the time. Ultimately, he decided that her situation was incompatible with the sort of biographies he sought to feature in this documentary. Here the objective was to shine a spotlight on an older generation of gays and lesbians, on the periphery of the queer community, whose lives might otherwise have slipped through the cracks. Lifshitz quickly realized Pruvot's prominent career in entertainment made her too famous for this group of "invisible" people. He furthermore concluded that the histories of homosexuality and transsexuality are too different to be lumped together, thus he conceived a separate film for her.[2]

In fact, Pruvot planted seeds for *Petite fille*, as well (see Lim and Lifshitz 2021; Zsombor and Lifshitz 2020; Ekchajzer 2020). During one of their conversations, Lifshitz asked Pruvot when she realized she was female. To his surprise, she replied that she had felt that way from the age of three or four onward. Lifshitz admits he had mistakenly assumed that trans identity was necessarily tied to a sexual awakening around adolescence, when in actuality, it often manifests in early childhood. Convinced that others shared his misconception, he believed it important to capture this dimension. Unable to rewind time, Lifshitz searched for a child whose story he could tell (Zsombor and Lifshitz 2020). He posted an announcement in an online forum for parents of trans children, which led him to Sasha's mother, Karine Kovac (Vié and Lifshitz 2020). The pair instantly developed a connection and Karine, weary from fighting battles on multiple fronts in her conservative provincial town, was relieved to have someone else on her side (Lim and Lifshitz 2020; Vié and Lifshitz 2020).

Lifshitz is interested in investigating what he describes as the construction of a person, or a life, and the material traces of that process (ARTE 2020). He defines his films as an encounter, one that combines self-narration and an exploration of the images that mark that journey (Gesbert and Lifshitz 2020). He has an affinity for collecting discarded photographs at flea markets and rummage sales, and has built a documentary aesthetic that is an extension of this practice, where his obsession with the private archive underpins and becomes the substance of his films. Lifshitz characterizes his photo-collecting as a "geste mémoriel" that aims to save the images from oblivion or destruction. Repurposing them in the creation of another narrative and putting them back into circulation is a means of reanimating or reactivating them (Gesbert and Lifshitz 2020).[3]

In 2019, the Centre Pompidou held "L'Inventaire infini," a retrospective of Lifshitz's films paired with an exhibition of amateur photographs he curated. Alexandre Gefen, discussing the event, argues that Lifshitz's attempts to rescue various "vies minuscules" from obscurity is a Foucauldian gesture (Gefen 2020, 157). Indeed, obvious parallels spring to mind. Foucault was himself preoccupied with the notion of *écriture de vie*, which we see in works like *La Vie des hommes infâmes*, *Moi, Pierre Rivière . . . , and Herculine Barbin.* Barbin's story is, moreover, one of transition, albeit involuntary.[4] However, it is worth noting a couple critical distinctions between Foucault's and Lifshitz's methods. First, Foucault's projects posthumously exhumed autobiographical accounts, whereas Lifshitz's living subjects actively collaborate in their portraits. Second, Lifshitz's films are a carefully concerted relationship between the visual and the verbal. Foucault, on the other hand, consistently privileged text over image.

What does seem Foucauldian about Lifshitz's filmmaking is the banality yet singularity of these narratives, which serve to crystalize something much greater. Bambi came to symbolize trans femininity before there was even a conceptual framework to speak about it, ushering in a new era of possibility for trans expression. *Petite fille* encapsulates the daily trials of a child who is unremarkable in that we would never know she was trans if we spotted her walking down the street, but exceptional in her astounding maturity beyond her years, her determination, and unshakeable sense of self. Her story also exemplifies public education's inept handling of trans students. Lifshitz monumentalizes these ordinary yet extraordinary lives by bringing them to the big screen.

Having visual documentation of one's lived existence was a prerequisite for participants in *Les Invisibles* and was important for *Bambi* and *Petite fille*, as well. In *Petite fille*, the archival component is limited to two short segments near the beginning and end of the film. The first is composed of a few scenes taken from faded home movies capturing Sasha's earliest moments, from newborn to toddler. The second contains approximately a dozen photos, picking up roughly where the video camera leaves off. Sasha shows off a framed photo of herself in a stroller, then holds it up next to her face, remarking how much she has changed. The camera hovers over her shoulder as she studies the image before cutting to a montage of photos picturing Sasha alone or with her siblings, the majority in black and white, except for three color snapshots, ending with her fifth birthday. They show her pre-girlhood, with short hair and boyish clothes, in place of the pink, ruffles, and glitter she gravitates toward later. Though Sasha has cultivated a more feminine appearance, she does not reject these other images of herself, but instead concentrates on her evolution.

Bambi presents a wider array of media, woven throughout the film, rather than being condensed into two discrete episodes. Paired strategically with specific anecdotes, they often serve an illustrative function. From Pruvot's personal collection, Lifshitz incorporates still and moving images spanning from childhood to her cabaret years and later teaching days. These are supplemented by additional content indirectly linked to Pruvot, such as clips from Jacques de Casembroot's *Jocelyn* (1952), Alessandro Blasetti's *Europa di notte* (1959), and press coverage of Coccinelle's wedding.[5] Found and new footage are assembled in a sort of "temporal collage," to borrow Romain Chareyron's term, where the sequencing is nonlinear, jumping between the present and different points in the past, allowing all the incarnations of Bambi to coexist (Chareyron 2019, 198).

In both films, Lifshitz allows the "external" images to occupy the entire frame, granting them the same status as the new material (Jonquet 2017, 69). While the inclusion of these personal artefacts is unsurprising in documentary film, the same technique is employed in his fiction films. Like *Petite fille*, in *Presque rien* (2000), the camera peers over protagonist Mathieu's shoulder as he flips through family photos before they begin to fill the screen. *Wild Side* presents a similar sequence of snapshots from Djamel's youth, which look like they could be the actor's own.

As Chareyron, Jonquet, Caillard, and others have observed, despite Lifshitz's preoccupation with archival documents, his approach to documentary filmmaking is unmistakably infused with a fictional aesthetic, borrowing many of its conventions, which he openly acknowledges (Jonquet 2017, 69). Lifshitz notes, in particular, his preference for medium to long shots instead of the expected close-ups. We can add to the list his penchant for fixed shots and use of a wide-screen format, which Caillard underscores (Caillard 2013, 18). Several have remarked that the views of Pruvot aboard a ship entering the harbor of Algiers are purely cinematic. Lifshitz's fluid integration of the two genres is no doubt because he sees them as equivalent, since in his estimation, documentary film produces its own form of fiction that nevertheless aims at truth (Jonquet 2017, 68–69). The influence he derives from fiction extends to literature as well. This much is clear when he describes Pruvot's story as a kind of novel and when he speaks about the notion of the *roman d'une vie* in relation to *Les Invisibles* (Lifshitz and Pruvot 2014; Caillard 2013, 18). The convergence of life, the novel, and cinema are perfectly summarized in the extended cut of *Bambi*, where Pruvot identifies with Laurence's situation in Lamartine's *Jocelyn*, which is then reinforced by inserted scenes from Casembroot's adaptation.

WHERE DRAG AND TRANS-IDENTITY CONVERGE

For Pruvot, the imbrication of performance and lived identity stems from her simultaneous first encounter with drag and transness, when at sixteen she saw Coccinelle perform with the Carrousel de Paris in Algiers. Afterward, she formulated a plan to move to the city with her boyfriend Ludo and start a fresh life as a woman. To her dismay, Ludo brutally spurned her, calling the new look a "déguisement" and hypocritically mocking her sexuality. His cruel reaction awakened her to the reality that she had no future in Algeria. Brushing aside passing thoughts of suicide, she determined that leaving for France was necessary to her survival.

Once in Paris, Pruvot approached the Carrousel's owner about joining the troupe and was told to earn her spot by training up at its sister club, Madame Arthur. In the cabaret, the boundary between life and art began to blur. Although the eye-opening burlesque show prompted her epiphany and subsequent transformation, the desire it sparked was not to simulate femininity on stage but to embody it full-time. The drag revue aspect followed because it provided her with a community and a space in which to exist, though not without judgment, as other performers tried to dissuade her from transitioning. They brought up the daunting administrative, legal, and social obstacles, but also seemed to disapprove of the departure from what they understood drag to be—men masquerading as women. These female impersonators presumably believed that if she and Coccinelle ceased to be men, then what they were doing was no longer drag but something else. Yet they themselves failed to maintain a distinct division between the stage and the outside world when they would go out to bars in drag in their off hours. Despite the discouragement of her peers, Pruvot, like Coccinelle, was undeterred and started a regimen of injections and pills, before proceeding with surgery.

STATIC VERSUS SHIFTING IMAGES

While presenting *Bambi* at the Berlin Film Festival, Lifshitz recounts how Pruvot, for a long time, did not own a still camera, only a Super 8. When asked why, she replies that it just seemed natural for her. Lifshitz hypothesizes that she gravitated toward the moving image because it was a better medium to capture her transformation, a theory which she confirms.[6] This exchange suggests that something about her essence eludes or exceeds the static image. Lifshitz postulates that it is too rigid. Perhaps after emerging from her cocoon, Pruvot disliked the idea of being pinned down like the anesthetized butterflies Barthes evokes in *Camera Lucida* (Barthes 2010, 57). This "intense immobility" or fixity might be thought of as a flattening of the image, tantamount to death, *flat death* in Barthesian parlance (Barthes 2010, 49, 92). As a mere slice of time, the photograph precludes the full emergence of the trans subject whose being and becoming is contingent upon duration.

In trans narratives, photographic documentation of early life often departs from lived experience, testifying to a disconnect between interior and exterior, a gap that is only bridged by an eventual transition. Jay Prosser characterizes pre-transition photos as representing "an absented presence," a reflection of something that was but is no longer, although the same could be said of any photograph (Prosser 1998, 213). As Susan Sontag famously wrote: "A photograph is both a pseudo-presence and a token of absence" (Sontag 1977, 12). Yet, for trans subjects, there is another layer to this absence, by virtue of the reconstruction or reframing of the body that once served as referent. These images, where the once familiar is rendered foreign, expose a rupture in continuity between the pre-and post-transition self. Take Pruvot for example: there are no photographs of her as a girl, in her favorite red frock. The only feminine images of her from this era are memories of admiring herself in the mirror in dresses her sister had outgrown. The photographs she has picture her as a boy, then as a woman, together designating a lost past, the girlhood she was denied. The images of Pruvot as a little girl that she was never able to fully possess, that were never concrete, are on the same order as those in Hervé Guibert's *L'Image fantôme*, a book devoted to latent, invisible, and inexistent images.

While Pruvot's boyhood photos provoke self-estrangement, she is not motivated to destroy them, unlike Coccinelle or Stéphanie (*Wild Side*'s protagonist), who are intent on erasing all traces of their former existence (Prosser 1998, 220). For them, burning or shredding these images is a means of neutralizing them, of extinguishing their alter egos' potential to return. Prosser, drawing on Barthes's theorization of photography's threat to resurrect the dead, contends that "photographs of a pre-transition self threaten to incarnate a 'dead' self that one is not" (Prosser 217).

PETITE FILLE AND VISIBILITY

For Sasha, visibility is a matter of fighting to be seen for who she is once she steps outside her protective domestic bubble. She simply wants to be treated like any other girl her age. This means being called by the pronouns that suit her and being able to dress according to her gender at school and in ballet class. Because the respective institutions find these wishes incomprehensible, she attracts unwanted attention. Sasha's teachers and peers misgender her and she encounters shoving and bathroom-related harassment from other children. The greatest humiliation occurs at the dance conservatory, when Karine follows up on Sasha's request to attend class as a girl. The ballet mistress refuses before callously pushing Sasha out of the room and closing the door in her face, in front of numerous onlookers. Rejecting Sasha's request is especially senseless given that at her age, the issue is essentially reducible to attire. Lifshitz recollects that while they were filming, Sasha was understandably very focused on external signs of femininity that visually reaffirmed her identity at a time when it was contested (ARTE 2020).

The school's administration proves to be another formidable enemy for the Kovac family. Their protracted battle over Sasha's right to be recognized as a girl undergirds most of the film. The school is not only uncooperative but openly malicious. Administrators' tactics range from ignoring Karine's persistent attempts at dialogue to threatening to report her for child abuse.[7] When Lifshitz arrived on the scene, the relationship became even more strained. After unsuccessfully trying to deter the Kovacs from participating in the film, the school did everything in its power to impede production. The crew was barred from the school's grounds and served a letter threatening legal action if its name or image appeared in the documentary (Lim and Lifshitz 2020; Gesbert and Lifshitz 2020; Vena and Lifshitz 2020). The irony is that in seeking to suppress the story, they only amplified it. By pitting themselves against a darling little girl, they become villains, rendering Sasha and her crusaders heroes.

Sasha's predicament emblematizes an acute problem within the French public school system. National educational policies have failed to ensure adequate training to appropriately handle trans students, which has resulted in extremely heterogenous practices, sometimes with disastrous consequences. In 2021, Minister of Education Jean-Michel Blanquer published an official bulletin purporting to take steps to rectify this (Blanquer 2021). However, his directive that schools defer to parents in the recognition of trans children has dangerous implications for those in transphobic households, since they would be denied assistance. The tragic suicide of a trans teenager in Lille in December 2020 (the month *Petite fille* aired on ARTE) stands as a poignant reminder of the grave risks for trans youth who are unsupported at home and at school. More cases like Sasha's are surfacing, including that of Lilie, an eight-year-old trans girl from Aubignan, who received media attention in 2021 regarding clashes with the school and a rejected petition to legally change her name.

GIRL, ITS HISTORY, AND THE QUESTION OF AUTHENTIC TRANS REPRESENTATION

Contrary to many trans critics' charges that Dhont's *Girl* is divorced from reality, it was inspired and shaped by a real person. Upon reading a 2008 newspaper article about fifteen-year-old trans dancer Nora Monsecour, he became interested in the aspiring ballerina's struggle to access training (Clarke 2019). A pupil at Antwerp's prestigious Royal Ballet School, Monsecour's request to switch to the girls' classes was refused (Ghyselings 2018). The dancer's plight resonated with Dhont, who was wrestling to square his homosexuality with his Catholic education (Dhont and Polster n.d.). Monsecour's unwavering sense of self empowered him to wholly embrace his own identity (Fagerholm and Dhont 2019). He promptly approached her about making a documentary. When she finally agreed to speak with him, the two quickly developed a friendship (Dhont and Polster n.d.; Monsecour and Kilday 2018).

Yet, Monsecour was reluctant to appear on screen because she was transitioning and felt uncomfortable being filmed (Wiseman 2018). She was also afraid of the stigma of being so publicly outed as trans (Curry 2019; Dhont and Polster n.d.; Smith n.d.). Nevertheless, she was enthusiastic about having her story told through a fictional character. Monsecour actively participated in several aspects of the film's production, from supplying personal experiences that would form the bedrock of the narrative, to weighing in on casting, being present on set, and reading and revising version after version of the script (Monsecour and Kilday 2018). Despite her extensive engagement in the project, when it came time to release the film, she preferred to remain in the shadows (Monsecour and Kilday 2018; Ramos 2018; Clarke 2019). Unfortunately, her phantom role made it look as though no trans person was involved in the conception of the film, which angered lots of trans critics.

Much of the queer press coverage focused intensely on cis dancer and actor Victor Polster holding the leading role of Lara. Trans audiences' indignation over seeing Polster in this part is rooted in the long and problematic history of cis actors playing trans characters. Even when these representations are handled with complexity and grace, they are still seen as depriving trans actors of opportunities. However, this attitude does not align with Monsecour's casting priorities: "I didn't care at all if the actor was male, female, transgender, lesbian, gay;" instead, she emphasized the importance of Lara being played "by someone who had a lot of love and empathy for the character" as well as being "a very good dancer" (Dry 2018). A gender-open casting call brought in approximately 500 young people, including a handful of trans girls (Clarke 2019). Yet, they found it very difficult to cast Lara (Fagerholm and Dhont 2019). Fortunately, when they discovered Polster, all agreed he was an excellent choice (Fagerholm and Dhont 2019; Debruge 2018). Monsecour recalls feeling "that he was the one person that could give this role life in a way that would pay respect to [her] story" (Dry 2018). Although she clearly privileged strong dancing over gender in her vision for the character, many trans viewers seem indifferent to this facet, ignoring how choosing a non-dancer could impoverish the performance in other manners.[8] Furthermore, Polster's detractors overlook the implausibility of casting a trans girl as Lara, since none fit the role, and the team of psychiatrists who consulted on the film advised against it (Thomas 2018).

As Jack Halberstam remarks: "Transgender actors should play transgender roles, but that is not always possible," adding "we cannot always demand a perfect match between directors, actors, and the material in any given narrative" (Halberstam 2018, 103). Despite Dhont's ongoing dialogue with Monsecour, health experts in the field, and Berdache Belgium (a support group for parents of trans youth), for some, his diligent research did not translate to the screen. The underlying assumption is that, regardless of belonging to a sexual minority group, as a cis director, his perspective is inevitably distorted. By the time Monsecour stepped forward to defend Dhont, Polster, and the film, most people's minds were made up. One wonders whether *Girl* would have become so polemic had her involvement been clear from the outset. When posed the question, Dhont speculates that the film might have been seen as more legitimate, but clarifies that he does not believe only trans people can or should tell trans stories (Clarke 2019). Monsecour supports this position, accusing those who use this logic to discount the narrative of trying to negate her experiences (Monsecour and Kilday 2018). She affirms: "My story is not a fantasy of the cis director. Lara's story is my story" (Dry 2018).

BALLET AND THE TRANS BODY:
A SITE OF DIVISION AND DUPLICATION

The critiques leveled against *Girl* were not limited to the cis director, screenwriter, and lead, but also pertained to the camera's relationship to Lara's body, the depiction of physical suffering, and the violent scene of self-harm. Oliver Whitney claims: "The film isn't just another case of irresponsible casting or harmful stereotypes, like much of Hollywood's long, ugly treatment of the trans community; it's the most dangerous movie about a trans character in years" (Whitney 2018). K. Austin Collins, similarly condemnatory, calls *Girl* "a curiously unjust, myopic, even dangerous movie." (Collins 2019). He contends that the "focus on dance feels like an excuse to harp on the physical realities of Lara's transition" citing the way the camera "zeroes in on the bloodied tape on Lara's bruised and battered toes when she removes her shoes before peeking at the torturously irritating tape over her pelvis" (Collins op. cit.). Mathew Rodriguez finds her suffering excessively graphic, too: "there's no reason for a film to focus so much on watching a trans person bloody themselves, even if it's in pursuit of becoming a ballerina" (Rodriguez 2018). Collins concludes that "*Girl* fixates on these images until, at least symbolically, they start to feel like intractable parallels, markers of Lara's progress toward becoming who it is she wants to become." Implicit here is a desire to disarticulate Lara's status as a dancer from her transness, discounting that the two are inextricably linked. Monsecour went through her transition as a ballet dancer and the tensions between these two facets of her identity subtend the corporeal crisis she endured. Indeed, the combination is fraught, but this is precisely why it interested Dhont.

To better contextualize the rawness of these scenes and other contested elements like Lara's frequent lingering over her own reflection, or the camera's proximity to her body as she stretches, dances, and goes about her routine, we might consider Nils Tavernier's gritty close-ups and behind-the-scenes views of the Paris Opera Ballet in *Tout près des étoiles* (2001). The gruesome feet, overexertion, constant monitoring of one's appearance, and overdependence on mirrors are present in both films and inherent to the craft. The problem derives from their intersection with how trans bodies are represented on screen and the way ballet emphasizes a set of aesthetic codes imposed on the body, which necessarily brings morphology into relief.

Dhont indicates that ballet's rigid gendering—which he sees as metaphor for society more broadly—is part of what drew him to the narrative (Dhont and Polster n.d.). He found the combination of a young trans person in classical dance, where the body is central, to be incredibly cinematographic (Giuliani and Dhont 2021). He underscores the significant tension in her primary instrument of expression triggering a crisis that demands its transformation (Fagerholm and Dhont 2019). Monsecour remembers her world collapsing when she graduated to gender-specific training, because "It was very hard to dance like a boy and transition at the same time" (Smith n.d.). She was ultimately forced out of the ballet track at the age of fourteen (Wingenroth 2019). Although critics like Collins allege that Dhont emphasizes the limitations of trans bodies through ballet, one could argue that his film constitutes a more optimistic retelling of Monsecour's story, where Lara is admitted into the program as a girl (Collins 2019).

Despite the conservatory's inflexibility, Monsecour cites herself as her greatest antagonist, an aspect Dhont preserved by making Lara's corporeal malaise the main conflict (Monsecour and Kilday 2018; Fagerholm and Dhont n.d.). While Monsecour found acceptance from friends and family, she felt betrayed by her flesh (Monsecour and Kilday 2018). Passing, which is not a goal for all trans people, but is for Monsecour and Lara, is trickier within the ballet setting, where there are strict gendered expectations for how a body should look, and formfitting attire that shows off the body's every contour. Lara goes to great lengths to conceal her anatomy, tucking and duct-taping her genitals, and avoiding undressing in front of her peers. Despite efforts to blend in, she is distastefully outed on multiple occasions, including when a teacher indiscreetly asks the girls if they mind Lara using their changing room. Though she faces microaggressions in the locker-room and when her little brother deadnames her during a tantrum, along with enduring an episode of overt transphobic bullying at the sleepover, Lara's primary enemy is herself.

This inner conflict culminates in a jarring act of self-injury, where Lara tries to remove her genitalia with a pair of scissors. Though her back is turned to the camera, and neither the crude amputation attempt nor its doubtlessly gory outcome is shown, audiences were inflamed over the brutality and illogic of this gesture. Monsecour justifies the controversial scene's indispensability by insisting that "it's reality," before clarifying that she never executed the deed but contemplated it countless times, fantasizing that it would bring relief (Smith n.d.). Dhont maintains that this event is never presented as a form of resolution, despite viewers interpreting it as such (Fagerholm and Dhont 2019). As evidence, he cites the shots of Lara in the hospital, where she sees her reflection in double. For him, it suggests that "her actions didn't really alter that perception" and that there is part of her identity that can never be excised (Ibid).

The duplication of her image is not constrained to this scene but occurs repeatedly throughout the film. We see Lara carry out myriad activities before various mirrors: piercing her ears, fixing her hair, getting weighed at the doctor's office, swallowing her hormones, applying or removing tape, dressing and undressing, riding the elevator with a neighbor boy, studying her body after fleeing the sexual encounter she initiated with him, examining the bump on her head from fainting in rehearsal, crumpling to the floor in pain during the scissor incident, and of course, dancing. Whether she is looking at herself or not, it is as though she is perpetually performing to the mirror. The doubling that results might be read on multiple levels. First, it seems to be a continuation of Dhont's visual metaphor cited above. Second, it accentuates the schism between exteriority and interiority, the disparity between how she feels and how she looks, or how she sees herself and how she is seen. Third, it echoes her dual identity as Lara the trans girl and Lara the dancer. In all these cases, the competing entities of her fractured self-image act as an analogy for her transness.

The rupture between Lara's past and present is conveyed not only by the mirror but by the elimination of any visual or verbal reference to her pre-transition life (apart from the isolated instance of deadnaming). *Girl* being a fiction film, Dhont could have fabricated a past for his character with flashbacks and childhood photos, borrowed from Polster's personal archive, or created using a young actor resembling Lara, as Lifshitz did for Stéphanie in *Wild Side*. Whatever his reason for not doing so, it further severs her current existence from any prior one. While Pruvot lacks images of her stolen moments as a little girl, Lara has no material evidence of her history at all. It is only her enduring family bonds and her technical skills as a dancer that indicate a past.

Dhont observes that because of the scarcity of trans protagonists in cinema, there is a tendency to comprehend every depiction of a trans character as a portrayal of the whole community (Curry 2019; Fagerholm and Dhont n.d.). Given the perceived need for positive representations to counteract inaccurate or unjust ones that have dominated media for decades, there is pressure to produce images of trans experiences that are authentic and relatable, if not uplifting. However, Dhont pushes back against the idea that every queer character needs to be a role model, emphasizing Lara's line: "I don't want to be an example, I just want to be a girl" (Wiseman 2018; Clarke 2019). He and Monsecour reiterate on numerous occasions that *Girl* is an individual portrait and is in no way meant to be universal (Wiseman 2018). Monsecour's circumstances, being particular to ballet, perhaps resonate with a narrower subset of trans viewers, but there are nonetheless plenty of instances of trans dancers being excluded from the ballet world.[9]

CONCLUSION

Having explored this trio of films through the three sets of opposing terms—hypervisibility/invisibility, real/fiction, lived identity/performance—let us recall how they function. Beginning with the first pair, Pruvot's visibility fluctuates with her initial celebrity, subsequent disappearance into anonymity, and return to fame with *Bambi*. There is also the namelessness of inhabiting an identity not yet codified by language. *Petite fille* calls attention to Sasha's situation, to trans feelings in early childhood, and to a blind spot in national education. While Sasha yearns to fit in, she understands that going public with her story could benefit other children like her (Vié and Lifshitz 2020). In *Girl*, visibility operates on multiple levels: Lara's desire to stand out as a dancer but not for being trans, the initial concealment of Monsecour's role in the project, and the film's engagement with the larger debate over what kind of trans stories ought to be told and by whom. Next, concerning the second dyad, all three films create a sort of fiction of the real. Lifshitz achieves this through stylistic choices that straddle genres, whereas Dhont embellishes and dramatizes details of Monsecour's life. Last, as we have seen, lived identity and performance are tightly intertwined in Pruvot's experience. Drag cabaret helped her to recognize her transness and, in her career as an entertainer, gender masquerade and trans womanhood coalesce, making it difficult to determine where one ends and the other begins. For Sasha, after adopting a feminine identity at home, attending school and dance lessons as a boy is akin to donning a costume and delivering a forced performance of masculinity. Lara is preoccupied with presenting as female not only in day-to-day life but in classical ballet, too, where gender roles are especially circumscribed and aestheticized. Thus, the image of femininity she aims to cultivate requires a higher level of performance to produce. Beyond the fluid movement between the polar combinations, there is overlap among these groupings.

Let us now consider what the films collectively contribute to the landscape of trans representation in cinema. First, each offers a depiction of trans femininity that departs from ones we often see. *Bambi*'s and *Petite fille*'s subjects fall outside the age range generally privileged, which naturally decenters transition. The documentaries also decouple transness from sexuality. *Girl* takes up the unexpected theme of a trans ballet dancer, which proves to be risky but compelling. Second, they propose three original stories, based on lived experiences, that tap into an intricate web of gendered cultural norms. Specifically, they highlight gender policing within public schools, drag, ballet, and society more broadly. Third, regardless of what has been said about Dhont's disconcerting portrayal of transness, both directors provide real trans individuals a platform to share their personal stories. Fourth, they advance trans representation in key respects. Lifshitz's narratives help to normalize transness. The exoticism of Pruvot's burlesque days is counterbalanced by the ordinariness of becoming a schoolteacher and settling into a stable long-term romantic partnership. The Kovacs are an average family with no explicit political agenda, who justly defend a child's basic freedom of self-expression. Dhont's visual execution of Monsecour's story might be disturbing, but in presenting Lara not as an ideal, but as a person, who is intrepid but lost, is humanizing and still serves to complicate trans representation in a productive fashion.

NOTES

1. Examples include Alain Berliner's *Ma vie en rose* (1997), Patrice Chéreau's *Ceux qui m'aiment prendront le train* (1998), Sébastien Lifshitz's *Wild Side* (2004), Céline Sciamma's *Tomboy* (2011), Xavier Dolan's *Laurence Anyways* (2012), François Ozon's *Une Nouvelle amie* (2014), Valérie Mitteaux's *Fille ou garçon, mon sexe n'est pas mon genre* (2016), Lorène Debaisieux's *Devenir il ou elle* (2017) Nadir Moknèche's *Lola Pater* (2017), Clarisse Verrier's *Être fille ou garçon: Le Dilemme des transgenres* (2017), Laurent Micheli's *Lola vers la mer* (2019), and Ruben Alves's *Miss* (2020).

2. Sébastien Lifshitz, *Bambi* DVD bonus: Avant-première Festival de Berlin.

3. For a discussion of Lifshitz's reanimation of still images, see: Jonathan Devine, "Documenting the Trans* and Animating the Still in Sébastien Lifshitz's Bambi," *French Screen Studies* 21 (4) (October 2, 2021): 9.

4. After a series of medical examinations, Barbin, who was assigned female at birth, although technically intersex by today's terminology, was deemed at the age of twenty-one to be a man and ordered to live as such. Michel Foucault, *Herculine Barbin dite Alexina B.* (Paris: Gallimard, 2014), 170-71.

5. *Jocelyn* is an adaptation of Alphonse de Lamartine's 1836 novel where female love interest Laurence is disguised as a man. Blasetti's film is a tour of European nightlife, featuring Coccinelle, Pruvot's mentor, friend, and fellow trans icon.

6. Lifshitz, *Bambi* DVD bonus: Scènes inédites.

7. Despite the hurdles, they eventually succeed in securing accommodations for Sasha, with the aid of Dr. Bargiacchi, who provides the documentation required to appease the school.

8. One might think of Darren Aronofsky's *Black Swan* and Natalie Portman's dependence on her (under-credited) body double, Sarah Lane.

9. Even New York's Ballets Trockadero, a comedic drag ballet, had a recent public dispute with former principal Chase Johnsey, who resigned, alleging discrimination over his femininity and potential transition. Candice Thompson, "Chase Johnsey Talks About Those Allegations Against the Trocks," *Dance Magazine*, January 24, 2018, www.dancemagazine.com/chase-johnsey-interview-trocks-allegations -2528105578.html.

FILMOGRAPHY

Bambi, directed by Sébastien Lifshitz (2013; Paris: Epicentre Films, 2013), DVD.
Bambi: une nouvelle femme, directed by Sébastien Lifshitz (2020; Paris: Canal+).
Black Swan, directed by Darren Aronofsky (2010; Los Angeles: Fox Searchlight, 2011), DVD.
Europa di notte, directed by Alessandro Blasetti (1959; Paris: Cinédis).
Girl, directed by Lukas Dhont (2018; Paris: Diaphana Distribution, 2019), DVD.
Jocelyn, directed by Jacques de Casembroot (1952; Paris: Panthéon Distribution).
Les Invisibles, directed by Sébastien Lifshitz (2012; Paris: Ad Vitam, 2013), DVD.

Petite fille, directed by Sébastien Lifshitz (2020; Paris: Arte).
Presque rien, directed by Sébastien Lifshitz (2000; Paris: Ad Vitam, 2010), DVD.
Tout près des étoiles: Les Danseurs de l'Opéra de Paris, directed by Nils Tavernier (2001; Paris: Pyramide).
Wild Side, directed by Sébastien Lifshitz (2004; Paris: Ad Vitam, 2004), DVD.

REFERENCES

ARTE: 28 minutes. 2020. "Sébastien Lifshitz—*Petite Fille*: Pas Son Genre." December 2, 2020. www.youtube.com/watch?v=HY96sr1tuKc.

Barthes, Roland. 2010. *Camera Lucida: Reflections on Photography*. Translated by Richard Howard. New York: Hill and Wang.

Blanquer, Jean-Michel. 2021. "Pour une meilleure prise en compte des questions relatives à l'identité de genre en milieu scolaire." *Ministère de l'Éducation Nationale de la Jeunesse et des Sports*, September 29, 2021. www.education.gouv.fr/bo/21/Hebdo36/MENE2128373C.htm.

Caillard, Guilhem. 2013. "Le cinéma documentaire de Sébastien Lifshitz: les traces de la mémoire." *Séquences: la revue de cinéma*, n° 284: 17–19.

Chareyron, Romain. 2019. "Sébastien Lifshitz: Cinéaste des identités." *Modern & Contemporary France* 27 (2): 185–203.

Clarke, Cath. 2019. "'I Have the Right to Tell This Story': Lukas Dhont Defends His Trans Film Girl." *The Guardian*, March 12, 2019. www.theguardian.com/film/2019/mar/12/lukas-dhont-defends-his-trans-film-girl-victor-polster-dancer.

Collins, K. Austin. 2019. "There's No Good Reason to Watch Belgium's Controversial 'Girl.'" *Vanity Fair*, March 15, 2019. www.vanityfair.com/hollywood/2019/03/netflix-girl-review.

Curry, Thomas Adam. 2019. "Trans Ballet Dancer Nora Monsecour Speaks on Netflix's Polarising 'Girl.'" *AnOther*, March 15, 2019. www.anothermag.com/design-living/11592/trans-ballet-dancer-film-girl-controversy-nora-monsecour-lukas-dhont.

Debruge, Peter. 2018. "'Girl': Trans Drama Wowed Cannes, but Can It Impress American Audiences?" *Variety*, August 7, 2018. variety.com/2018/film/news/girl-cannes-trans-drama-american-audiences-1202896291/.

Devine, Jonathan. 2021. "Documenting the Trans* and Animating the Still in Sébastien Lifshitz's Bambi." *French Screen Studies* 21 (4): 333–49.

Dhont, Lukas, and Victor Polster. "Girl: Victor Polster x Lukas Dhont." *Issue Magazine*, n.d. issuemagazine.com/girl-victor-polster-x-lukas-dhont/.

Dry, Jude. 2018. "Netflix's 'Girl' Slammed by Trans Critics, but the Film's Subject Says They're Wrong." *IndieWire,* December 19, 2018. www.indiewire.com/2018/12/girl-netflix-transgender-ballerina-nora-monsecour-interview-1202028761/.

Ekchajzer, François. 2020. "'Petite Fille' sur ARTE, le portrait solaire d'une enfant unique en son genre." *Télérama*, December 2, 2020. www.telerama.fr/ecrans/petite-fille-sur-arte-le-portrait-solaire-dune-enfant-unique-en-son-genre-6747078.php.

Fagerholm, Matt, and Lukas Dhont. 2019. "Lukas Dhont on *Girl*, the Film's Controversial Casting, What Representation Means to Him and More." RogerEbert.com, January 14, 2019. www.rogerebert.com/interviews/lukas-dhont -on-girl-the-films-controversial-casting-what-representation-means-to-him-and -more.

Foucault, Michel. 2014. *Herculine Barbin dite Alexina B.* Paris: Gallimard.

Gefen, Alexandre. 2020. "Sébastien Lifshitz, L'Inventaire infini, textes Isabelle Bonnet." *Nouvelle revue d'esthétique* 25 (1): 157–158.

Gesbert, Olivia and Sébastien Lifshitz. 2020. "Sébastien Lifshitz: Qui suis-je? L'identité en questions." *France Culture: La Grande Table idées*, December 1, 2020. www.franceculture.fr/emissions/la-grande-table-idees/sebastien-lifshitz-qui -suis-je-lidentite-en-questions.

Ghyselings, Marise. 2018. "Girl, Vivement déconseillé aux personnes trans-genres." *Paris Match*, October 18, 2018. parismatch.be/culture/cinema/188731/ girl-deconseille-personnes-transgenres.

Giuliani, Morgane, and Lukas Dhont. 2021. "'Girl': Rencontre avec le réalisateur, Lukas Dhont." *Marie Claire*, February 3, 2021. www.marieclaire.fr/girl-lukas -dhont-victor-polster-interview-critique,1284470.asp.

Halberstam, Jack. 2018. *Trans*: A Quick and Quirky Account of Gender Variability*. Oakland, California: University of California Press.

Jonquet, François. 2017. "Sébastien Lifshitz: Fiction du réel." *Artpress*, n°466 (July–August 2017): 68–73.

Lifshitz, Sébastien, and Marie-Pierre Pruvot. 2014. *Berlin International Film Festival Teddy Award Interview Sebastian Lifshitz, "Bambi."* www.youtube.com/watch?v =h-0IH5JS6Do.

Lim, Dennis, and Sébastien Lifshitz. 2021. *Film at Lincoln Center: Little Girl Q&A with Sébastien Lifshitz.* www.youtube.com/watch?v=AIOnoaFUgcM.

Monsecour, Nora, and Gregg Kilday. 2018. "Belgium Oscar Submission 'Girl' Is a 'Message of Courage, Bravery and Compassion' (Guest Column)." *The Hollywood Reporter*, December 7, 2018. www.hollywoodreporter.com/news/general-news/ belgium-oscar-submission-girl-is-a-message-courage-1167532/.

Prosser, Jay. 1998. *Second Skins: The Body Narratives of Transsexuality.* Gender and Culture Series. New York: Columbia University Press.

Ramos, Dino-Ray. 2018. "Director Lukas Dhont Talks Netflix Drama 'Girl,' Opening a Dialogue with Trans Community—Awardsline Screening Series." *Deadline*, November 14, 2018. deadline.com/2018/11/lukas-dhont-netflix-drama- girl-transgender-lgbtq-representation-awardsline-screening-series-1202501468/.

Reeser, Todd W. 2007. "Transsexuality and the disruption of time in Sébastien Lifshitz's *Wild Side*." *Studies in French Cinema*, 7 (2): 157–168.

Rodriguez, Mathew. 2018. "Netflix's 'Girl' Is Another Example of Trans Trauma Porn and Should Be Avoided at All Costs." *INTO*, October 4, 2018. www.intomore .com/culture/netflixs-girl-is-another-example-of-trans-trauma-porn-and-should-be -avoided-at-all-costs/.

Smith, Mark. "Interview with Trans Twins Arno and Nora Monsecour: Born Identical Boys, Now Brother and Sister," *The Times Magazine*, n.d. www.thetimes.co.uk

/article/interview-with-trans-twins-arno-and-nora-monsecour-born-identical-boys
-now-brother-and-sister-qzzxb38zz.

Sontag, Susan. 1977. *On Photography*. New York: Farrar, Straus and Giroux.

Thomas, Ann. 2018. "In Defense of 'Girl,' the Trans Film Called 'Trauma Porn' by Critics." *Advocate*, December 13, 2018. www.advocate.com/commentary/2018/12 /13/defense-girl-trans-film-called-trauma-porn-critics.

Thompson, Candice. 2018. "Chase Johnsey Talks About Those Allegations Against the Trocks." *Dance Magazine*, January 24, 2018. www.dancemagazine.com/chase -johnsey-interview-trocks-allegations-2528105578.html.

Vena, Teresa, and Sébastien Lifshitz. 2020. "Interview: Sébastien Lifshitz, Réalisateur de *Petite fille*." *Cineuropa*, February 26, 2020. cineuropa.org/fr/interview/385969/.

Vié, Caroline, and Sébastien Lifshitz. 2020. "'La différence donne envie de se battre' clame Sébastien Lifshitz." *20 Minutes*, November 25, 2020. www.20minutes.fr/arts -stars/cinema/2915679-20201125-difference-donne-envie-battre-clame-realisateur -sebastien-lifshitz.

Whitney, Oliver. 2018. "Belgium's Foreign-Language Oscar Submission, 'Girl,' Is a Danger to the Transgender Community (Guest Column)." *The Hollywood Reporter*, December 4, 2018. www.hollywoodreporter.com/movies/movie-news/ belgiums-oscar-submission-girl-is-a-danger-transgender-community-1166505/.

Wingenroth, Lauren. 2019. "Girl Was Called 'the Most Dangerous Movie About a Trans Character in Years'—But It Helped Its Subject Learn to Love Herself." *Dance Magazine*, March 15, 2019. www.dancemagazine.com/nora-monsecour-girl -2631395713.html?rebelltitem=7#rebelltitem7?rebelltitem=7.

Wiseman, Andreas. 2018. "Oscar-Snubbed 'Girl' Director Lukas Dhont Responds to Tough Words from Trans Critics: 'The Biggest Strength of Art Is Empathy.'" *Deadline*, December 18, 2018. deadline.com/2018/12/ netflix-girl-oscars-trans-lukas-dhont-criticism-1202522069/.

Zsombor, Bobák, and Sébastien Lifshitz. 2020. *Berlin International Film Festival Teddy Award: Interview with Sébastien Lifshitz on "Petite fille."* www.youtube .com/watch?v=zUqUHZ5Ut34.

Chapter 7

Circus Freaks and Pretty Monsters

Fighting and Reclaiming a Transphobic Stigma

Arthur Ségard

As an opening to her seminal work on the representations of transidentities in contemporary France, trans scholar Karine Espineira quotes at length Tod Browning's 1932 film *Freaks*'s opening crawl:

> Before proceeding with the showing of the following HIGHLY UNUSUAL ATTRACTION, a few words should be said about the amazing subject matter. BELIEVE IT OR NOT. . . . STRANGE AS IT SEEMS. In ancient times anything that deviated from the normal was considered an omen of ill luck or representative of evil. [. . .] Occasionally, one of these unfortunates was taken to the court to be jeered at or ridiculed for the amusement of the nobles. [. . .] The majority of freaks, themselves, are endowed with normal thoughts and emotions. Their lot is truly a heart-breaking one. They are forced into the most unnatural of lives. Therefore, they have built up among themselves a code of ethics to protect them from the barbs of normal people. Their rules are rigidly adhered to and the hurt of one is the hurt of all, the joy of one is the joy of all. The story about to be revealed is a story based on the effect of this code upon their lives. [. . .] With humility for the many injustices done to such people, (they have no power to control their lot) we present the most startling horror story of the ABNORMAL and THE UNWANTED. (Espineira 2015, 13)[1]

The meaning of this reference is left open as Karine Espineira offers no reflection upon it. Nor does she establish a relationship between this opening remark about freaks and her own reflection on the media treatment of a social group that is also considered *abnormal* by not conforming to dominant gender norms. Here, "freak" is a historical reference to "abnormal" people who were exhibited "for fun and profit" (see Bogdan 1985)—mostly in nineteenth-century United States, but also in France. One can easily identify some implicit similarities between the two marginalized groups, their conflicting relationship to institutions, and the creation of strategies to "protect them from the barbs of normal people."[2] What is the meaning of this connection between freaks and trans people for a trans scholar and activist? Is it a way to reclaim a relatively widespread and *pointed* slur? "There are such pointed slurs about being trans: crime against nature, freak, monster . . . ,"[3] ("6 personnes trans . . . " 2021)[4] says the famous trans activist Lexie (@aggressively_trans); but what is specifically transphobic about these slurs? How have they been sharpened over time in relation to a hatred and dread of transidentity? Most importantly, why would trans figures want to reclaim these terms, as Paul B. Preciado notably did in a recent, well-publicized and well-received book *Je suis un monstre qui vous parle* (2020)? This chapter proposes 1) to study the "discursive formation" (Foucault 1969, 53) that has associated trans people with monsters or freaks, especially from the nineteenth century onward, 2) to briefly trace the reversal of this stigma in contemporary trans discourses, and 3) to highlight the advantages, but also the paradoxes and limitations, of such a strategy. In the context of this work, we make ours the question Pierre Bourdieu once asked: "When stigmatized groups claim stigma as a principle of their identity, should we speak of resistance? And when, on the contrary, they work to appropriate what would allow them to assimilate, should we speak of submission?" (Bourdieu 1983, 101).[5]

GENEALOGY OF A TRANSPHOBIC STIGMA

From the outset, it must be emphasized that "the mixture" ("le mixte") has been a primordial category of the monstrous at least since the Middle Ages, and that the hermaphrodite—meaning a being that mixes masculine and feminine body gender signifiers[6]—constitutes a particular occurrence of this. As Michel Foucault expresses in one of his lectures at the *Collège de France*:

> From the Middles Ages to the eighteenth century [. . .] the monster is essentially a mixture. It is the mixture of two realms, the animal and the human: the man with the head of an ox, the man with a bird's feet—monsters. It is the blending, the mixture of two species: the pig with a sheep's head is a monster [. . .] *It is the mixture of two sexes: the person who is both male and female is a monster.* (Foucault 2003, 63; *emphasis added*)

While it is possible to express reservations about the relevance of the notion of gender binary and thus on the truly monstrous character of the mixed masculine and feminine in the period of which Foucault speaks,[7] the late nineteenth century sees a multiplication of scientific works on sexuality. Such works develop a very precise taxonomy of sexual practices and deviant, pathological, or monstrous physical structures.[8] Within this new scientific and disciplinary paradigm, anything and anyone that contradicts the gender binary is perceived as *monstrous*: unnatural, disturbing, and spectacular (in the etymological sense of the term: *worthy of being watched*).

Many of Rachilde's novels play on the intermingled feelings of fear and fascination caused by bodies that escape gender norms, transitioning at will, subverting and inverting social relations of domination. Such experiments often end in the death of the protagonists, which always seems to symbolize a punishment for their unnatural wanderings. We see a similar ending in Jane de la Vaudère's novel *Les Demis sexes* (1897), in which the young and innocent Camille is persuaded by the mysterious Nina to undergo an oophorectomy in order to escape her duty to be a mother and, together with it, the patriarchal norm. Irreversible changes take place in Camille's body; she becomes virilized and joins the strange community of the "half-sexes." This community is made up of "women" who have undergone the same operation and who are presented as a group of monstrous witches who have escaped womanhood and whose gender is now an enigma. While Camille initially enjoys this subversive company, she changes her mind when she meets a charming young man with whom she falls in love. She quickly wants to marry him and have children, but there is no turning back. The heroine dies brutally at the end, burnt like a witch, her dress accidentally catching fire as she walks close to a chimney hearth. It is as if she was struck by a divine punishment or condemned to death by a disciplinary and sexist court from the Middle Ages. The ideological underpinnings of this story correspond to the natalist policy that was in force in France at the time, following the defeat of 1870, in which the birth rate became a major political issue.[9] Any deviation from gender and sexual norms, especially among women, for whom reproduction had become a national duty, was then considered monstrous.

Monstrous, and thus appealing: it is precisely these social injunctions that made so popular, at the time, the exhibition of "monstres humains" (freaks), such as "bearded ladies." However, the thrill that accompanied this kind of show was never subversive from a political standpoint. Dr. Edgar Bérillon, who observed and interviewed many of them at the beginning of the twentieth century, noted that they all remained *real women*. For example, of one of them he says "[s]he was menstruating every month and showed a marked inclination for the stronger sex"[10] (Bérillon 1904–1905, 40)[11] and of another "[s]he proved that to be bearded, one is no less a woman. The result was the birth of a child who died thirty-six hours after its birth" (74).[12] As long as they complied with the heterosexual order, desired men, and could procreate, bearded women were not considered pathological. Moreover, he relates that, in his consultations with bearded ladies, he always advised them "to be virile only by the physiognomy and to remain women by the taste, by the heart and by the spirit" (327).[13] At a time when the entertainment industry capitalized on the disturbance caused by non-conforming bodies, the medical institution made sure that these bodies did not cause any real trouble to the binary gender order, even if it meant performing some kind of gender orthopedics (such as advising bearded ladies to adopt a more feminine attitude, pushing them to have children, and so on). If gender trouble already appeared as freakish, one suspects that any idea of a real transition at the time was still unthinkable.

In France, the first real media exposure of trans people has been linked to what Karine Espineira calls the "transgender cabaret culture." She uses this expression when commenting on a text by Maxime Foerster, that compares the exposure of the first trans celebrities in France and in the United States in the 1950s. Foerster writes:

> Both Jorgensen and Coccinelle[14] concretized transgender issues within the public eye through their work in transgender cabaret culture. The differences between them become apparent when examining their performance styles [. . .] Whereas Jorgensen aimed for bourgeois respectability by portraying the common woman, Coccinelle adopted an erotic and flamboyant persona full of humour and pluck. (Foerster 2012, 50)[15]

Although it was certainly not a premeditated political strategy, Coccinelle did not adopt a rhetoric of *normalization*, but rather a strategy of *visibility* based on extravagant performances, whose success could be due to an interest in the bizarre and freakish among the audience. Even if the transvestite shows of the 1950s were very different from the freak shows of the end of the nineteenth century, similar affects may have been manifested in both types of performance. Bambi, another famous trans cabaret performer slightly younger than Coccinelle, states: "Back then [in the 1950s] people would go to the Carrousel [a Parisian cabaret famous for its trans performers]; people would go to see the circus freaks; it was great; we loved it" (*Bambi* 2013, 0:43:00).[16]

Aware of the troubled and fascinated gaze that was being cast upon them,[17] the trans personalities of the time nevertheless decided to take advantage of it, mostly in terms of money and fame, making themselves visible in the public arena, be it only in the Parisian night life and in the tabloid press. Even if some people might have found a form of empowerment in these cabaret shows, the question remains as to whether they still functioned as some disciplinary apparatuses, relegating the possibility of transgressing the gender binary to a freakish and exuberant show. For a trans person, is staging themself as a "pretty monster"[18] a way to explore and express a new, non-conforming gender identity? Is it a way to comply to the normative cis gaze, or is it both?

PRETTY MONSTERS' PRIDE

From the nineteenth century to their first public appearances in mainstream media, trans people were constructed as both monstrous and spectacular beings—two aspects that some trans intellectuals and activists started to reclaim from the 1990s onward. However, it must be stressed that, before becoming a political strategy, being a monster (or feeling like one) has been a modality of existence imposed on trans people by the hetero-patriarchal society. Maud-Yeuse Thomas discusses this in an article in which she analyzes Kafka's *Metamorphosis* (Thomas 2016). For her, the alteration of Gregor Samsa's body—turned into an insect—is a metaphor of the violence exerted by the capitalist and industrial society on a body. Her rereading of Kafka's seminal work allows her to reexamine the violence exerted on trans people by a society where gender binary is considered the norm. Thomas draws a parallel between Gregor Samsa's morphed body and that of trans people because of "the deeply ambiguous dualism that holds sway over our modes of existence and produces pariah lives and vile bodies, as Grégoire Chamayou wrote (2011), or infamous lives, to quote Foucault" (109).[19] Thomas notes that Gregor Samsa's body is not the result of some magical thought, like other morphed bodies we can think of in myths or legends, but is instead linked to a specific social order, with its own institutional, political, and epistemological structure: his metamorphosis is a logical consequence of the time he lives in, and of the capitalist alienation of bodies that is part of it.

> Kafka's insect is a deeply historicized figure, brought about by a grand history of structural transformations. Modernity is the culmination of the human saga, wielding absolute control over its environment. The next logical chapter can be found within these mutant subjects, who are enumerated and transmuted in a political sense. They find their place under the microscope of new disciplines such as medical law and criminal—and therefore colonial—anthropology. Kafka's insect is the black hole of our worldly consciousness, a matrix of "untranquility" that underlies everything. (112)[20]

The act of reclaiming the stigma can thus be read as embracing a pre-existing reality that has not been produced by the trans person themself, but that is rather a collective, political, and social production. Being-a-monster is not only about willingly performing one's queerness for the benefit of the scandalized cis majority. It can also be a phenomenological fact for some trans people. In this case, embracing it has less to do with a political staging of one's life and body than with a personal approach, linked with one's individual affects. As Karine Espineira writes, when drawing a comparison between trans people and "mutants," like those in the *X-Men* comics and movies:

> Calling oneself a "mutant" is an act that positions the individual relative to the majority and is a type of resistance that is both real and felt. Considered marginal by virtue of their shapeshifting bodies, mutants oppose by their very existence the bodily limitations that apply to ordinary humans. (Espineira 2015, 17)[21]

Beyond the public showing of a reversed stigma, feeling like a mutant or like a "monster" encapsulates the feelings of inadequacy and rebellion against a particular political and epistemological order, its "stillness" that rigidifies one's gender identity, and an externally applied essentialization.

It is precisely against the "stillness" of the patriarchal epistemological order that Paul B. Preciado uses the figure of the monster. Preciado claims that "[t]he monster is the one who lives in transition. The one whose face, body and practices cannot yet be considered as true in a determined regime of knowledge and power" (Preciado 2020, 49).[22] Interestingly, Preciado also refers to Kafka, "the master of all metamorphoses"[23] (15) at the beginning of *Je suis un monstre qui vous parle.*[24] He quotes *Eine Bericht für eine Akademie* (1917), a short story in which a monkey that has learnt the language of humans speaks in front of an assembly of Darwinian scientists to let them know its thoughts on evolution. The object of knowledge and of discourse suddenly becomes a subject. Here, the reference to Kafka is not only used to understand an existential discomfort, but as a strategic model. Preciado reproduces this discursive structure in his own text when he says: "Today, the once monstrous bodies produced by the patriarchal-colonial regime of sexual difference speak and produce knowledge about themselves" (117).[25] *Je suis un monstre qui vous parle* originated from a speech Preciado gave at the *École de la Cause freudienne* (School of the Freudian Cause)[26] on the theme "Women in psychoanalysis," where he had been invited to speak. Instead of addressing this topic, Preciado challenged the very notion of sexual binarity, from his own perspective as a trans person (that is, as he says, neither really a woman nor a man), hailing the assembly of Freudian psychoanalysts, whom he makes the representatives of an oppressive, patriarchal, and colonial scientific institution. He addresses them as a trans man, which, in a strictly Freudian framework, is in itself a deviance, an aberration.

Rather than criticizing and deconstructing the images of monsters and human spectacles that have been associated with trans people throughout history, Preciado chooses to fully embrace these clichés in order to give more power and resonance to his words:

> I should add that the clichés that follow would not have been possible for me to say if I were not totally sure of myself or if my position as a trans person had not already been confirmed beyond a shadow of a doubt by means of a digital spectacle for all the civilized world to see. (22)[27]

When Preciado says, "I made my body a showroom"[28] (57), the structure of this sentence and the agent position of the subject indicate that this is a fully deliberate choice. After all, "monster" or "freak" are socially constructed categories into which nobody falls *naturally*. According to Robert Bogdan, "'[f]reak' is a frame of mind, a set of practices, a way of thinking about and presenting people. It is the enactment of a tradition, the performance of a stylized presentation" (Bogdan 1985, 3). One is not born, but rather becomes, a monster. This is also the case for Preciado, who could never have been seen as one without a series of social and discursive apparatuses. He is fully aware that this is a choice he made, and that it would have been easier for him, in some ways, to fully "pass" as a cis man. After receiving his PhD—which guaranteed him a certain symbolic status and greatly facilitated his relationship with the medical institution to accompany him in his transition—he realized that:

> Two paths lay before [him]: the first offering the privacy of normative masculinity through the pharmacological and psychiatric rituals of domesticated transsexuality. The second, a more contrarian path, and certainly showier: political writing. (36–37)[29]

Becoming a monster and a (freak?) show is thought of as an opposition to the act of passing, which is, after all, a silent acceptance of the binary gender divide. This is precisely what Bambi chose after spending approximately twenty years working for the Carrousel transvestite show: the anonymity of unchallenged womanhood.[30] Recently interviewed in a documentary series,[31] she appears a bit out of touch with recent queer activism, not understanding why some people would publicly claim they are trans, and not simply wish to pass as a man or a woman. It is true that showing oneself as trans and, even more so, showing oneself as a monster, is an uncomfortable—even dangerous—strategy. Interestingly, Preciado explains that this is not the choice he made at the beginning of his transition:

> However, the most important thing I realized was that as a so-called white man in a patriarchal and colonial world, I could for the first time in my life access privilege and universality. A place of quiet and privacy where people finally

left you the hell alone. [. . .] If I stopped publicly identifying as "trans" and simply let myself be recognized as a man, I could finally shed the weight of identity. (41)[32]

This identity strategy of reversing and reclaiming stigma is particularly peril-ous in France, where any assertion of belonging to a minority group can be perceived as a direct attack on republican universalism, and sometimes on the Republic itself,[33] whereas being "normal" (e.g., fitting dominant gender, sexual orientation, race, and disability norms, or at least trying to erase as much as possible one's particularities) allows one's speech to be considered as universal. It is also this structure, this organization of speech and of its legitimacy, this reduction of the minoritized to bodily difference, and the "bodylessness" of the dominant that Preciado intends to question. He does so by addressing the psychoanalysts in the audience, reminding them that they too have a body, and by wondering whether a trans psychoanalyst is among them, addressing "to this dear mutant [his] warmest greetings" (13).[34] It also has to be noticed that Preciado does not only consider himself as being part of a show, as he says for instance that the hetero-patriarchal binary regime is a "circus" (27).[35] The intense discomfort that was felt when this speech was delivered is certainly due to this direct address to the assembly. As a matter of fact, Preciado did not only say "I am a monster" to abstractly analyze his abnormal condition: he said "I am a monster who speaks to you," insisting on this interpellation of the audience. It is this interpellation that makes his text a political one since, in his speech, Preciado indicates that he speaks "as a citizen, as your monstrous equal" (17):[36] the monster *as such* claims a place in the agora. Embodying the failure and the violation of the gender binary's epistemological order, he asks for its abolition. The political goal of this text is utopian in nature and Preciado's individual transition is a mere symbol for a more general transition that society as a whole has to operate: "I prefer this new form I have taken—that of a monster—to that of a man or a woman, for in this form I can step into the void, forging the way towards a new world" (47).[37]

Although it is rooted in Preciado's autobiography, the most important part of this text is the performative interpellation it aims to produce that allows everyone to receive it personally and to identify to it. Reading this text, every-one is invited to identify as a monster, as a being who lives in transition and who wishes to operate a transition in society, even those who are not trans. This is precisely what is conveyed by the scenography Preciado chose for a public reading of his text. Four voices (including his own) take turns reading. The sentence "I have the honor to appear before the Academy to report on my life as a trans man" is repeated and adapted accordingly by each reader: "I have the honor to appear before you to report on my life as a trans woman,"

"I have the honor to appear before you to report on my life as a faggot," "I have the honor to appear before you to report on my life as a woman" ("Paul B. Preciado—Je suis un monstre qui vous parle" 2020, 1:41). Every person living in opposition to the hetero-patriarchal society can become a monster. This is at once the great advantage and the limit of the political identification as a monster, the latter being, by definition, outside all categories (Foucault 1999, 57). To create a politically relevant group of "monsters" would mean to unify people who might only share the attribute of not fitting into social norms. As the authors of *The Emergence of Trans* put it playfully:

> It is precisely the monster's ambivalent ability to speak to oppression and nega-
> tive affect that appeals to trans* people reclaiming the monster for their own
> voices. [. . .] This multiplicity of voices is important, for we do not have to be
> the same monster; while many of us may find ways to embrace our strangeness
> and aberration, monsters come in different shapes with different configurations
> of skin and teeth. (Pearce, Moon, Gupta and Steinberg 2019, 6)

Indeed, choosing the figure of the monster to spearhead a political move-ment means accepting to include in one's speech a multiplicity of voices and experiences. This would entail, for instance, for a FtM activist like Paul B. Preciado, to take into account MtF, women (especially lesbians) or gay voices. Monster politics also operate on an affective level. If the monster has the "ability to speak to oppression and negative affect," (Koch-Rein 2014, 135) it is also important, when reclaiming this figure, to go beyond shame and to cultivate fearlessness. As Preciado states, "during my transition, the number one rule that became obvious to me was to abolish the fear of being abnormal, planted in my heart since childhood" (45).[38]

THE LIMITS OF A SPECTACULAR STRATEGY

To conclude this analysis, it must be emphasized that while the strategy of reclaiming the stigma can be very rewarding in terms of visibility, it is not widely endorsed among trans people. As a matter of fact, this rhetoric, which can take the form of an injunction to accept and showcase a non-conforming body that is socially perceived as abnormal, can be overtly criticized.[39] Many trans people see it as creating a fantasized idea of what transition is, by dis-playing it as a strange and appealing fairytale that erases the most difficult aspects of trans people's lives. While he cultivates this exciting narrative of a fantastical transgender metamorphosis, Preciado is also aware of the risks it poses, undermining it from time to time: "But I would like to avoid the heroic account of my transition. There was nothing heroic about it. I am not a werewolf, and I don't have the immortality of a vampire" (56).[40] He even explains that he in fact did not want to be a "gender freak" at the beginning of his transition:

> When I learnt that leaving the gender binary meant leaving humanity in order to be plunged into a space dominated by violence and control, I did everything necessary to hold on to a better life, claiming my place within the binary structures of "sexual difference." (32)[41]

In order not to be totally crushed by this oppressive regime of sexual difference, Preciado had to pretend, at least for some time, to be a normal (cis) man. This biographical detail shows that, before a trans person is able to publicly present themself as trans, and before they are able to publicly present themself *as a monster*, they have to reach a certain level of economic, political, and symbolic security; otherwise, they can put themself in danger. After all, we live in a time when the insult "monster" can be accompanied with death threats.[42] It is thus a privilege to be able to reclaim this slur without putting one's life at risk. It also has to be noted once again that the monster is a socially constructed category; typically, a stage and a set of discourses would be necessary to make someone a monster. Thus, if Paul B. Preciado can appear as a monster when talking about his transidentity in front of old school Freudian psychoanalysts, it is certainly not the case when he walks the street or when he is confronted by disciplinary institutions. As he puts it, even when one is a trending topic, "in reality you are alone when you have to present yourself to the psychiatrist, the border guard, the doctor, or the judge" (21).[43] It is self-evident that in these situations there is no strategic interest in stating, "I am a monster talking to you."

This strategy is also fraught with danger since reclaiming the stigma—as confusing as it can be for transphobes—does not prevent said stigma from being reactivated. An example of this could be found in the issue 1461, dating from July 2020, of French satirical weekly newspaper *Charlie Hebdo*, in which Alice drew a cartoon depicting *Je suis un monstre qui vous parle*.[44] In one of the panels is written, "And so, I made of my body and my mind, of my monstrosity, of my desire and of my transition, a public spectacle." Freud is shown eating popcorn in front of a box reminiscent of both a freak show and a peep show. On the box appears Preciado, naked, with a sign reading, "Insert a coin here." An arrow placed at the lower belly suggestively points to a coin slot. Above, the title of the show: "The man who didn't understand a thing about psychoanalysis." Preciado's goal has been to take control of his own image, displaying himself as a monster on his own terms. This has allowed him to present a strong political discourse. However, this strategy leaves open the possibility for his opponents to resurrect the old, normalizing representation of the trans person as a freak and a public spectacle as a means of degradation. The main problem of reclaiming a stigma is that the latter is subsequently recycled and manipulated, never erased. As such, it can still be weaponized by any party. Reclaiming a stigma is a gutsy move, precisely because it leaves the reclaimant exposed to attack. However, while it is essential that pride and fearlessness be valued as positive affects within a stigma reclaiming strategy, the vulnerability and the risks it involves must also be acknowledged.

NOTES

1. Espineira quotes *Freaks*'s opening crawl in English and then proceeds to translate it in French. The French version is as follows (cuts in the text are mine): "Avant notre film sur cette extraordinaire attraction nous aimerions vous entretenir du sujet du film. Croyez-le ou pas . . . Aussi étrange que cela paraisse. Jadis tout ce qui déviait de la normalité était considéré comme un mauvais présage ou un signe diabolique. [. . .] Parfois, un de ces misérables se retrouvait au tribunal pour y subir sarcasmes et railleries au grand amusement de la noblesse. [. . .] La plupart des monstres ont un esprit sain et des émotions normales. Leur sort est véritablement pathétique. Ils sont forcés de vivre un destin peu naturel. Ils se sont donc bâti un code de conduite pour se protéger des gens normaux. Leurs règles sont strictement observées. La blessure de chacun est portée par tous; la joie de chacun partagée par tous. L'histoire qui va vous être révélée raconte l'impact de ce code sur leurs vies. [. . .] Avec humilité devant les maintes injustices subies par ces êtres qui n'avaient aucun espoir d'infléchir leur destinée, nous vous présentons l'histoire la plus horrible des anormaux et des indésirables."

2. Espineira chose not to keep this animal metaphor in her translation, and puts it more bluntly: "pour se protéger des gens normaux" ("to protect themselves from normal people").

3. Unless otherwise specified, all English translations of French texts are mine.

4. "Il y a des insultes tellement spécifiques sur le fait d'être trans: erreur de la nature, bête de foire, espèce de monstre . . . "

5. "Lorsque les groupes stigmatisés revendiqu[ent] le stigmate comme principe de leur identité faut-il parler de résistance? Et quand, à l'inverse, ils travaillent à s'approprier ce qui leur permettrait de s'assimiler, faut-il parler de soumission?"

6. It is possible that some "hermaphrodites" from the past would be described today as trans persons.

7. Even if Ambroise Paré already includes the hermaphrodites among the monsters, for Thomas Laqueur it is only in the eighteenth century that the Galenic model of the unique sex is abandoned (see Laqueur 1992). A recent work by Clovis Maillet (2020) shone light on gender fluidity in the Middle Ages.

8. See Sylvie Chaperon, *Les Origines de la sexologie (1850–1900)*; Evanghélia Stead, *Le Monstre, le singe et le foetus: tératogonie et décadence dans l'Europe fin-de-siècle*.

9. See Francis Ronsin, *La Grève des ventres. Propagande néo-malthusienne et baisse de la natalité française, XIXe-XXe siècles*.

10. "Elle était régulièrement réglée tous les mois et témoignait d'un penchant marqué pour le sexe fort."

11. Bérillon published his observations on "bearded ladies" in a series of articles that appeared in the *Revue de l'hypnotisme et de la psychologie psychologique* over the course of 2 years.

12. "Elle prouva que pour être barbue, on n'en est pas moins femme. Il en résulta la naissance d'un enfant qui mourut trente-six heures après sa naissance."

13. "[. . .] n'être viriles que par la physionomie et de rester femmes par le goût, par le cœur et par l'esprit."

14. Christine Jorgensen (1926–1989) was the first person to become widely known in the United States for having had gender reassignment surgery. Jacqueline Charlotte Dufresnoy (1931–2006), better known as Coccinelle, was a French actress, entertainer, and singer. She was the first person whose gender reassignment surgery became widely publicized in post-war Europe.

15. "Le point commun entre Jorgensen et Coccinelle, c'est d'avoir cristallisé aux yeux du grand public la condition transsexuelle mais aussi d'avoir poursuivi une carrière basée sur la culture du cabaret transgenre. Les différences relèvent du style de la performance [. . .]. D'autre part, Jorgensen visait une respectabilité bougeoise en inspirant à incarner Madame tout-le-monde, alors que Coccinelle assumait une personnalité érotique et flamboyante, pleine d'humour et d'audace."

16. "À l'époque, on allait au Carrousel, on allait voir les bêtes de cirque, ce qui était très bien, ce qui nous plaisait beaucoup."

17. A striking example of this can be found in Claude Lelouch's *cinéma verité* documentary *La Femme spectacle* (1964), in which a voice-over comments on a transvestite cabaret show, using an oversimplified and mainstream psychoanalytical language to do so: "The fascination toward femininity is so powerful that it can make weak minds, disconnected from reality, give in to the pitiful perversion of a dream. It would be hypocritical to pass over in silence these monstrous inversions. These deviant beings are indeed in need of medical assistance" ("La fascination de la féminité est telle qu'elle peut faire basculer des esprits faibles et sans attache avec le réel vers la lamentable perversion d'un rêve. Il serait hypocrite de passer sous silence ces inversions monstrueuses. Ces êtres dévoyés auraient besoin en fait du secours de la médecine"). Even if this part of the documentary deals with "transvestites," their lifestyle can be legitimately described as "transgender practices" (Bourcier 2018, 133–46), which exceed both the space and the temporality of the cabaret show. A street interview is shown in which a person with a very feminine gender expression refers to themself as "a transvestite." They are asked, "Do you always live like this?" to which they reply, "Always, yes: in the street, in everyday life . . . " Another performer, who "has breasts," states that they resort to "a particular kind of injection" ("des piqûres particulières") and shares their strong desire to be a woman.

18. We are borrowing this expression from cis author Julien Dufresne-Lamy, whose novel on the New York City ball culture is titled *Jolis jolis monstres* (2019).

19. "L'ambiguïté profonde du dualisme de nos normes produisant des vies parias, des corps vils, écrit Grégoire Chamayou (2011), des vies infâmes, écrira Foucault, confortant un ordre social selon des représentations ordonnées."

20. "L'insecte kafkaïen est une figure profondément historicisée, induite par l'Histoire d'une transformation structurelle: la modernité est le fruit de la geste humaine, qui prend le contrôle absolu de son environnement. Sa phase suivante, logique, est en ces sujets mutants, politiquement décomptés et métamorphosés, qui prennent place sous le microscope des nouvelles disciplines que sont la médecine légale, l'anthropologie criminelle s'ajoutant et s'ajustant à l'anthropologie coloniale. Sa figure est le trou noir de notre conscience au monde, cette 'intranquillité' matricielle et fondamentale."

21. "Se dire 'mutant' tient lieu de positionnement personnel et collectif face à la majorité dans un contexte et un sentiment de résistance. Les mutants considérés comme des marginaux aux corps métamorphes ou métamorphosés, s'opposent par leur simple existence contre le corps-limite considéré chez l'humain *lambda*."

22. "Le monstre est celui qui vit en transition. Celui dont le visage, le corps et les pratiques ne peuvent encore être considérés comme vrais dans un régime de savoir et de pouvoir déterminés."

23. "le maître de toutes les métamorphoses."

24. We want to specify that our references to Preciado's text correspond to the French edition, and all English translations are our own. A translated version of this text was released in 2020, called *Can the Monster Speak? Report to an Academy of Psychoanalysts* and translated by Frank Wynne.

25. "Aujourd'hui, les corps autrefois monstrueux produits par le régime patriarco-colonial de la différence sexuelle parlent et produisent un savoir sur eux-mêmes."

26. *L'École de la cause freudienne* is a French psychoanalytic body.

27. "Il convient d'ajouter que je ne pourrais pas vous dire les banalités qui vont suivre si je n'étais pas totalement sûr de moi-même, si ma position de trans n'avait été déjà affirmée de manière incontestable dans tous les grands spectacles numériques du monde civilisé."

28. "[. . .] j'ai fait de mon corps un showroom."

29. "[. . .] devant moi s'ouvraient deux possibilités: d'une part le rituel pharmacologique et psychiatrique de la transsexualité domestiquée, et avec lui l'anonymat de la masculinité normale ou, d'autre part et en opposition aux deux, le show de l'écriture politique."

30. After performing at Le Carrousel, Bambi—whose real name is Marie-Pierre Pruvot—became a teacher of French literature after earning a university degree from La Sorbonne in Paris. She taught French literature in the cities of Cherbourg and Garges-lès-Gonesse for over 25 years.

31. "Les transidentités, racontées par les trans." Hosted by Perrine Kervran. *France Culture—La Série Documentaire*, August 27–30, 2018. www.franceculture.fr /emissions/series/les-transidentites-racontees-par-les-trans

32. "Mais la chose la plus importante que j'ai comprise, c'est qu'en tant que soi-disant 'homme' et soi-disant 'blanc,' dans un monde patriarcal-colonial, je pouvais accéder pour la première fois au privilège de l'universalité. Un lieu anonyme et paisible où l'on vous fout sacrément la paix. [. . .] Si je renonçais à m'affirmer publiquement comme 'trans' et acceptais d'être reconnu comme un homme, je pourrais abandonner une fois pour toutes le poids de l'identité."

33. See Mame-Fatou Niang, *Identités françaises. Banlieues, féminités et universalisme*; Alice Coffin, *Le Génie lesbien*.

34. "[. . .] à ce cher mutant mes salutations les plus chaleureuses."

35. "Eh bien, puisque dans le cirque du régime binaire hétéro-patriarcal [. . .]"

36. "Je suis le monstre qui se lève du divan et prend la parole, non pas en tant que patient, mais en tant que citoyen, en tant que votre égal monstrueux."

37. "Je préfère ma nouvelle condition de monstre à celle d'homme ou de femme, car cette condition est comme un pied qui avance dans le vide en indiquant la voie vers un autre monde."

38. "La première loi que j'ai considérée comme allant de soi pendant tout mon processus de transition a été d'abolir la terreur d'être anormal qui avait été semée dans mon cœur d'enfant."

39. Such oppositional attitudes are especially visible on social media, such as Twitter: "I hate being trans, it makes me want to die so much. I hate people who like being gender freaks [. . .]"/("Je déteste être trans ça me donne tellement envie de mourir je déteste les gens qui aiment être des freaks du genre.") @cloporte, Twitter, June 4 2021; "Maybe in a small LGBTI safe space it's perfectly acceptable to be a bearded woman but in the street it's an ordeal and a danger. But there is a whole discourse about brave trans people who defy gender norms that can become an injunction to accept oneself."/("Peut-être que dans un petit safe space LGBTI c'est tout à fait accepté d'être une femme à barbe mais dans la rue c'est une épreuve et un danger. Mais voilà on a tout un discours sur les braves personnes trans qui défient les normes de genre qui peuvent devenir une injonction à s'accepter.") @DaisyLetourneur, Twitter, January 27 2022.

40. "Mais je voudrais éviter le récit héroïque de ma transition. Il n'y avait rien d'héroïque à cela. Je ne suis pas le loup-garou et je n'ai pas l'immortalité d'un vampire."

41. "Quand j'ai compris que quitter le régime de la différence sexuelle signifiait quitter la sphère de l'humain et entrer dans un espace subalterne de violence et de contrôle, j'ai fait [. . .] tout ce qui était nécessaire pour pouvoir continuer à vivre le mieux possible et j'ai exigé une place dans le régime du genre binaire."

42. @LJPizza1 made public on Twitter private messages they received on May 6, 2021: "vous allez tous crever bande de grosse merde sale violeurs / Raclure humaine des monstres à enfermer / Espèce de travelo de merde."

43. "[. . .] en réalité on est seul lorsqu'on doit se présenter devant le psychiatre, le garde-frontière, au cabinet médical ou au juge."

44. The cartoon can be accessed at the following link: charliehebdo.fr/2020/07/culture/lu-pour-vous-le-livre-de-paul-preciado/

REFERENCES

"6 personnes trans vs clichés." *YouTube* video, 34.42. December 12, 2021. www .youtube.com/watch?v=YwUUW73VGgc

Bérillon, Edgar. 1904–1905. "Les Femmes à barbe: Étude psychologique et soci-ologique." *Revue de l'hypnotisme et de la psychologie psychologique*. Paris.

Bogdan, Robert. 1985. *Freak Show: Presenting Human Oddities for Amusement and Profit*. Chicago: University Press of Chicago.

Bourcier, Sam. 2018. "Des 'femmes travesties' aux pratiques transgenres: repenser et queeriser le travestissement." In *Queer Zones redux*, 133–46. Paris: Amsterdam.

Bourdieu, Pierre. 1983. "Vous avez dit 'populaire'?" *Actes de la recherche en sciences sociales*, vol. 46: 98–105.

Chaperon, Sylvie. 2007. *Les Origines de la sexologie (1850–1900)*. Paris: Audibert.

Coffin, Alice. 2020. *Le Génie lesbien*. Paris: Grasset.

Dufresne-Lamy, Julien. 2019. *Jolis jolis monstres*. Paris: Belfond.

Espineira, Karine. 2015. *Transidentités: Ordre et panique de genre. Le Réel et ses interprétations*. Paris: L'Harmattan.

Forester, Maxime. 2012. *Elle ou lui? Une Histoire des transsexuels en France*. Paris: La Musardine.

Foucault, Michel. 1969. *L'Archéologie du savoir*. Paris: Gallimard.

Foucault, Michel. 2003. *Abnormal. Lectures at the Collège de France 1974–1975*. Translated by Graham Burchell. London and New York: Verso.

Koch-Rein, Anson. 2014. "Monster." *Transgender Studies Quarterly*, vol. 1 (1–2): 134–35.

Laqueur, Thomas W. 1992. *Making Sex. Body and Gender from the Greeks to Freud*. Cambridge, MA: Harvard University Press.

Maillet, Clovis. 2020. *Les genres fluides. De Jeanne d'Arc aux saintes trans*. Paris: Arkhê

Niang, Mame-Fatou. 2020. *Identités françaises. Banlieues, féminités et universalisme*. Leiden: Brill.

"Paul B. Preciado—Je Suis un monstre qui vous parle." *YouTube* video, 1:00:20. December 3, 2020. www.youtube.com/watch?v=0iL0yAE4sAE

Pearce, Ruth, Igi Moon, Kat Gupta, and Deborah Lynn Steinberg. 2019. *The Emergence of Trans. Cultures, Politics and Everyday Lives*. London: Routledge.

Preciado, Paul B. 2020. *Je Suis un monstre qui vous parle. Rapport pour une académie de psychanalystes*. Paris: Grasset.

Ronsin, Francis. 1980. *La Grève des ventres. Propagande néo-malthusienne et baisse de la natalité française, XIXe–XXe siècles*. Paris: Aubier.

Stead, Evanghélia. 2004. *Le Monstre, le singe et le foetus: Tératogonie et décadence dans l'Europe fin-de-siècle*. Genève: Droz.

Thomas, Maud-Yeuse. 2016. "*La Métamorphose* de Franz Kafka. Pour une épistémologie philosophique des transidentités." In *Corps vulnérables, vies dévulnérabilisées*, edited by Jean Zaganiaris, Ludovic-Mohamed Zahed, Maud-Yeuse Thomas and Karine Espineira, 107–18. Paris: L'Harmattan.

FILMOGRAPHY

Bambi, directed by Sébastien Lifshitz. Featuring Marie-Pierre Pruvot. Epicentre Films, 2013. 0:58.

Chapter 8

Peau d'homme

A Different Kind of Happy Ending

Annick Pellegrin

The death of the *bande dessinée* scriptwriter and colorist Hubert in February 2020 (Roure 2020) was followed by a flurry of posthumous releases: *Peau d'homme* [A Man's Skin] (Hubert and Zanzim 2020); *Première née* [First Born] (Hubert and Gatignol, 2020)—the fourth and final installment of the series *Les Ogres-dieux* [The Ogre Gods]; *Joe la pirate* (Hubert and Augustin 2021); and the first installment of the diptych *Ténébreuse* (Hubert and Mallié 2021).[1] Some of these albums were still being drawn at the time of Hubert's passing, which resulted in certain difficulties for the artists in finishing their respective works without him (Augustin 2021a; Mallié 2021a, 71; Mallié 2021b, 70).[2] However, it appears that *Peau d'homme* had been largely completed prior to Hubert's death: the website of the publisher, Glénat, mentions that Hubert passed away a few weeks prior to the release of the book. In addition, journalist Frédéric Bosser recounts that the author's passing was announced on the very day Bosser was planning to call Hubert to set up an appointment for an interview, and that he had almost finished reading the album at the time (Glénat, n.d; Bosser 2020, 60).

Peau d'homme was warmly received by the French specialized press, and its release was covered by most magazines dedicated to *bande dessinée*. In addition, it received numerous awards in the months following its release, including the Fauve des lycéens at the Angoulême comics festival ("Palmarès 2021" 2021) and the Bédélys étranger at the Montreal comics festival ("Les 22e prix Bédélys"), becoming the most acclaimed French *bande dessinée* album in 2021 in terms of number of awards won (Zanzim 2021b). Hubert and Gatignol's *Première née*, for its part, was also nominated for a prize at the Angoulême comics festival the same year (Pasamonik 2021). It was not long before *Peau d'homme* was translated to Italian, Portuguese and English (Hubert and Zanzim 2021). The album had an original print run of 15,000 copies and has been reprinted several times since, selling more than 100,000 copies by November 2020 ("Monique Younès" 2020). *Peau d'homme*'s success is especially noteworthy as it reaches beyond the regular *bande dessinée* readership: Zanzim reports meeting several readers at book signing events who confessed to not usually being interested in *bandes dessinées* but having been drawn to the work because of the topic itself ("Monique Younès" 2020; Zanzim 2021a).

With a clear reference to the fairy tale "Peau d'âne" [Donkey Skin] both in its title and in its premise, Hubert's first posthumously released work, set in the Cinquecento (Zanzim 2020b, 74), tells the story of Bianca, the young daughter of a rich merchant, who is promised to Giovanni, a young man she has never met, in exchange for money. As Bianca is unhappy with such a transaction and laments the fact that she did not get to know her fiancé prior to the engagement, her godmother gives her a male bodysuit that is passed down to women in her family and that enables her to transform into a man, Lorenzo, with fully functional body parts. Through Bianca's eyes, as she moves between male and female sex *and* gender at a time of religious fanaticism spearheaded by her own brother, readers are presented with a strong critique of contemporary gender injustice.

What does the traditional form of the fairy tale bring to Hubert's work and what does Hubert bring to the traditional form of the fairy tale in return? Through a close reading of Hubert's first posthumous *bande dessinée*, taking into consideration its place within Hubert's *œuvre* as a whole, I will explore how, through the use of the traditional form of the fairy tale, Hubert offers a critique of contemporary social issues linked to LGBTQ+ rights in France, rewriting the prescribed "happy ending" of fairy tales in the process.

HUBERT, THE FAIRY TALE, AND GENDER ISSUES

Both gender and sexuality issues on the one hand and the traditional form of the fairy tale on the other hand are recurrent in works scripted by Hubert. For instance, issues pertaining to gender and sexuality are at the forefront of *La Ligne droite* [Adrian and the Tree of Secrets] (Hubert and Caillou 2013), which tells the story of a young boy discovering same-sex attraction while oppressed by religious dogmas and a strict upbringing; *Les Gens normaux* (Hubert 2013), which is a non-fiction collection of interviews with LGBT people conducted by Hubert and illustrated by a variety of artists; and *Miss Pas Touche* [Miss Don't Touch Me] (Hubert and Kerascoët 2014b), in which a conservative virgin starts living and working in a brothel, but does not understand that playing the role of the dominatrix is a form of sex work (Hubert and Kerascoët 2007). Homosexual characters can also be found in several of Hubert's works, from Jo (the male prostitute and Josephine Baker impersonator) and the persecuted Prince Charming, Antoine (the lead character's love interest), who suffers from severe mental health problems after being forced to undergo conversion therapy in *Miss Pas Touche*; or the lead male couple of *La Nuit mange le jour* (Hubert and Burckel 2017) who explore their sadomasochistic side; to *Joe la pirate* (Hubert and Augustin 2021), which offers a biography of Marion Barbara Carstairs, a colorful British-US citizen who liked women and enjoyed dressing in men's clothes but was *not* transsexual, according to the artist, Virginie Augustin (2021a; 2021b). As a side note, it is also worth mentioning that Zanzim himself scripted and illustrated an album that is reminiscent of mythological tales and that comments on gender inequalities by reversing them: *L'Île aux femmes* (2015), for which Hubert was the colorist.

The archetypal structure of the fairy tale can be found in many of the works scripted by Hubert, such as the trilogy *Beauté* [Beauty] (Hubert and Kerascoët 2014a), the séries *Les Ogres-dieux* (Hubert and Gatignol 2014–2020) or *Ténébreuse* (Hubert and Mallié 2021) to name but a few. Even the sexually explicit *La Nuit mange le jour* has been likened to the tale "Bluebeard" by journalist Loraine Adam (Hubert 2017). However, although fairy tales, gender and sexuality are common and often intersect in Hubert's body of work, *Peau d'homme* stands out as it presents the reader with a lead character who, through magic, can *alternate* at will between sexes and genders.

WHAT DOES THE FAIRY TALE GENRE BRING TO *PEAU D'HOMME*?

Marina Warner, known for her extensive work on fairy tales, argues that "A reversal of animal and other metamorphosis, leading to the recognition of the protagonist's value and virtue, provides the determining structure of classic fairy tales" (Warner 2014, 39). She also asserts that in her rewriting of "The Beauty and the Beast," Jeanne-Marie Leprince de Beaumont:

> [S]wung the fairy tale more toward an ideal alliance, evoking a bourgeois romance designed to soothe young women facing arranged marriages; the tale invites them to accept the match their father proposes, however unappealing they find the prospective husband. They will come to love him the story reassures them. (39)

Peau d'homme resorts to known tropes and devices commonly found in fairy tales in order to set the scene in remote and make-believe times. Bianca, a fair maiden from a rich family, is betrothed to a man she has never met because it serves her father's interests. Bianca bemoans her fate of not knowing her fiancé prior to their engagement and it is her godmother who offers a solution in the form of a magical object: a "peau d'homme," that is to say, a man's skin. So far, very recognizable stock figures and plotlines have been employed—a rich maiden with marriage-related preoccupations, a rich young man presented as an apparently highly eligible bachelor, parental abuse of power, the fairy-like godmother who provides magical solutions and the existence of magical objects readily accepted as such. Moreover, as mentioned previously, the narrative is particularly reminiscent of "Peau d'âne," in which the eponymous lead character seeks advice from her godmother and hides her identity under a donkey's skin in order to escape from her father's pursuits until, one day, a prince finds out her real identity and marries her. Thus, the happy ending of "Peau d'âne," like that of numerous fairy tales, is one that involves a heterosexual marriage to one considered an equal once someone's true self has been revealed and/or someone has been freed. Aside from the aforementioned "The Beauty and the Beast," fairy tales such as "Cinderella," "Riquet à la houppe" [Ricky of the Tuft], "The Princess and the Frog," "Sleeping Beauty," "Snow White," "Rapunzel" and even "Bluebeard," in which the heroine finds marital bliss after being freed from her bloodthirsty first husband, spring to mind.

However, once traditional fairytale tropes have been used to set the scene, the story of *Peau d'homme* takes a different turn, as when she starts wearing the man's skin, Bianca has to learn to become a man so that she can inconspicuously follow her future husband around the city. As a result, the authors are able to comment on the differences between the accepted and *expected* behaviors of men and women. For instance, Bianca must learn to walk and talk like a man to go unnoticed and to gain access to places she could not enter previously, such as what is essentially a gay bar rendered in a fairytale setting. This is a place where only men go to drink, brawl, and be with other men within the safe confines of its walls (Hubert and Zanzim 2020, 19, 33–36). This gives her the opportunity to get to know Giovanni as an equal. As she does, she also comes to learn that men, too, act a certain way around each other and are not necessarily being themselves, but play a gender role. As Bianca's godmother puts it: "Those are the social codes of men, my dear. We're more delicate in our ways. Theirs are rude and even disgusting. He wasn't the only one acting that way, right? [. . .] So, he was just being a boy"[3] (Hubert and Zanzim 2021, 25). Although Bianca is initially disappointed by Giovanni's behavior, they gradually grow closer to each other (Hubert and

Zanzim 2020, 25). Unfortunately for both, however, their love is an impossible one because, although Giovanni clearly appreciates the person under the man's skin, he only likes men and feels nothing more than friendship for Bianca as a woman, even when she cross-dresses as a man (95–101). Bianca finds herself increasingly confused not only because it is Lorenzo with whom Giovanni fell in love, but also because she sometimes forgets that she is expected to walk in a ladylike fashion when she is not in Lorenzo's skin (40) and therefore starts feeling lost in her back-and-forth between her two bodies, two personas and two gender roles, dreaming that she is a man who owns a woman's skin rather than the opposite (49).

It is worth noting, however, that even before she was introduced to the man's skin, Bianca already found it burdensome to behave in socially prescribed ways for women, such as in her gait. For example, when she spots Tomaso, she lifts her skirt up high enough for her pantalets to become visible and runs down a flight of stairs in order to talk to him and is scolded by her mother for her unladylike demeanor (11). While it is not explicitly said what Tomaso's role is, their short interaction reveals that they have known each other for many years and that Tomaso loves Bianca, although she claims to consider him like a brother. It is also made clear that Tomaso is an employee of the house and that it is considered socially inappropriate for them to spend time together (12). Starkly aware of social norms, Tomaso changes his behavior toward Bianca after her wedding night, using titles and maintaining a respectful distance although this makes them both sad (78). Near the end of the album, Tomaso states that in Bianca's father's household he was "the steward's son"[4] (Hubert and Zanzim 2021, 157) and that he could not have married her because of class differences.

While Bianca enjoys her newfound freedom in the skin of Lorenzo, acting recklessly at times, her brother Angelo leads a religious war against all earthly and bodily pleasures, with a particular interest in oppressing women. In church, for instance, he preaches: "All I see is indiscreet breasts, the nipples almost escaping from corsages, ambiguous men, more woman than man, with expectant codpieces and soft bottoms! [. . .] This whole town is a loose woman"[5] (Hubert and Zanzim 2021, 92). This string of assertions is representative of Angelo's rhetoric throughout the work. Bianca thus witnesses her brother's attempt to ban the town's carnival because of the cross-dressing it entails, destroying artifacts as well as inflicting heavy physical punishments on her friend Rubina for cheating on her repeatedly unfaithful husband Alessandro while the latter initially suffers no consequences for his behavior (Hubert and Zanzim 2020, 105–7, 18–30). Women are also increasingly depicted as evil sources of temptations and are eventually forced to wear a veil in public lest men be led to lecherous thoughts (106). Although the contrast between the freedoms men enjoy and the control imposed on women's bodies becomes particularly jarring, in reality men controlled women's lives even prior to Angelo being put in a position of power. Giovanni himself is not devoid of all manner of prejudices against women and until quite late in the work he objects to the idea of Bianca being able to take a lover even though he does not love her and wants to have affairs with men himself (143).

Bianca's switching between two sexes and two genders (including, as mentioned earlier, cross-dressing as a man while in her female body) puts her in a unique position, as she can experience both sides and is therefore able to see for herself how social norms dictate behaviors. The fact that she reacts to injustices in very vocal ways and that her becoming Lorenzo is readily accepted as a plausible metamorphosis in a fairytale world make it possible to comment on the situation of women and LGBT persons in that fictional society.

Here is where yet another layer of meaning can be identified within Hubert's work. When presenting *Peau d'homme*, the journalist Monique Younès (2020) observed that: "Hubert often used tales, fantasy and the absurd to gently broach difficult topics" (my translation).[6] Hubert proceeded the same way with this album. While some connections between Bianca and Giovanni's fictional world and contemporary societal issues might be inferred by the reader, Zanzim provides additional contextual information in numerous interviews elucidating the social commentary that Hubert set out to make. Indeed, just as resorting to stock characters and fairy tale plots and devices that can easily be recognized as such makes it possible to subsequently diverge from that format and engage with socially determined inequalities based on sex and gender, the Cinquecento serves as a supposedly remote setting only to better comment on present-day society.

Zanzim explains on numerous occasions that after having collaborated with Hubert on his early works (2002; 2004; 2006; 2012; 2013), he had expressed the wish to be given the opportunity to illustrate a more personal work, should Hubert ever choose to write one. Zanzim recounts that in the wake of the *mariage pour tous* debate (to which I will return shortly), Hubert had contacted him, both angry and scared, and offered him a "scathing attack" (my translation)[7] titled *Débaptisez-moi* [Unchristen Me] (my translation) to illustrate. Zanzim was hesitant to accept because it felt too "trashy" (my translation),[8] but when Hubert came back to him two or three months later with an entirely rewritten work now titled *Peau d'homme*, Zanzim was glad to take on the task of illustrating it (2020a; 2020c, 58; 2021b; 2021c).

THE *"MARIAGE POUR TOUS"* DEBATE

Le mariage pour tous [Marriage for all] is a French law that was first presented as a bill to the cabinet in November 2012, voted for in Parliament in
April 2013 and issued in May of the same year, making it possible for people
of the same sex to get married and conjointly adopt ("Le Mariage pour tous"
2017). These legal milestones, however, were overshadowed by the resultant
backlash of protests, particularly in the formation of a group, *Manif pour
tous* [Protest for all] (my translation), that "represented a protest movement
consisting of hundreds of thousands of people marching through the streets
of Paris" ("La Manif pour tous" n.d.; my translation).[9] While today the
group focuses on other laws pertaining to the family and sexuality—namely
surrogate pregnancy and medically assisted reproduction ("La Manif pour
tous" n.d.)—it is the group's earliest actions that hold the most significance
insofar as this is what originally motivated Hubert to write the script for
Peau d'homme. The plans for the initial January 2013 demonstrations against
marriage equality were sizeable, with the use of forty-five sound trucks,
a podium, and giant screens (Seguin 2013). It is estimated that between
350,000 and 800,000 people were present at the protest (Leray 2013). While
those associated with *Manif pour tous* asserted that they simply wanted to
defend family values and children and that they were not homophobic per
se (Leray 2013), the religious group Civitas formed an independent protest,
separate from that of the *Manif pour tous* collective, with some 40,000 to
80,000 people chanting prayers and slogans referencing, amongst others,
Sodom and Gomorrah ("Mariage contre le mariage gay" 2013). A second,
larger demonstration was held in March 2013, with an estimated 300,000 to
1.4 million participants, thirty-three sound trucks, sixteen giant screens and a
podium (Politi 2013).

While Bruno Perreau's book *Queer Theory: The French Response* (2016)
focuses on the reception of queer theory in France, it also deals with its
reception in connection with the *mariage pour tous*. Indeed, his first chapter
"retraces the fixation on gender theory in contemporary debate on marriage
and the family" (20). Perreau writes that:

> [. . .] despite legal reforms, the "straight mind"—that is, a mode of thought
> based on a reification of the differences between the sexes—continues to func-
> tion as a political totem in France and that the majority conceptualization of citi-
> zenship is as operative today as it was prior to marriage-for-all. Preventing any
> change to that conceptualization caused opponents of the law to pour into the
> streets—and they continue to do so. Ultimately, performing homosexual mar-
> riages is not the key issue behind their struggle. Even the staunchest opponents

have never tried to disrupt a wedding ceremony. Their activism targets above all
the idea of marriage as a vector of meaning and moral values. (6)

He also argues that while the passing of the law did allow for same-sex marriage, "the marriage-for-all did not [. . .] constitute a complete success for
sexual minorities but was a kind of concession to their struggle" (5) because
it did not extend the same rights to married same-sex couples as it did to
married heterosexual couples. Indeed, he points out that medically assisted
procreation was not made legal "for single women and lesbian couples" and
that gay men's access to procreation was also limited as surrogate pregnancy
was not made legal (5). By late 2020, Perreau's assessment was still accurate
inasmuch as many groups that had united under the banner of "Marchons
Enfants" [Let's Walk, Children] (my translation), including *Manif pour
tous*, had taken to challenging the extension of access to medically assisted
procreation and surrogate pregnancy to all women. Their main arguments
revolved around the traditional family structure, maintaining that medically
assisted procreation outside of the married heterosexual couple would deprive
children of a father, and that it would in essence legalize the commodification of women's bodies ("contre la GPA et la PMA pour toutes" 2020; "Paris,
Toulouse, Lyon" 2020). These preoccupations are by no means new as
Perreau traces similar concerns raised at the time of the passing of the French
law for marriage equality. As he puts it, "[t]hey fear that children will be 'con-
verted' to homosexuality and that transsexuality will become widespread. All
these movements [. . .] described the Taubira Act[10] as an attack on 'the' family
and 'their' children" (40). He also notes that these groups went even further,
relying on a "subtext associating homosexuality with pedophilia" (53), suggesting that children were at risk of being physically and sexually abused
(40), and bringing minors to the protests, "sometimes going to questionable
lengths such as gagging children to protest the arrest of an activist or placing
'children up front' to use them as a shield when the police sought to disperse
a demonstration" (52). Finally, Perreau asserts that for all the insistence on
a distinction between religious groups and *Manif pour tous*, the latter group
"was not a classic mobilization of French right-wing forces but was primarily
based on religious convictions" (37).

Peau d'homme was a way for Hubert and Zanzim to comment on the
"mariage pour tous" debate, in particular the demonstrations and the religious
arguments put forward to prevent LGBT people from being able to enter a
marriage contract as well as the preoccupations with the traditional family
unit. With the acceptance that Bianca is magically able to alternate between
sexes and genders in the familiar world of make-believe, the lead character
becomes relatable, and it becomes possible to understand Bianca's essence as
distinct from her physical attributes; Bianca is still the same person, no matter

how many times she switches back and forth (Zanzim 2020a). Similarly, religious impositions on everyday life—be it related to restrictions on access to marriage or orders to veil women—that echo contemporary preoccupations in France and the Western world in general, are presented under the guise of inequalities in a temporally remote fictional society. It also leads one to reflect on the medievalism of the power of state being in the hands of fanatical religious leaders and the impacts it can have on individual lives.

In addition, the choice of referencing "Peau d'âne" is in no way fortuitous. This story is one that is becoming rarer in collections of fairy tales, perhaps due to its incestuous thematic content, although it clearly speaks of a father's incestuous propositions to his daughter in order to condemn them. Commenting on this tale as well as several others that follow similar plotlines, Warner (1988) observes that "The Donkeyskin group of fairy tales mirrors the legal and religious subjection of daughters to their father's authority with polished accuracy" (155).[11] The parallels with the attempts to determine the legal rights of LGBTQ+ citizens based on semi-covert religious values on the part of groups such as *Manif pour tous* are quite clear. What is more, given the preoccupations with the potential for abuse of children put forward by opponents of marriage equality, the decision to reference a cautionary tale about a father's incestuous desire for his daughter could serve as a noteworthy reminder that inappropriate behavior toward children is not inherent to homosexuality, nor is homosexuality synonymous with pedophilia.

Furthermore, the Peau d'âne type of heroine is not obedient but rather rightfully rebellious and Warner suggests that this might be the reason why fairy tales like "Peau d'âne" have become rare:

> These medieval narratives, with their interest in the strains and problems of young women on the threshold of the mature erotic life, these tales about a longed-for escape from an ordained fate, have proved unpalatable, and in the medievalizing fiction, disseminated as children's morality tale in the last century and in this one, the heroine's virtue requires that she be represented according to the conventions of maidenly modesty and filial duty. Her good behavior earns her a reward: beauty, sex appeal, the very desirability the stories used to dramatize as so painful and problematic. (162)

Relying on a plot of the "Peau d'âne" type therefore makes it possible to posit a more empowered female character than one such as Sleeping Beauty (who is the epitome of the passive main female character) (Pellegrin 2017, 141) and to suggest that righteousness does not mean blind obedience to abusive rules such as the ones imposed by Bianca's brother. Just as it is wrong to use religion to pre-emptively punish women for supposedly tempting men merely by existing, it is wrong to banish Giovanni for being caught with a "man" who is really his wife. Similarly, when caught by her mother walking around the city in Lorenzo's skin, Bianca is rebuked and ordered to fall back in line, but she rebels, yelling that "I haven't killed anyone! I haven't hurt anyone! [. . .] It's my life" (Hubert and Zanzim 2021, 113).[12] The social and political background that inspired *Peau d'homme*, however, is not approached in a direct manner and readers are left to draw their own conclusions rather than having arguments pushed on them (Zanzim, 2021b). Thus, the authors never suggest that punishing Giovanni for his sexual orientation is wrong; rather, they let readers reflect on this matter on their own. The work also relies on the safe distance provided by the world of fairy tales, which is likely to ensure a more receptive readership than the original text Hubert had submitted to Zanzim. As Younès points out, as readers become attached to the lead characters and feel for their tragically impossible love story, they come to wish that Bianca could reveal her true self to Giovanni but this is not how the story goes ("Monique Younès" 2020). In any case, Bianca and Giovanni's problem would not have been solved had Bianca's double identity been revealed. Marc Szyjowicz of CanalBD makes a similar remark in an interview with Zanzim (Zanzim 2021c). Through the couple's fairytale love story, it is possible to change more conservative readers' minds because Bianca shapeshifts so often that it becomes irrelevant which body she inhabits (Zanzim 2020a; Zanzim 2021b) and readers just want her to be happy (they have, after all, been conditioned to expect a happy ending from most fairy tales). Indeed, Zanzim asserts "in the end we don't really care about the packaging that we come in . . . what matters well it's love, right, love between beings and that is what this album shows" (Zanzim 2021a; my translation).[13]

WHAT DOES *PEAU D'HOMME*
BRING TO THE FAIRY TALE?

The traditional fairy tale has been criticized at length for presenting only one possible happy ending in the form of marriage. Although Bianca and Giovanni are eventually able to find their own marital bliss, it is by no means the one that is typically found in fairy tales such as "Cinderella," "Snow White," "Sleeping Beauty" or "Donkey Skin." While such tales end with the princesses marrying a young prince and living a happy life after a number of hardships, Bianca and Giovanni are married off against their will for economic reasons. Although Bianca is not opposed to marrying Giovanni per se, the latter, being drawn to men, does not feel any love for her. Their married life does not go well at first, as Bianca yearns to be loved and held while Giovanni becomes increasingly attached to Lorenzo and avoids any unnecessary physical contact with his wife. As a result, Giovanni engages in sexual intercourse with Bianca, as a woman, out of duty and in order to produce an heir but remains cold and distant as a lover. Moreover, Bianca knows that revealing her true or dual identity would not be the solution to her problems. They eventually learn to find happiness in their married life, long after their daughter Chiara is born and Bianca is able to obtain a pardon for Giovanni who had been caught in her company as Lorenzo and sent to live in exile for some time. This happiness is achieved by living as a regular married couple in public but as co-parenting roommates behind closed doors, each with their own chosen romantic partner. While Giovanni picks Hans, a man he met while in exile, Bianca chooses Tomaso, whom she always liked but would likely not have been allowed to marry because of class differences. Using each other as a cover, Bianca and Giovanni are able to raise the child they have together and get along amicably while enjoying the company of a partner of their choice. More importantly, they are happy because they are free to live as they wish inside their home although they must still maintain appearances for society to leave them alone.

The very existence of Chiara is also significant: she grows up in an unconventional family, cared for and loved by all, surrounded by happy adults. In light of the concerns for children's wellbeing that were raised and discussed at length in the debates about how marriage equality might affect the traditional family structure, it is perhaps no accident that the authors chose to include a child being raised in such circumstances. Giovanni and Bianca's family structure does not represent the only possible unconventional family structure, but it is a positive example of how a child might fit into a family outside of the traditional format, with a homosexual father and his partner being responsible caregivers for a young child while co-parenting with a woman who has now taken a lover of her own choosing.

CONCLUSION

Peau d'homme turns to the reassuringly familiar form of the tale so often tied to readers' childhood experiences to address an issue that has brought much anguish both to those who felt they needed to protest *en masse* in order to protect the traditional family structure and to people who, like Hubert, felt targeted and unsafe as a result of the virulent rejection of their way of life. Concurrently, *Peau d'homme* subverts the fairy tale form and redefines its traditional happy ending. By framing Bianca and Giovanni's unconventional marriage within the traditional form of the tale, it offers an alternative to the "happily ever after" trope that typically excludes the possibility of finding happiness outside of marriage, whether heterosexual or homosexual, since Bianca and Giovanni can be said to be happy *in spite* of their (poorly) arranged marriage rather than because of it.

In the process, this album brings our attention back to a type of fairy tale that is becoming rarer in favor of those that depict submissive female characters and supports a more empowered lead female character. In the end, *Peau d'homme* modernizes the fairy tale by injecting contemporary issues and ways of being into this make-believe world. The reception of the work—both in terms of the acclaim and multiple prizes it garnered and in relation to the fact that it drew in readership outside of the usual comic-reading circles— suggests that its creators were able to strike a suitable balance between relying on tradition and redefining it in relation to family structures and the fairy tale form.

NOTES

1. The official translated titles of works that are available in English are provided between square brackets.

2. In the case of *Ténébreuse*, Mallié reports that he had almost finished the art for the first volume and that Hubert had seen most of it at the time of his death. As regards the second volume, Hubert had written its entire script although it still required some final touches. Although Mallié considered abandoning the project at the time of Hubert's passing, in the end he brought the final touches to the script of the second volume with the help of his editor and the release date is set for September 2022. (Mallié 2021a, 70–71; Mallié 2021b, 70) As for *Joe la pirate*, Virginie Augustin mentions that Hubert had completed the full script and that he saw about half of the finished work before his passing. However, she also states that it was difficult to finish the album on her own although she does not specify the nature of the difficulties (Augustin 2021a).

3. While the official translation provided between square brackets gives a general idea of the godmother's words, it does not do justice to the original. Indeed, while the official translation suggests that men just are rude and disgusting, the original rather suggests that men force themselves to be ruder and more disgusting than they are naturally inclined to be in order to conform to social codes. In addition, in the original text, the godmother concludes that she was right in saying that Giovanni was acting like a boy, almost like it was a children's game where one pretends to be a boy while the English translation almost seems to refer to the saying "boys will be boys" as if the behavior displayed by Giovanni was intrinsic to men and boys. The original version is as follows: "Ce sont les codes sociaux du monde des garçons, ma chérie. Nous nous faisons plus délicates que nous sommes, eux se font plus grossiers, quitte à se forcer. Il n'était pas le seul à se comporter ainsi, n'est-ce pas? [. . .] Voilà. Il jouait au garçon."

4. "le fils de l'intendant"

5. "Je ne vois que seins impudiques, mamelons dressés s'échappant des corsages, jeunes hommes ambigus, plus filles que garçons, la braguette arrogante et la fesse trop moulée! [. . .] Toute cette ville est femelle et luxurieuse."

6. "Hubert utilisait souvent le conte, le merveilleux, l'irrationnel pour entrer en douceur dans des débats périlleux."

7. "un brûlot"

8. "trash"

9. "[s]ymbolisait un mouvement de contestation fort de centaines de milliers de personnes, défilant dans les rues de Paris."

10. The Taubira Act is the Mariage pour tous Act. Christiane Taubira was the French Minister of Justice and Keeper of the Seals when the law was passed. Together with Dominique Bertinotti (the Minister for Family at the time) Taubira presented the bill to the Parliament in 2013 and defended it (see Guerrier 2014; Mallaval 2016).

11. Examples provided by Warner include "The She-Bear," "Cap-o'-Rushes," *La Manékine* (by Philippe de Beaumanoir), the stories of Saint Uncumber, Saint Barbara and Saint Dympna.

12. "Je n'ai tué personne! Je n'ai fait de mal à personne! [. . .] C'est ma vie."

13. "Finalement on s'en fout un p'tit peu de l'enveloppe qu'on a . . . c'qui compte ben c'est l'amour hein, l'amour entre les êtres et c'est ça que cet album révèle."

REFERENCES

Augustin, Virginie. 2021. "Rencontre live—Joe la pirate." *YouTube* video, 40:40. May 7, 2021.https://youtu.be/lH0Vz9Ls0h4.

Augustin, Virginie. 2021b. "'Joe est ce que l'on pourrait appeler une butch'—Rencontre avec Virginie Augustin." *YouTube* video, 25:57. June 29, 2021. https://youtu .be/gvAT8PIHXR4.

Bosser, Frédéric. 2020. "Hubert: Tragique destin." *dBD*, n°142 (April 2020): 60–64.

"Festival de la Bande Dessinée d'Angoulême. Palmarès 2021." July 28, 2021. www .bdangouleme.com/palmares-2021.

Guerrier, Sophie. 2014. "Le discours de Christiane Taubira pour le mariage pour tous." *Le Figaro*, March 27, 2014. www.lefigaro.fr/politique/le-scan/2014/03 /27/25001-20140327ARTFIG00079-le-discours-de-christiane-taubira-pour-le -mariage-pour-tous.php.

Hubert et al. 2013. *Les Gens normaux: Paroles lesbiennes gay bi trans*. Tournai: Casterman.

Hubert. 2017. "Hubert: Barbe bleue et moi." Interview by Loraine Adam. *dBD*, n°115 (July–August 2017): 80–83.

"Hubert." Glénat. n.d. January 15, 2022. www.glenat.com/auteurs/hubert.

Hubert and Burckel. 2017. *La nuit mange le jour*. Grenoble: Glénat.

Hubert and Gatignol. 2014. *Petit*. Paris: Soleil.

Hubert and Gatignol. 2016. *Demi sang*. Paris: Soleil.

Hubert and Gatignol. 2018. *Le Grand Homme*. Paris: Soleil.

Hubert and Gatignol. 2020. *Première-née*. Paris: Soleil.

Hubert and Kerascoët. 2007. "Hubert & les Kerascoët: 'Joann Sfar est l'arbre qui cache la forêt.'" Interview by Nicolas Anspach. *ActuaBD*, March 30, 2007. www .actuabd.com/Hubert-les-Kerascoet-Joann-Sfar-est-l-arbre-qui-cache-la-foret.

Hubert and Kerascoët. 2014a. *Beauté: L'Intégrale*. Marcinelle: Dupuis.

Hubert and Kerascoët. 2014b. *Miss Don't Touch Me: The Complete Story*. Translated by Joe Johnson. New York: NBM.

Hubert and Mallié. 2021. *Ténébreuse*. Marcinelle: Dupuis.

Hubert and Marie Caillou. 2013. *La Ligne droite*. Grenoble: Glénat.

Hubert and Virginie Augustin. 2021. *Joe la pirate: La Vie rêvée de Marion Barbara Carstairs*. Grenoble: Glénat.

Hubert and Zanzim. 2002. *La Politesse des monstres*. Paris: Carabas.

Hubert and Zanzim. 2004. *Capitale des enfers*. Paris: Carabas.

Hubert and Zanzim. 2006. *La Sirène des pompiers*. Paris: Dargaud.

Hubert and Zanzim. 2012. *Ne m'enterrez pas trop vite*. Grenoble: Glénat.

Hubert and Zanzim. 2013. *Anisette et Formol*. Grenoble: Glénat.

Hubert and Zanzim. 2020. *Peau d'homme*. Grenoble: Glénat.

Hubert and Zanzim. 2021. *A Man's Skin*. Translated by Ivanka Hahnenberger. Portland: Ablaze.

"La Manif pour tous, collectif né de l'opposition à la loi sur le mariage homosexuel." *L'Express*, n.d. https://www.lexpress.fr/actualite/societe/la-manif-pour-tous -collectif-ne-de-l-opposition-a-la-loi-sur-le-mariage-homosexuel_1841714.html.

"Le mariage pour tous." 2017. Last modified August 15, 2021. https://www .gouvernement.fr/action/le-mariage-pour-tous.

Leray, Pascale. 2013. "Manifestation contre le mariage gay: 'Nous attendons un référendum.'" *L'Express*, January 13, 2013. www.lexpress.fr/actualite/societe/ video-manifestation-contre-le-mariage-gay-nous-attendons-du-debat-et-surtout-un -referendum_1209182.html.

"Les 22e prix Bédélys." September 1, 2021. www.fbdm-mcaf.ca/prix-bedelys/22e -bedelys/.

Mallaval, Catherine. 2016. "Taubira, le mariage pour tous pour toujours." *Libération*, January 27, 2016. www.liberation.fr/france/2016/01/27/taubira-le-mariage-pour -tous-pour-toujours_1429262/.

Mallié, Vincent. 2021a. "Princesse pas du tout en détresse." Interview by Klervi Le Cozic. *Casemate*, Hors-série été n°149 (August-September 2021): 70–75.

Mallié, Vincent. 2021b. "Un conte classique?" Interview by Frédéric Bosser. *dBD*, n°155 (July–August 2021): 69–75.

"Mariage contre le mariage gay: les intégristes de Civitas ont défilé à part." 2013. *L'Express*, January 13, 2013. www.lexpress.fr/actualite/societe/mariage-contre-le -mariage-gay-les-integristes-de-civitas-ont-defile-a-part_1209207.html.

"Monique Younès nous dévoile le nom de l'album qui reçoit le Grand Prix RTL de la Bande Dessinée 2020." *YouTube* video, 22:01. November 30, 2020. www.youtube .com/watch?v=CE2AbBu9RPI

"Paris: la 'Manif pour tous' a manifesté contre la GPA et la PMA pour toutes." 2020. *L'Express*, March 8, 2020. www.lexpress.fr/actualite/societe/paris-la-manif-pour -tous-a-manifeste-contre-la-gpa-et-la-pma-pour-toutes_2120368.html.

"Paris, Toulouse, Lyon . . . pourquoi des manifestants anti-PMA ont battu le pavé." 2020. *L'Express*, October 10, 2020. www.lexpress.fr/actualite/societe/paris -toulouse-lyon-pourquoi-des-manifestants-anti-pma-ont-battu-le-pave-ce-samedi _2136146.html.

Pasamonik, Didier. 2021. "*Première Née*, le final flamboyant de la tétralogie noire de Hubert et Gatignol." *ActuaBD*, January 11, 2021. www.actuabd.com/Premiere-Nee -le-final-flamboyant-de-la-tetralogie-noire-de-Hubert-et-Gatignol.

Pellegrin, Annick. 2017. "Feroumont's, Hubert's, and Kerascoët's Heroines: Debunking the Myths of Happiness in Romantic Fairy Tales and Romance Novels." In *Heroes, Heroines, and Everything in Between: Challenging Gender and Sexuality Stereotypes in Children's Entertainment Media,* edited by CarrieLynn D. Reinhard and Christopher J. Olson, 139–57. Lanham, Maryland: Lexington Books.

Perreau, Bruno. 2016. *Queer Theory: The French Response*. Stanford: Stanford University Press.

Politi, Caroline. 2013. "Combien a coûté la manif' pour tous?" *L'Express*, March 25, 2013. www.lexpress.fr/actualite/societe/combien-a-coute-la-manif-pour-tous _1234698.html.

Roure, Benjamin. 2020. "Hubert est mort." *BoDoï*, February 13, 2020. www.bodoi .info/hubert-est-mort/.

Seguin, Amandine. 2013. "Antis mariage gay: la manifestation soutenue par une importante logistique." *L'Express*, January 12, 2013. www.lexpress.fr/actualite /politique/antis-mariage-gay-la-manifestation-soutenue-par-une-importante -logistique_1208803.html.

Warner, Marina. 1988. "The Wronged Daughter: Aspects of Cinderella." *Grand Street* 7 (3): 143–63.

Warner, Marina. 2014. *Once Upon a Time: A Short History of Fairy Tale*. Oxford: Oxford University Press.

Zanzim. 2015. *L'Île aux femmes*. Grenoble: Glénat.

Zanzim. 2020a. "BD—Interview Zanzim—Planches de BD—Peau d homme [*sic*]." *YouTube* video, 6:04. September 28, 2020. youtu.be/dJPA0kdO5Ss.

Zanzim. 2020b. "De l'homme, de l'âme, de l'amour." Interview by Sonia Déchamps. *Casemate*, n°135 (June 2020): 70–75.

Zanzim. 2020c. "Une tranche de vie." Interview by Frédéric Bosser. *dBD*, n°143 (May–June 2020): 53–59.

Zanzim. 2021a. "Comment Zanzim explique le succès incroyable de sa bande-dessinée, 'Peau d'homme.'" Interview by Nathalie Rossignol. *YouTube* video, 7:00. January 22, 2021. youtu.be/Gc-gl7Fi84w.

Zanzim. 2021b. "*Peau d'Homme*: un succès au goût d'amertume." Interview by Didier Pasamonik and François Rissel. *ActuaBD*, April 6, 2021. Podcast, 40:25. podcasts.a pple.com/be/podcast/peau-dhomme-un-succ%C3%A8s-au-go%C3%BBt-damertum e/id1559845569?i=1000515987342.

Zanzim. 2021c. "Rencontre live Peau d'Homme à 19h." Interview by Marc Szyjowicz and Jean-Pierre Nakache. *YouTube* video, 59:08. January 28, 2021. youtu.be/S7J-Q7XMUX0.

Index

About the Editor

Dr. Romain Chareyron is an assistant professor of French at the University of Saskatchewan (Saskatoon, Canada). He specializes in contemporary French and Francophone cinema. His current SSHRC-funded research investigates the representation of disabilities in French cinema. His other fields of interest include: the concept of "film genre" (with a focus on horror and pornography) in mainstream cinema, sexuality and gender, youth in film. He recently co-edited the volume *Screening Youth: Contemporary French and Francophone Cinema* (Edinburgh University Press, 2019). His most recent publications include: "Créer pour mieux voir: Image(s) du sida et enjeux de la représentation dans 120 battements par minute" (*Hybrida—numéro spécial: SIDA/S – 40 ans*, n°3: 35–60); "Le Handicap dans le cinéma français contemporain: Quelles représentations? Quels discours?" (*Nouvelles études francophones* 36 (1–2): 9–28); "Off the Beaten Path: Non-Metropolitan Representations of Homosexuality in Three French Films" (*Screen Bodies. An Interdisciplinary Journal of Experience, Perception, and Display,* 3 (2): 17–38); "Sébastien Lifshitz: Cinéaste des identités" (*Modern and Contemporary France—special issue: LGBTQ Politics and Identities in France Since 1968*, 27(2): 185–203).

About the Contributors

R. Cole Cridlin (he/him/his) is a recent graduate from the University of Pittsburgh's Department of French & Italian where he received his PhD in French Language and Literature. His research situates itself at the intersections of contemporary French studies and queer/sexuality studies. He is most interested in the relationship between sexual subjectivity formation/iteration as it relates to notions of rural and urban spaces. Titled "Redrawing the Lines: Queer Metronormativity in French Contexts," his dissertation project considers a corpus of novels and films spanning from 2004 to 2017 (including Sébastien Lifshitz' *Wild Side*) that complicate models of queer metronormativity by considering it in French literary and filmic contexts.

Charlie Fabre (he/they) is an LGBTIQ+ advocate. They are currently working on a project about trans representation on screen, through the website *representrans.fr*, while being actively involved in local LGBTIQ+ organizations. Their master's thesis focused on the construction of the cis gaze in the movie industry and the ways trans characters and bodies are portrayed in order to reassure and confirm cis centered biases.

Dr. Justine Huet is an associate professor of French at Mount Royal University (Calgary, Canada) in the Department of English, Languages, and Cultures. She is coeditor of *Convergences francophones*, a pluridisciplinary Francophone peer-reviewed online journal indexed in the DOAJ. Her research interests are the dubbing of both animated and non-animated TV series and cinema in France and Quebec.

Dr. Laurel Iber received her PhD in romance studies from Duke University (USA) in May 2020, after defending her dissertation, "Troubles in Representation: (Con)figuring Non-Binary Sex in 19th-Century French Literature, Art, and Medicine." Her research focuses primarily on the construction, representation, and conceptual articulation of gender, sex, and sexuality in nineteenth-century France. Dr. Iber is currently an independent researcher in Paris, where is she is preparing her first book, an interdisciplinary study that explores the ways in which specters of Greco-Roman antiquity haunt nineteenth-century French articulations of androgyny and hermaphroditism.

Dr. Annick Pellegrin is a graduate of The University of Sydney. Her PhD thesis is a comparative study of representations of Latin America in Franco-Belgian, Mexican, and Argentinean comics. She is a columns and articles editor for the *Comics Forum* and sits on the editorial board of *Studies in Comics*. Her research has been published in French, English and Spanish, most recently in *The Journal of Comics & Culture*, the journal *Atlantide* and *The Routledge Companion to Gender and Sexuality in Comic Book Studies*. She also guest edited (with María Celina Bortolotto) an issue of JILAR dedicated to the Argentine Roberto Fontanarrosa.

Arthur Ségard is a PhD candidate at New York University (French/French Studies). He works on the multimedial spectacularization of abnormal bodies (literature, cinema, performance), from 19th century to the present time.

Dr. Brian J. Troth earned his PhD from The Ohio State University in the United States of America. His dissertation was entitled "Amour à risques: A Reworking of Risk in the PrEP Era in France." He is an LGBTQ+ advocate and scholar whose work converges at the intersection of French Studies, Visual Studies, and Queer Studies. His current research interests include the dangers of medication, risky behavior, palliative care, and digital spaces and identities.

Leah E. Wilson is a PhD candidate in literary studies at Washington State University. Her dissertation evaluates the transnational relationship between American and French sex-positive and queer feminisms as exhibited in the works of Virginie Despentes, Paul B. Preciado, Maggie Nelson, and Michelle Tea. She has published articles on Preciado, Despentes, and Tea in *French Cultural Studies*, *The Rocky Mountain Review*, and *Gender Forum*.

www.ingramcontent.com/pod-product-compliance
Lightning Source LLC
Chambersburg PA
CBHW031135270326
41929CB00011B/1635